THE TOWNSCAPE OF
DARLINGTON

THE TOWNSCAPE OF DARLINGTON

by Gillian Cookson

With contributions by
Christine M. Newman and Graham R. Potts

V C H

First published 2003

ISBN 978 1 90435 621 9

A Victoria County History publication
in association with The Boydell Press
an imprint of Boydell & Brewer Ltd
PO Box 9, Woodbridge, Suffolk IP12 3DF, UK
and of Boydell & Brewer Inc.
668 Mt Hope Avenue, Rochester, NY 14620-2731, USA
website: www.boydellandbrewer.com
and with the
University of London Institute of Historical Research

Our Authorised Representative for product safety in the EU is Easy Access System Europe
– Mustamäe tee 50, 10621 Tallinn, Estonia,
gpsr.requests@easproject.com

A CIP catalogue record for this book is available
from the British Library

Typeset by Joshua Associated Ltd, Oxford

Contents

Contents

Preface

The Townscape of Darlington is the first publication to emerge from the revived Victoria County History of Durham. It is also the first of a new series of VCH studies, well-illustrated paperbacks which aim to appeal to a wide audience.

The Durham VCH was reborn in 1999 after a gap of 80 years. Three of the traditional red VCH volumes had been completed for County Durham by the time of the First World War, and more material reached proof stage but was never published. This work, much of it meticulously researched and written by our predecessor, the eminent scholar Madeleine Hope Dodds, has been invaluable as a starting point for our modern project, especially as a guide to medieval sources. To Madeleine Dodds we owe a great debt.

The opening chapter of this volume, 'Medieval Darlington', was written by Christine M. Newman. Chapter 4, 'The Architects of 19th-century Darlington', is the work of Graham R. Potts. Elizabeth Williamson made additional contributions to chapter 4 and wrote sections on the architecture of St Cuthbert's church and the Friends' meeting-house. The remainder of the book was written by Gillian Cookson.

Additional research was carried out by Philip Darragh, with the support of the Marc Fitch Fund. Thanks are also due to Robin Coulthard for producing supplementary material and references. We are grateful to David Blair of the Darlington Building Society; Robin Coulthard; Brenda Flynn; George Flynn; David Howlett; and John Smith, for information, advice and comments on draft text.

We would like to thank Katherine Williamson, Kimberley Bennett, Lisa Bowe, Brian Myers, Gillan Wilson and Margaret White, all of Darlington Library, for their continuing help. We are also much indebted to Jennifer Gill, David Butler and staff of the Durham Record Office for their patient assistance. Linda Drury, Margaret McCollum, Beth Rainey and Richard Higgins, past and present staff members of Durham University Library, have also been extremely helpful. Roger Norris has been a mine of information about the holdings of the Durham University and the Durham Chapter libraries. We are grateful to the patron of the Durham VCH, Lord Barnard, for granting access to his archive at Raby Castle, and to Clare Simpson, the curator there, for her help with research.

Our thanks go to Stuart Muckle and his staff in the building control section, to Andrew Cockburn and Jim Gordon, all of Darlington Borough Council. We thank Patrick Conway, Iain Watson and his successor Alistair Bowden, and Geoff Pratt, of Durham County Council, and the former Durham county archaeologist, Niall Hammond, and Fiona McDonald, who succeeded him. Peter Ryder has been immensely helpful on St Cuthbert's church and other aspects of the early archaeology and topography of Darlington.

We acknowledge with thanks the various contributions to our work made by colleagues at the University of Durham, Helen Dunsford and Simon Harris, Adrian Green and Sam

Lucy, and by Tony Pollard and Linda Polley of the University of Teesside. We also wish to thank David Brown of Latimer, Hinks, solicitors; Jessie Campbell of Barclays Bank archives; Constance Fraser; Barbara Harbottle; Chris Lloyd of the *Northern Echo;* Charles McNab; and Revd Robert Williamson of St Cuthbert's church.

Illustrations of the bridge with St Cuthbert's church beyond; of Darlington from the road to Yarm; of the bishop's palace and deanery; and Westall's view of the market place, are reproduced with the permission of the Durham University Library Archives and Special Collections. Whitworth's plan of the Tees and intended canal, the south-east aspect of Darlington in 1760, and the view of Trinity church, are published by permission of the Durham Chapter Library, Durham Cathedral. Durham county libraries gave consent for the publication of Richardson's view of Darlington, *c.*1830, and for the drawing of Elm Ridge. Photographs of the construction of council housing and of St Cuthbert's Way appear by courtesy of the *Northern Echo*, and that of the demolition of Brunswick Street, taken by Joseph Coulthard, by permission of Robin Coulthard. All other pictures from the Durham Record series are reproduced by permission of Darlington Borough Council, as is the Local Board of Health plan of *c.* 1850.

We are grateful to English Heritage for taking the modern photographs in this volume. These and other views of buildings and street scenes taken by English Heritage on behalf of the VCH in the autumn of 2001 can be seen in the National Monuments Record, Swindon. Plans of Darlington before 1600 and of 19th-century estates and suburbs were drawn by Cath d'Alton of the University of London.

Finally, we thank Bernard Newman and Neil Cookson, who have helped and supported us enormously in many ways.

List of illustrations

Introduction

It is exactly a thousand years since Darlington first appeared in written records, when granted in *c.* 1003 by Styr the son of Ulf to the see of Durham. During the following millennium, the small Anglo-Saxon settlement grew into today's thriving town, its history now generally linked in the public mind with entrepreneurial Quakers and the birth of railways.

This book traces one aspect of Darlington's long history, its physical development from early foundations, to medieval borough, to modern town. Medieval growth came as a result of Darlington's position in the bishopric, building on a market serving a prosperous agricultural hinterland, and on traffic passing through on the Great North Road between London and Edinburgh. A borough was established around the modern market area, separate from the vill or manor of Bondgate, by the end of the 12th century. Around St Cuthbert's church there grew an ecclesiastical complex, including a bishop's palace, and trade flourished so that by the 1530s Darlington was described as the best market town in the bishopric outside Durham itself.

Later in that century, in 1585, came a great misfortune, a catastrophic fire which destroyed most of Darlington's medieval housing, though not the larger buildings. The town's rebuilding took place within the medieval streets and burgage plots, maintaining the earlier pattern of central yards and wynds which largely survives today. In the 17th and especially the 18th centuries, freehold lots within the borough were subject to intensive infilling with cottages and workshops. It had taken some time for Darlington to fully regain its previous size after the fire, but between the late 17th and late 18th century the number of dwellings approximately doubled. Much of this expansion was in yards and garths behind the market place frontages, and connected with marketing activities and services for long-distance travellers. Even by 1825, when the Stockton and

Darlington railway arrived in the town, there had been little building beyond the confines of the medieval settlement. The main exception was the mansions and parks of Quaker industrialists on the fringes of the urban centre.

The railway reinforced Darlington's prosperity, particularly after a main north-south line opened in the 1840s, and the town's steady growth continued. Yet it was not until after 1851 that the town underwent spectacular expansion, its population multiplying two and a half times in 20 years to reach 27,700 by 1871. This mushrooming was not a direct result of railways, rather a by-product, as iron and engineering companies settled near the lines at Rise Carr and Albert Hill to serve and use the railway. Darlington acquired suburbs, including a polite middle-class area on the former glebe land of the west end. As the wealthier Quakers left the spreading town, their former estates were built over with terraced housing. Throughout the 19th century the town centre developed to reflect the growth around it, acquiring features designed by significant provincial and local architects, as well as by one nationally acclaimed figure, Alfred Waterhouse.

The 20th century saw large-scale housing development on the outskirts of town and the fusion of the centre with its suburbs. Council house building started in the 1920s, and a decade later the demolition commenced of terraces which had been built for the first influx of workers in the mid 19th century. A number of schemes to re-develop municipal buildings and the market area came to nothing, and not until 1965 did a long awaited bypass take the Great North Road traffic away from Darlington's town centre. Heavy industry disappeared at a rate which alarmed civic leaders during the late 1960s and 1970s, but Darlington's diversity, and position on main communication routes, proved her salvation. Some new businesses did move in, although many former industrial sites became housing areas. Much of Darlington today is residential, dormitory suburbs surrounding a town centre where Victorian and 18th century buildings populate medieval streets.

The story of Darlington's physical growth casts a light across many other aspects of the town's history. This is a town with historical depths extending far beyond the well-worn tales of railways and Quakers.

1. DARLINGTON BEFORE 1600

The market and industrial town of Darlington occupies a relatively favoured and strategically significant site in the lower Tees valley. It lies on well-drained land immediately to the west of the river Skerne, about a mile north of the Tees and some four miles upstream of the confluence of the two rivers at Croft bridge. Its protected environment attracted comment from 18th-century agriculturalists, who remarked that the town's 'fortunate inhabitants' enjoyed a warmer climate than those of other parts of the county, since the Skerne valley declined to the south, rather than from west to east. As a result it was spared the ravages of the north-easterly wind which so 'annoyed' its neighbours.[1] The productive soils of the surrounding terrain also undoubtedly attracted settlers,[2] and there has been considerable agricultural activity in the area since the early neolithic period.[3]

The geography of the Skerne valley dictated the position of early settlement, which was located at the first point where the river narrowed sufficiently to allow a crossing place avoiding the low-lying marshlands further downstream.[4] Darlington's strategic position is illustrated by the fact that no other major bridges have emerged to challenge its dominance as the natural crossing point over the Skerne before that river meets the Tees.[5] The small stream of Cocker beck flows through the town from the west, meeting with the Skerne at Northgate.[6]

The course of the river has altered over time, with the old watercourse lying to the east of the modern one. That the land on the eastern bank of the old river bed was lower lying and more prone to flooding influenced the siting of the town on the western rather than the eastern bank of the Skerne.[7] The site of settlement slopes quite steeply eastwards down to the Skerne. The main streets of High Row, Bondgate and Skinnergate stand at the top of the rise, with the market place and adjacent streets sloping down towards the river. In geological terms, the town sits on a foundation

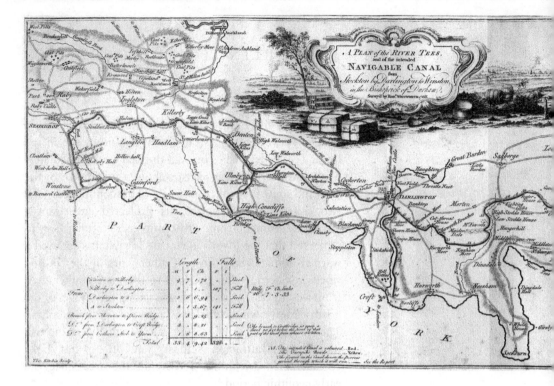

of boulder clays, post-glacial sands, gravels and clays, which provide a well-drained area for settlement.[8] Boulder clay is more prevalent in the area east of the Skerne, whilst the west bank has a finer subsoil made up of pure sand and gravel.[9] Physical evidence of the glacial and post-glacial upheavals that created this foundation is to be found in the shape of the Bulmer Stone, a boulder of red granite carried down from Shap Fell, in Westmorland, during the Ice Age. This stood in the Northgate, marking what was once the northern boundary of the town, opposite the old cobblestone cottages known collectively as Darlington House which were subsequently replaced by the technical college.[10] The stone remained in position until 1923 when it was removed and placed behind the college railings, where it still stands.[11]

Whilst there is clear evidence of prehistoric and later Iron Age activity in the vicinity of Darlington, the Romans chose a fresh site at Piercebridge, at the junction of the Tees with the major thoroughfare of Dere Street, as their base. Although the Roman presence was predominantly military,

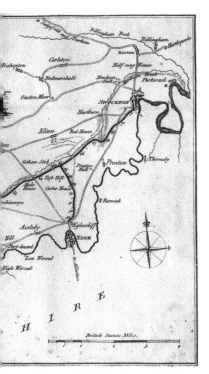

1. *Part of a plan drawn by Robert Whitworth in 1768, showing main routes through the town including alternative roads south to the Tees. The proposed canal linking to the Tees, drawn in black, was never built*

after its decline Darlington itself emerged as a site of domestic habitation. An Anglo-Saxon settlement, focused upon an important church, developed into a bustling centre of religious, administrative and economic activity in the middle ages.

PREHISTORIC DARLINGTON

Excavations in the area to the west of Five Arches bridge and Hutton Avenue footbridge at the time of the River Skerne restoration project in 1995 revealed information about the landscape 7,000 to 10,000 years ago. The finds related to local plant and animal life, with an elk bone being unearthed during the excavations, but no evidence was found of human habitation.[12] Nevertheless, there is considerable indication of early settlement by the early neolithic period, with prehistoric artefacts of a later date found within the vicinity of the modern town.[13] Several flints have been excavated during the past century, including finds from the Cleveland Avenue and Elton Road areas of the town.[14] Flints dating from the mesolithic or neolithic periods were found during excavations undertaken in the market place in 1994. A sherd of pottery and a number of stake holes, possibly relating to some type of temporary structure, were also discovered during this operation.[15] Evidence of prehistoric activity, possibly from the same period, has been identified in Morton Palms, on the eastern outskirts of Darlington.[16] In 1974 an arrowhead dating from the Bronze Age was discovered on the Hummersknott housing estate.[17]

Complementary archaeological evidence shows similar levels of prehistoric activity in Darlington's rural hinterland.[18] Flints have been found in and around the Piercebridge area,[19] with others recorded in Newton Ketton.[20] Moreover, studies of fossil pollen, taken from nearby Neasham Fen, show evidence of woodland clearances occurring at the beginning of the neolithic period, between 4178 and 4020 BC. A series of further clearances occurred during the early and late Bronze Ages, 1670–1640 BC; 1034–994 BC; and 800–550 BC. Towards the end of this period, which extended into the early Iron Age, relatively large tracts of land were being cleared and cereal cultivation undertaken which provides further indication of permanent human settlement.[21] There is firmer evidence of settlement somewhat later, within the vicinity of the town.[22] Cropmark sites at Morton Palms, for instance, have been identified as possible Iron Age or Romano-British enclosures.[23] Excavations at Holme House, Piercebridge, some six miles west of Darlington, have also revealed evidence of continuous occupation from the middle or late Iron Age, pre-dating the Roman settlement in that locality. This may have been the site of a Brigantian homestead, since the Brigantine stronghold of Stanwick was situated only some five kilometres to the south-west.[24]

ROMAN INFLUENCE

The major focus of Roman activity was at Piercebridge, where the Romans built a fort, strategically placed near Dere Street, at the point where that major thoroughfare running northwards from York to Hadrian's Wall crossed the river Tees.[25] The Piercebridge settlement was substantial. In addition to the fort and its surrounding *vicus*, or civilian settlement, the site included the Roman villa of Holme House and a stone bridge which spanned the Tees.[26] The known fort, which extended across more than 10 a., dated from the later Roman period, around AD 300. Its surrounding settlement pre-dates this by some 150 to 200 years, indicating earlier Roman military occupation of the site.[27] The adjacent villa of Holme House, one of the most northerly of known Roman villas, was certainly of earlier origin, dating probably from the latter part of the first century AD. This was erected on the site of an existing Iron Age settlement and possibly stood at the centre of an agricultural estate. It had been extended to relatively 'opulent proportions' by the middle of the 2nd century, and stood at the height of its prosperity in the 3rd and 4th centuries, declining thereafter as Roman influence withered.[28]

At least two Roman bridges were erected across the Tees at Piercebridge. The first, probably of combined timber and masonry construction, followed the route of the original Dere Street, whilst the second, a stone bridge, was built some 200 metres downstream of the original, on a later diversion of the Roman road.[29] The remains of the first bridge were in evidence until 1771, when they were washed away during the great flood of that year.[30] Parts of the second, stone, bridge are still visible. One or other of these bridges seems to have survived until *c.* 1500, although it was replaced in the early 13th century by a new structure.[31] This long remained an alternative route into the bishopric, since the bridge was rebuilt in the early 16th century and widened in 1781.[32] With the growth of Darlington as a staging post on the route north, however, a more commonly used crossing point over the River Tees came increasingly to be Croft bridge, situated further downstream and only three miles from the town.[33]

Despite the proximity of the Roman settlement in Piercebridge, no firm evidence has emerged of any similar settlement in Darlington, although several finds of Roman coin have been made in the vicinity of the town. In 1790 a large collection of silver coins was taken from the Tees near Darlington.[34] Later, in the mid 19th century, another hoard of possible 3rd century date was unearthed in Baydale Beck, near Mowden bridge. Finds have also been recorded in Cockerton and in Cobden Street, off Yarm Road, Darlington.[35] A further discovery took place on a site to the south of the Cleveland Bridge company's works near Yarm Road.[36] There is also evidence of continued native occupation in the town's hinterland, following the decline of Roman influence in the area. In Piercebridge, finds of Anglian pottery and the discovery of a cruciform brooch suggest post-Roman inhabitation of the area.[37] A number of horse-man burial sites, discovered at Piercebridge in the mid 19th century, may also date from this period.[38] Moreover, as the discovery of an Anglian burial site on the Greenbank estate indicates, some form of settlement was certainly in evidence in Darlington itself by the latter part of the 6th century.

ANGLO-SAXON SETTLEMENT

The name of Darlington appears to be Anglian in origin. Its early forms, 'Dearthingtun' or 'Dearnington', may have been derived from 'Derne', probably an alternative name for the River Skerne. 'Derne' or 'dierne' in old English meant hidden or secluded, a reference perhaps to the nature of the river at that time.[39] An alternative suggestion is that this was the settlement or 'tun' of 'Deornod' or 'Deornoth', a local headman.[40] Such evidence, together with that pertaining to other place-names in the locality, suggests that the town was probably settled in the early Anglian period.[41] An Anglo-Saxon burial ground, discovered during building excavation work on the Greenbank estate in 1876, provides further evidence of settlement in the town by the 6th century.[42] The cemetery, which proved to be one of the largest and richest of its kind to be discovered in the area north of the Tees, was sited on the summit of a hill, occupying the area between what is now Dodds Street and Selbourne Road.[43] It was adjacent to Bondgate, giving rise to speculation that the focal point of the earliest settlement was there, and transferred only later to the central area around the church and market place.[44] Excavation of the burial ground revealed six skeletons of males, females and a child. The graves were aligned west-east, in what later became the standard Christian fashion. However, the site appears to be pre-Christian in origin as grave goods and weapons were present.[45] The grave goods included brooches, a quantity of pins, bronze tweezers, spearheads, two shield bosses and two swords, with the bulk of the finds dating from the later 6th and the early part of the 7th centuries.[46] Several of the objects bore close similarities to Anglian artefacts found in north Lincolnshire and Humberside, suggesting links with early settlers in that part of the country.[47]

The discovery of a ditch during excavations in Feetham's

2. *Bondgate, thought to be the focal point of Darlington's earliest settlement, photographed after the rebuilding of the King's Head, 1890–3.*

field in 1912 has led to speculation that, by the late 9th or early 10th centuries, the settlement at Darlington may have developed into one of the most northerly of the late Anglo-Saxon 'burhs' set up by Alfred the Great as a defence network against the encroachments of the Danes.[48] The evidence for this is flimsy, since the precise findings of the excavation were not recorded.[49] Outlines of the supposed earthwork fortification appeared to fall within the scheme of the town's early street plan.[50] However, whilst there is some evidence that this bore similarities to those of other pre-conquest 'burhs', such street layouts were also common in later planned towns of the 12th century. Given the lack of solid evidence, the notion of Darlington as an Anglo-Saxon 'burh' remains largely hypothetical.[51]

Nevertheless, the discovery of several Anglo-Saxon sculptures in or near St Cuthbert's church suggests that Darlington was in continuous occupation throughout this period.[52] Two cross heads, found during restoration work undertaken in the church in 1862–5,[53] and a decorated slab, now incorporated into the outside south wall of the south transept,[54] have been identified as dating from the later 10th or early 11th centuries. Another sculpture, located in the north wall of the church, dates from slightly earlier in the 10th century.[55] This is of the 'hogback' design, indicating Scandinavian influence[56] and perhaps linking the early settlement more firmly with Scandinavian estate holders such as the Yorkshire nobleman, Styr, the son of Ulf, who reputedly granted Darlington to the See of St Cuthbert in the early 11th century.[57] A sandstone sundial, now located in the church, which was formerly regarded as Anglo-Saxon, is now thought to be of a slightly later date.[58]

The sculptural artefacts and other remains show that there was clearly a church in Darlington long before Bishop Hugh du Puiset founded his in *c.* 1192.[59] The aisleless structure he incorporated in the west end of his building may not have been the first and perhaps was not the only church.[60] Unfortunately, no adequate record survives of the foundations, which were uncovered beneath the present church during 19th-century restoration work and presumed at that time to be Anglo-Saxon, and which may have supplied useful additional evidence.[61] Ditches and a graveyard containing burials of the 11th to the 14th centuries, found west of du Puiset's church, may have been associated with a church on the present site or with another, perhaps earlier, Anglo-Saxon church in the vicinity of the market place.[62]

The fact that a church with burial rights was located in the town at this period lends weight to the view that Darlington was not merely a parochial centre, but had developed into the administrative and economic focal point, or 'chief place', of one Durham's pre-conquest shires.[63] The earliest surviving documentary reference to the town dates from this period and concerns a grant of land made to the newly established see of Durham by one Styr, the son of Ulf. [64] It was by virtue of this grant, made in *c.* 1003, that the bishop of Durham acquired the vill called Dearthingtun, together with its dependent townships and the sac and soc of the same.[65] The landed extent of Darlington's dependencies is not specified. However, Styr's grant does mention other gifts of adjacent lands in Cockerton, Coniscliffe, Haughton-le-Skerne and Little Ketton, which may have formed part of the dependent area, although Haughton-le-Skerne and High Coniscliffe were, or later became, parishes in their own right. Blackwell, Oxenhall, Whessoe, Skerningham and Barmpton may also have been amongst the dependencies.[66]

Darlington's connections with the Cuthbertine community may have pre-dated Styr's grant, although the link is tenuous. The town's geographical position on the main route from Ripon to Durham, combined with the later dedication of its church to St Cuthbert, has given rise to speculation that it may have provided one of the resting places for the saint's body during the wanderings of the monks of Lindisfarne before they finally settled in Durham at the end of the 10th century.[67] The link was perhaps reinforced during the episcopate of William de St. Calais (1080–96), when the secular clergy of the monastery were replaced by the regular order of Benedictines. In order to maintain the dispossessed seculars, colleges of priests were reputedly founded in Darlington and three other localities within the bishopric.[68] Again, however, there is little direct evidence of this and it is only from the time of the episcopate of Bishop du Puiset, whose building work laid the foundations of the medieval town, that the history of Darlington can be charted with confidence.[69]

THE EARLY MEDIEVAL TOWN

By the end of the 12th century, the vill of Darlington, as granted to the bishop of Durham in c. 1003, was subdivided into two entities, the borough of Darlington and the vill of Bondgate.[70] The earliest mention of the borough appears in Boldon Book, Bishop du Puiset's survey of the Durham bishopric estates, compiled in c. 1183.[71] However, the information provided is sparse. Moreover, the original Boldon Book has not survived, with historians being forced to rely upon later medieval copies of the text, the earliest dating from the 13th century. These copies contain material added after the original survey,[72] so that some, if not all, of the detail concerning the borough of Darlington may have been added at a later date.[73] Nevertheless, the borough was certainly in evidence by 1197, when it was mentioned in the pipe roll of 8 Richard I detailing the revenues of the bishopric during the vacancy of the see following du Puiset's death.[74] The market may well have been in existence since at least the time of the conquest, although firm documentary evidence survives only from the 13th century.[75]

Boldon Book does not provide a full account of the numbers and classes of the bishop's tenants. The free tenants of the bishopric, for instance, do not figure largely in the survey.[76] It was concerned primarily with the enumeration of those services, customs and dues that the bishop could expect to draw from the bond and demesne lands which formed the major part of his estates at that time.[77] As such, the borough of Darlington and its burgesses received scant mention, with du Puiset's survey focusing upon the customary (non-freehold) tenures, which were dominant within the vill of Darlington. At this time, the bulk of the land enumerated for the vill of Darlington, some 48 bovates, was held by bond tenants who rendered payments in a combination of cash and services. The number of these is not given; there may have been 48, with each holding one bovate, although 24 seems more likely, given that the usual bond holding comprised two bovates.[78] In Darlington the bovate, or oxgang, was composed of 15 a.[79] This was the usual acreage as given in Boldon Book, although measurements could vary in extent, according to locality and terrain.[80] The services required of the bondmen as a group included mowing the lord's meadow, making and carrying hay, enclosing the lord's courtyard and copse, as well as customary service at the lord's mill. Boldon Book confirms the existence of mills on the Skerne at Darlington, Haughton and Ketton, grouped together under the entry for Darlington and noted as jointly worth 30 marks.[81]

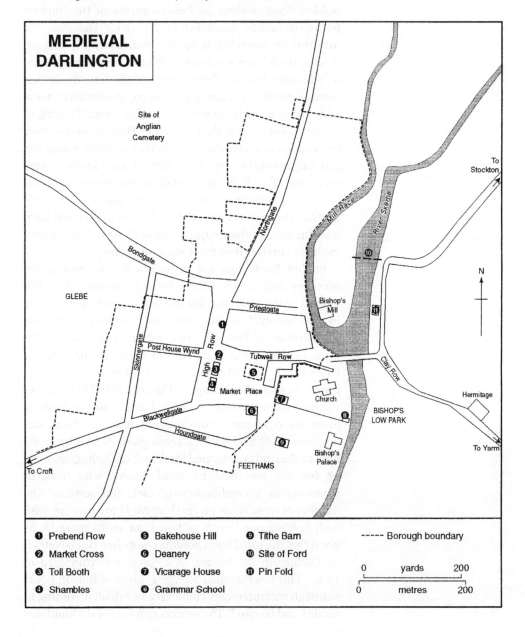

MEDIEVAL DARLINGTON

Site of Anglian Cemetery

To Stockton

Northgate

Mill Race

River Skerne

GLEBE

Bondgate

Priestgate

Bishop's Mill

10

11

N

Skinnergate

Post House Wynd

High Row

❶

Tubwell Row

❷

❸

❺

❹

Market Place

Church

Hermitage

Blackwellgate

❼

❻

❽

BISHOP'S LOW PARK

Houndgate

❾

To Yarm

FEETHAMS

Bishop's Palace

Clay Row

To Croft

❶ Prebend Row	❺ Bakehouse Hill	❾ Tithe Barn
❷ Market Cross	❻ Deanery	❿ Site of Ford
❸ Toll Booth	❼ Vicarage House	⓫ Pin Fold
❹ Shambles	❽ Grammar School	

- - - - - Borough boundary

0   yards   200

0   metres   200

Other classes of customary tenure existed within the vill. Twelve lessees, or *firmarii*, each held one bovate of land, paying the same rent as the bondmen but without other services or obligations. Four cottagers with tofts were also noted in the survey in Darlington, as well as a smith, who held eight acres of land in return for maintaining ironwork on the ploughs of Haughton and carrying out small ironworking tasks within the lord's court. A village official, the pinder, who was the keeper of the village pound, or pinfold, where stray animals were contained, held a further nine acres.[82] Later records indicate that the pinfold, enclosed in the early 19th century by a brick wall of unknown date, was located on the eastern bank of the Skerne in Clay Row.[83] Five other named individuals also held lands within the vill.[84] The tenant of the Manor of Oxenhall, now Oxen-le-field, physically separate from that of Darlington although the property formed an outlying territory of that vill, held one carucate and two cultures of land, including a horse-mill.[85]

It was only at the end of the Darlington entry in Boldon Book that mention of the borough was made, noting only that it was at farm – or leased out – for the sum of £5. It possessed a dyeworks, providing early evidence of the town's cloth industry. It also had a mill and a common bakehouse, the latter feature which, in the bishopric, occurred only in boroughs at this time.[86] It has been suggested that the borough of Darlington, like others in the bishopric, had been founded in order to complement an episcopal palace which had been built in the vicinity. Not only would this have provided a suitable focal point for the provision of foodstuffs, goods and services, but it would also have served to create extra revenue in terms of rents, tolls and market dues.[87] Bishop du Puiset is credited with building the episcopal palace, or manor house, in Darlington in *c.* 1164 and it was certainly in existence by 1183.[88] It is likely that he was also responsible for the creation of the borough, although it seems to have held this status rather by prescription than charter.[89] If, as appears to be the case, Darlington was already a 'place of consequence' by the time of the Norman Conquest, it is hardly surprising that a vigorous and politically ambitious bishop such as du Puiset should seek to impose his influence there more

3. *Schematic plan of the main features of medieval Darlington and their presumed locations, with the borough boundary marked, based on documentary sources.*

effectively.[90] This he did through the enhancement of the town's role within the locality, but also in visible terms, through the building of his episcopal palace and church and the development of the borough.[91]

In administrative terms, Bondgate encompassed those lands within the vill of Darlington that did not fall within the confines of the borough. Included in this was the bishop's palace, together with the episcopal parklands situated on the eastern bank of the Skerne. In topographical terms, Bondgate was the area centred on the two-row settlement, or street, of bond holdings, still known by that name, which led westwards from the north end of High Row towards the vill of Cockerton.[92] To the west, the Tees bounded the township for a short distance. The area lying on the north bank of the river was known as Bathel, now the site of Baydale woods and Baydale beck.[93] Other variations of the name include Baddel, Battle, Bathely and Bathela. The leper hospital of Bathel, later the free chapel of Battlefield, was situated here.[94] The fields of Bathel lay close to Blackwell, and both the Boldon Book and Hatfield's survey included details of the herbage of 'Bathela' with the entry for that township.[95] In 1525, however, an injunction of the palatine chancery decreed that the inhabitants of Bondgate, who were in dispute with the burgesses of Darlington over the use of the common pastures, should have to farm 'a ground called the Battlefield, with the pasture to the same belonging'.[96]

It is impossible to be certain that Bondgate was the original settlement in the locality, with the site of the borough developing alongside it, or whether it was re-planned as a rural settlement adjacent to the borough at the time of the division of the vill.[97] The existence of the Anglian cemetery near Bondgate points to this locality as an early settlement site. Whether it remained the main focus of the town through to the 12th century is unclear, since a later settlement may have grown up around the site of the pre-conquest church. If so, some rationalisation may well have taken place at the time of the borough's creation. Mention in Boldon Book of the existence of old and new villein tenures suggests that some re-planning and relocation had occurred.[98] In terms of layout, the two entities had separate, clear-cut characteristics. The Bondgate site was arranged as a typical vill settlement, with two rows of plots facing a green area. The borough, in contrast, had as its focal point a rectangular market area that was surrounded on three sides by burgage plots and on the fourth by the church and manor house. In common with many boroughs, the market place stood at the junction of the main roads out of the town.[99]

The division of Darlington into the separate entities of the borough and the vill of Bondgate, was clearly defined in Hatfield's survey completed *c.* 1382.[100] The entry for Darlington was headed 'Darlington with Bondgate', although, as in Boldon Book, the borough received scant mention beyond the fact that it was at farm for the sum of £90. This sum was amended at a later date to £93 6s. 8d.[101] The survey did, however, clearly illustrate how patterns of landholding within the township had developed during the two centuries that had elapsed since the compilation of the Boldon Book.

Some holdings had changed little since 1183. The bondlands, for example, were largely unaltered, with the rents, services and labour dues still as those enumerated in Boldon Book. The number of bond holdings had, however, decreased, with only 14 tenants holding a total of 34 bovates.[102] The nine-acre holding of the pinder noted in Boldon Book was still in evidence, although held jointly by the bond tenants of the vill, who rendered 53s. 4d. yearly for the lands and meadows appertaining to this. These lay in Nestfield, Dodmersfeld, Westfield, Ellyng and Polumpole. The first three fields, which lay on the eastern banks of the Skerne, were noted in other records as the common fields of the borough.[103] The meadow identified as Polumpole is now known as Polam. The manor of Oxen-le-field had come into the possession of the Neville family, in whose hands it was to remain until the attainder of the 6th earl of Westmorland in the wake of the Northern Rebellion of 1569.[104]

In other respects, however, major changes had occurred. The period between the later 12th and early 14th centuries was one of considerable growth in County Durham, in terms of the expansion of settlements and increased land cultivation.[105] A considerable number of new holdings was created, with an increase in the number of new freehold tenures as fresh land was taken in from the waste.[106] Another aspect of the expansion was the emergence of a new form of tenure, apparently free in status, which was known as 'exchequer land', since its rents were originally collected by officials of the bishop's central exchequer. Such development had clearly taken place in Darlington during the period of expansion, for Hatfield's survey records the existence of some 35 free tenants and a further 25 tenants who held exchequer land.[107]

The free tenants of the vill held between them a total of 57 parcels of lands and tenements, for which they mostly owed money rents.[108] Unfortunately there is no enumeration of the burgage holdings in the borough. Landmale, as the usual rent for burgages was called, was a perquisite of the farmers of the borough and was not paid directly to the bishop, hence its omission from the survey.[109] Consequently there is little indication of the size of the borough at this time. Nevertheless, the names of some of these lands are still recognisable in the street and estate names of the modern town. They included Le Crosseflat, Bekfield, Cramelbotham, Ravensnab, Hundhawe and Holkerre. Dodmorefeld, Dentensland and Milnerland were all mentioned as lying in the hands of free tenants. Two holdings in the street of Northgate were also identified, as were the meadows called Fyton (Feethams) and Ellyng. The latter, sometimes written as 'Hellyngs' was later known as the Ings, the water meadow of Darlington, which lay at the junction of the Cocker beck and the Skerne to the north of the town.[110] The free tenants also held between them certain other lands. These were known as Calfhous, Swatergate, Elfebankes, Sadberigate, Cokyrtongate, Bathelgate, Duresmgate, Croftgate and Hurthworthgate. Of these, Bathelgate was certainly Blackwellgate, whilst Cokyrtongate seems to have been an alternative name for Bondgate.[111] Others were obviously named after the roads to outlying townships, and were probably situated close to those roads. In the survey, they were described as parcels of the lord's ancient and proper waste, suggesting that these were lands brought under cultivation during the period of expansion.

Yet by the time of Hatfield's survey, in c. 1382, the period of growth and expansion which had characterised the 12th and 13th centuries had given way to one of economic and demographic decline, the legacy of the Black Death and plagues which followed in its wake. Whilst the halmote rolls of the bishopric survive for Darlington ward from 1349, they contain little direct evidence of the impact of the Black Death in the township. The borough did not of course come under the jurisdiction of the halmote. Nevertheless, evidence from nearby townships and vills suggests that the impact of the plague was severe. It was first noticed in the bishopric in the summer of 1349, and had reached Darlington by September. A surviving bailiff's account from the adjacent vill of Coatham Mundeville noted that the epidemic had killed four ploughmen by Michaelmas of that year.[112] Analyses of Durham Priory properties, for which better evidence survives, suggest that other adjacent townships suffered badly in the initial outbreak of the plague. Aycliffe lost between 50 and 59 per cent of its tenants, whilst in the Teesside vills of Billingham and Wolviston, death rates stood at 47 and 45 per cent respectively. The vill of West Thickley, in the western part of Darlington ward, lost all its tenants.[113] Durham as a whole was badly hit by the Black Death and by the subsequent outbreaks of plague. It has been suggested that the county's population was some 45 per cent lower at the end of the 14th century than it had been before the first outbreak of 1349.[114] The records of the bishops' halmotes show that the administration sought to bolster declining revenues by pressurising tenants into taking on additional holdings and other obligations.[115] However, the force of demographic decline was too great. In Darlington and its adjacent vills, developments such as the leasing of the bishop's demesne, the commutation of labour services for cash payments and the incidence of decayed and decreased rents indicated that the locality was suffering the same problems of depopulation as other areas.[116]

THE LATE MEDIEVAL AND EARLY MODERN TOWN

Economic decline and the fall in population which followed the Black Death led to a long period of stagnation in Darlington, as in other parts of the region,[117] with no major new buildings started and no evidence of the town's expansion. Nevertheless, the town's trading life continued to function throughout the period, attracting business from across the region. Indeed, in the late 1530s, the Tudor antiquary, John Leland, on his travels through the county was able to describe Darlington as 'the best market town in the bisshoprick, saving Duresme'.[118] Yet the main characteristics of the mid 16th-century town, as described by Leland, had been in evidence for much of the town's medieval history and would have been equally familiar to visitors travelling through Darlington at any time during the preceding 300 years.

BRIDGE, CHURCH, MANOR AND MILL

The outstanding features noted by Leland were the stone bridge which was 'as I remembre, of 3 arches'; the 'exceding long and fair altare stone' in the collegiate parish church; and the 'praty palace in this toune', which belonged to the bishop of Durham.[119] A market place is recorded from the 13th century.[120] The earliest evidence concerning the bridge dates only from the same period. However the topographical layout of the town suggests that this structure stood upon the site of what had been, from earliest times, the natural crossing point across the Skerne.[121] The construction of the town's most important buildings, the collegiate church of St Cuthbert and the bishop's palace or manor house, was undertaken during the episcopate of Bishop du Puiset, which extended from 1153–95.[122]

Bridge

The bridge over the Skerne can be securely dated to at least the 14th century, and probably earlier. A wardrobe account of Edward I, dated 1299, noted how the sum of 45s. 2d. was paid to Adam de Sutton, bailiff of Darlington, for repairs to a bridge in the town which was to be reinforced in order to bear the weight of carriages transporting provisions and treasure northwards during the king's campaign against the Scots. Nails and planks were used for this operation, suggesting that the bridge was then made largely of wood.[123] Whether this reference was to the Skerne bridge or to that over the Cocker beck at Northgate, on the Durham Road, is not clear. However, a direct reference to the bridge over the Skerne was made in 1343, in the will of Cecilia Underwood, the wife of William de Durham, a leading Darlington merchant. She bequeathed the sum of 13s. 4d. towards the upkeep of the bridge, 'ultra aquam de Skyrryn'.[124] The bridge mentioned in Bishop Hatfield's survey of c. 1382 seems to have been a different one, connecting the Neville properties on either side of the Skerne.[125] By the time of Leland's journey through the town in c. 1538, the bridge was a three-arched structure, made of stone.[126] By the latter part of the 16th century it was in a state of disrepair. From 1575 onwards, bequests for repairs to the bridge, providing sums ranging from 4d. to 2s. 6d., appeared in the wills of 10 Darlington testators, and in 1587 a rate of 2d. in the pound was levied, raising £62 2s. 8d. to repair the bridge, although the extent of any work undertaken at this time is not known.[127] However, by 1615, Darlington bridge was amongst a number of Durham bridges noted in an inquiry by the Durham Justices of the Peace as 'very ruinous and in need of repair for wheeled traffic'.[128] At this stage the bridge was not sufficiently wide to permit travellers a dry passage across its full extent. Indeed, even in the 18th century the river was wider and more shallow than it later became, forming as a consequence 'a vast morass along its banks on the eastern side'.[129] As a result, a causeway was constructed, leading eastwards from the river up to the Hermitage, near to what is now Bank Top.[130] Matthew Lambert, a cordwainer who died in 1603 and Michael Jeffrayson, a tanner, who died in 1612, left sums of money, 5s. and 3s. 4d. respectively, to 'the mending of the carswe going to the Armytage'.[131]

Church

Immediately to the south of the bridge lay the parish church of St Cuthbert, one of the most important in the diocese. The property of the bishop and served by a college of priests, comprising the bishop's deputy or vicar and four prebendaries, it was of exceptional size and architectural grandeur.[132] Its foundation probably dates to the closing years of the episcopate of du Puiset, and belongs to a group of ambitious buildings – and the first in early Gothic style – commissioned by the bishop. The chronicler Geoffrey of Coldingham, writing before 1214, indicated that building was in progress by 1192, but comparison with the stylistic

4. THE PARISH CHURCH OF ST CUTHBERT

(a). *From the south west c. 1774 or earlier*

The large cruciform church begun c. 1192 by Hugh du Puiset was built in local sandstone to a design of great dignity. Unity is established by the equal height of the four tall arms and by the syncopated rhythm of blind wall arcade and lancet windows. The only major additions to the original design were made in the 14th century when the tower was raised above the level of the aisle roofs and a spire (at first perhaps of timber) was built. The aisles were also raised and traceried windows inserted then. This view shows the church before extensive restoration in the 1860s. The scar of the high medieval roofs can be seen above those of c. 1547–53 (chancel) and 1707 (nave and transepts) and the outline of the south doorway over the 17th- or 18th-century porch. The embattled parapets were added to the nave in 1707 and to the tower in 1750 after a lightning strike.

(b). *Plan in 1907*

Although the majority of the fabric is late 12th and 13th century, du Puiset incorporated an aisleless church of unknown date into the west end, as the thicker walling on this plan suggests. That church may have still been in use as rebuilding began to its east, only to be replaced by an aisled nave in the second quarter of the 13th century, after the chancel, crossing and at least part of north transept had been built. The choir stalls seem to have sealed off a door to a previous vestry on the north side of the chancel; it may have been replaced by the present south one c. 1500. South of it is the choir vestry added in the 19th century.

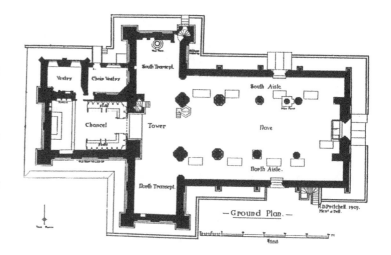

— Ground Plan. —

(c). *Interior looking south from the crossing.*

The eastern part of the interior, including the first bay of the nave, is more elaborate than the west end and the chancel and the south transept (background centre) *have the richest decoration. The pulpitum* (foreground bottom left) *may have been inserted between the east crossing piers for extra support when the stone spire was built in the 14th century. The organ* (foreground top left) *was installed in 1879, after an extensive restoration by Sir G. G. Scott in 1862–5.*

traits of du Puiset's other buildings and the consistent use of lancets and of ornament characteristic of the transition between the Romanesque and early Gothic styles suggests that work probably began on its east end in the 1180s and that the whole church was complete by 1250.[133] The west end, executed in a plainer style, seems to have incorporated the remains of an earlier aisleless church.[134] The original structure was relatively little altered in the succeeding centuries, though a major addition – a taller tower with a spire – was made in the 14th century, perhaps necessitating the construction between 1381 and c. 1407 of the stone screen (pulpitum) to brace the crossing and enable it to carry the extra weight, and the strengthening of the crossing piers. [135] Other 14th-century work was more superficial: the raising of the aisle walls and the insertion of traceried windows in them, and the provision of sedilia, the three 'bold and beautiful' stone seats for clergy, situated on the south side of the chancel.[136] The chancel continued to be embellished by successive bishops during the 15th century, with stalls for the prebends bearing the insignia of Thomas Langley, bishop of Durham, 1406–37,[137] with an Easter sepulchre, created in the north wall of the chancel perhaps during the episcopate of Robert Neville (1438–57),[138] and with a large south vestry c. 1500.[139] By the 16th century the high altar was covered with an 'exceeding long and fair altare stone' which was made of black marble, spotted with white.[140] Any medieval character lost during the 17th and 18th centuries was restored in the 19th and 20th, chiefly in the 1860s by J. P. Pritchett (chancel) and Sir G. G. Scott (the rest).[141]

A central feature of late medieval religious devotion was the preoccupation with provisions for the redemption of the soul and its relief from the pains of Purgatory. The proliferation of chantries, set up to endow masses for the souls of the founder and other nominated individuals, bore witness to this concern.[142] There were two chantries within the church of St Cuthbert.[143] That dedicated to the Blessed Virgin Mary, founded in the early 13th century, received mention in Hatfield's survey of c. 1382. Its later history is unclear. In the Chantry Commissioners' return of 1548, its revenues were entered with those of the chantry of St James, which was situated in the bishop's manor house.[144] The chantry of All Saints, which stood in the north transept of the church, was founded by Robert Marshall, clerk, in order to find a priest to pray for his soul and to maintain the free grammar school of Darlington. A foundation date of 1530 has been suggested for this, although the precise date is unclear. Following the dissolution of the chantry in 1548, its possessions were used to endow Darlington grammar school.[145] The grammar school, which was re-founded in 1563, was situated in the south-east corner of the churchyard, adjacent to the River Skerne. The school remained on this site until 1813, when the burial ground was extended. A new building was subsequently erected to the south of the churchyard.[146]

In 1439, Bishop Robert Neville revised the church's collegiate constitution, ordaining that the vicar should thereafter enjoy the title of dean. An extra prebend was created in order to support his enhanced status.[147] As part of his revised endowment, the newly created dean was allowed to retain his 'ancient manse', the medieval vicarage, which had been granted to the church in 1309 by charter of Bishop Bek. By the terms of this grant the vicar held one messuage together with its appurtenances, which stood near to the gate of the bishop's manor house, to the south west of the church. Included in the grant was an adjacent vennel that led to the well in Houndgate. In 1312, the vicar was given the further grant for life of a flat of land between the manor house and the vicarage. This extended from the gate of the manor down to the meadow of 'Fycton', as Feethams was then known.[148] At some point in the 15th century a new and grander residence was constructed for the use of the dean. The old vicarage survived to become the residence of the curates of the living. Robert Hope, curate from 1622–40, resided there but it had fallen out of use by 1712.[149]

Manor

To the south of the church and skirting the banks of the river beyond the borough boundaries, lay the bishop's palace, or manor house. The episcopal manor house, a long, low building made of stone,[150] stood within parklands that had reputedly been enclosed during the episcopate of Bishop Bek (1283–1311),[151] with the whole enclosure being known as the Hallgarth.[152] The chantry of St James was attached to the building.[153] Within the enclosure was the house of the janitor and keeper of the manor, who also held the position of bailiff of the bailiwick of the manor of Darlington and often that of bailiff of Coatham Mundeville, whose role was to oversee the management of the bishop's estates within the locality. The existence of this official is noted as early as 1183. In Boldon Book, mention is made of one Adam de Selby, the farmer of the demesne in Little Haughton, who was charged with keeping the house and the court of the bishop in Darlington. In return for this, de Selby held the piece of arable land called Hacdale, situated in the fields of Darlington on the eastern side of the river, adjacent to the hall.[154] Beyond the confines of the manor house, across the river on the eastern bank of the Skerne, lay the episcopal parklands that later became known as the High and Low parks. These encompassed the modern Lakeside and Parkgate, extending towards Neasham Road to the east.[155] The parklands, which included both meadow and pasture, had been let to tenants from an early stage. A lease of 1391, for instance, notes the granting of the lord's park for the term of three years. The practice of leasing these lands continued throughout the period and beyond. In the parliamentary survey of the bishopric, made in 1647, the High and Low parks, together with the meadow of Feethams, were leased for the sum of £10 13s. 4d. a year with the improved rent given as £40.[156]

The manor house, by then converted into the town's poor-house, was described in the mid 19th century by Longstaffe. The building had been extensively altered so that the precise plan of the early mansion was impossible to determine. Nevertheless, Longstaffe came across several medieval features such as the 'neat little early English arch . . . the remnant of [du Puiset's] work' which had once formed the entrance to a long arched passage leading reputedly to the dungeon. Upstairs he saw the remains of the banqueting room, which retained its traceried windows and an early stone fireplace. The walls of the upper chamber were constructed of rushes and plaster.[157] To the outside, Longstaffe noted three surviving Norman lights in the eastern gable dating, he suggested, from c. 1160, and a high square chimney which retained 'an early corbel table, formed of minute arches'.[158]

5. *The bishop's palace or manor house in the late 18th century.*

The manor house was not in permanent occupation, although it was probably used on a regular basis by the bishop's officials and by prominent visitors to the town as well as by the bishop himself when he was in, or travelling through, the locality. The situation of the town, on the main northern route between York and Durham and thence to Scotland, ensured that Darlington received its fair complement of important visitors. King John passed through the town on five occasions between 1209 and 1216.[159] Henry III visited in 1227.[160] During the Anglo-Scottish wars of the later 13th and early 14th centuries, the town became a frequent halting place for royal armies. Edward I came to the town in 1292 and 1302. His grandson, Edward III, visited Darlington in 1335 and 1338.[161] The manor house was probably the only appropriate lodging within the vicinity capable of accommodating such visitors. Margaret Tudor, daughter of Henry VII, certainly spent a night there on her journey north to marry the Scottish king, James IV, in 1503.[162] Other visitors to the manor house may have included members of the Council of the North, which met in Darlington in 1538, and the lieutenants-general appointed to command the royal armies, for whom Darlington became a base during the Anglo-Scottish wars of the early 1540s.[163]

During the times it was unoccupied, the manor house, or at least part of it, appears to have been let to tenants. An account of Thomas Popely, bailiff of the manor of Darlington, dated 1457–8, notes a rent of 6s. 8d. for one stable and one chamber called 'Whitechaumber' within the manor of Derlyngton. The rent of this had not been received that year because it was lying in the hands of the lord for want of a tenant.[164] In 1564 the inventory of the Darlington dairyman, Edward Acrige, provided a description of a dwelling which was possibly the manor house. Two of the rooms mentioned therein were noted as chambers belonging, respectively, to 'the lord' and 'the steward'.[165] By this time the manor house may have been sliding towards that 'state of complete dilapidation' from which it was rescued by Bishop Cosin who oversaw its restoration in 1668.[166]

Deanery

The deanery, which stood in the south-eastern corner of the market place, was also prominent.[167] It was probably constructed at some point in the 15th century, following the reorganisation of the church's collegiate constitution, but evidence from the 16th century suggests that the deans of Darlington were often non-resident. A visitation of the church, undertaken in 1501, noted how the dean, Ralph Lepton, 'does not reside, but is in the service of the bishop'.[168] Whether the property was let to tenants at this time is not clear but it was certainly farmed out by the last incumbent of the living, Cuthbert Marshall. He, at some point in the 1530s, granted the lease of the deanery to William Wytham, who had been appointed bailiff of the borough of Darlington in 1528–9 by Cardinal Wolsey.[169] By 1538, Marshall was seeking to re-occupy the premises with the result that the lease became a matter of dispute between the two men. Wytham, a gentleman usher of the King's Chamber, sought the support of his royal master in the

6. *The deanery in the late 18th century*

dispute. Marshall, who received a communication from the king on the subject, subsequently laid out the details of his complaint in a letter to the king's chief minister, Thomas Cromwell.[170] At this time the deanery was valued at £36 8s., although Wytham was paying an annual rent of only £20 plus £8 in corn.[171] From Marshall's correspondence on the subject it seems that the property was in need of repair. A survey of 1548 noted that the deanery was unoccupied.[172] It was in this year that the Chantry Commissioners undertook their survey in Durham, and the collegiate church was subsequently dissolved.[173] Its landed possessions and tithes then passed into the hands of the Crown, with only a small stipend being reserved for a vicar and curate.[174] A 21-year lease of the site of the deanery, together with the dean's prebend and tithes, was granted to Thomas Windsor in 1548.[175] In 1564 a grant of the reversion of the deanery, upon the expiration of Windsor's lease, was made to Thomas Brickwell, and renewed in 1567.[176] At some earlier stage, however, the deanery lease seems to have passed into the hands of Henry, 5th earl of Westmorland, since by his will dated 1564 he left this to his stepdaughter, Margaret, the daughter of Sir Henry Gascoigne of Ravensworth.[177] The inventory of her possessions within the bishopric, made after her death in 1567, makes mention also of the grant made to her by the earl of the lease of Oxen-le-field.[178] Margaret Gascoigne died intestate, and her rights and properties descended to her brother Thomas, who became embroiled in a dispute with Charles, 6th earl of Westmorland, over these properties.[179] The earl apparently retained control since Oxen-le-field passed into the hands of the Crown following Westmorland's attainder for his part in the Northern Rising of 1569. In 1574 Thomas Brickwell, together with one Andrew Palmer, acquired Oxen-le-field, which was held by the fortieth part of a knight's fee.[180] By this time, the lease of the deanery had also passed into Brickwell's hands, in accordance with the terms of his grant.[181] A Crown survey of the deanery in 1570–1 gave details of a 'mansion house or burgage in Darlington' which comprised a hall, parlour, buttery, great chamber over the parlour, two little chambers and a low gallery.[182] In the late 18th century it was depicted with an asymmetrical hall and symmetrical cross-wings in a conventional H-plan, and had a timber-framed first floor, perhaps somewhat tidied up, above a lower storey of stone.[183] In addition to the deanery and the glebe land belonging to this, Brickwell's grant specified other profits including the tithes of corn and hay in Darlington, Cockerton, Blackwell and Archdeacon Newton, together with the property in that part of the borough known as Prebend Row.[184] Another Crown survey of 1580 noted that the holding in Prebend Row comprised 'nine cote houses and barns in Priestgate Street'.[185] Brickwell, a captain in the garrison at Berwick, was still the farmer of the deanery at the time of the 1580 survey and it remained in his possession up to the time of his death in 1586.[186]

Thomas Brickwell's will and inventory, dated 1586, noted that he had left Henry Brickwell, his nephew, some of the wool and hangings of 'the mansion house of the deanery of Darlington'. However, he bequeathed his letters patent of the deanery and prebends to other beneficiaries. These were Elizabeth Nelson, Brickwell's sister, and Richard Prescot, another of his nephews. Elizabeth, noted as a singlewoman, was bound by the terms of the bequest to take the advice of Henry Brickwell and one William Bower 'touchinge the bestowing of hirself in marriage'. If she failed to do this, she would be 'void' of any benefits of the letters patent.[187] It is not clear whether Henry Brickwell eventually acquired the lease of the deanery after his uncle's death. The inventory of his residence, made in February 1590 after Henry's death, provides extensive details of a spacious, extremely well-furnished property. This may well have been the deanery although the property mentioned here does appear to be rather larger than that described in the sparse Crown survey of 1570–1.[188] Whilst no records survive of the transaction, it seems likely that the deanery was later sold to two Yorkshiremen, Sir Thomas Crompton of Driffield and Robert Crompton of Skerne. In 1619 Sir Thomas's daughter and heiress, Katherine, together with her husband, Sir Thomas Lyttelton of Frankley, Worcestershire, sold the property to Sir Richard Darley of Buttercrambe, and his brother Thomas, of Halnaby, both in Yorkshire. This sale included the site of the deanery, together with eight oxgangs of land in the parish of Darlington, and their tithes and profits. However it excluded the corn and hay tithes of the

7. *The glebe land, part of the deanery possessions, ran west from Skinnergate to Carmel Road, bounded on the north by lanes later called Woodland and Milbank Roads, and to the south by Coniscliffe Lane and the Black Path, later Cleveland Terrace. The Glebe farm is pictured on the still undeveloped Milbank Road in 1930.*

towns of Cockerton, Newton and Blackwell and the houses called Prebend Rowe, all of which had previously been attached to the property.[189] The Fletcher family later acquired the deanery property. A deed of 1634 notes the bargain and sale of a burgage in South Row, between Richard Fletcher's tenement called the deanery on the east and Oswald Fawcet's tenement on the west. By 1640, however, the deanery was in the hands of the Vanes.[190]

Mill

Darlington's 'ancient water corn mill', commonly called the bishop's mill,[191] was certainly in existence by the end of the 12th century, on the west bank of the Skerne, north of the church and the stone bridge. The eastern boundary of the borough followed precisely the meandering course of the mill race, confirming that there was a mill before the borough's foundation.[192] The mills of Darlington, Haughton and Blackwell, mentioned in the Boldon Book, had been let to the borough freeholders by 1382.[193] In the later middle ages there was only one mill in the town itself.[194] An episcopal commission of 1586 decreed that a bridge, sufficiently wide for carts to pass over, should be made over the mill dam at the north end of Northgate.[195] This was to be maintained by the tenants of Bondgate, an obligation that gave rise to numerous disputes over the years.[196] By 1634, two mills were in existence in the town. According to a decree enrolled in the Palatine Chancery in that year, the burgesses of the town, the free tenants of the manor and the customary tenants of Bondgate and Cockerton were all bound to grind their grain at the bishop's mills.[197]

THE MARKET PLACE AND STREETS

The market place stood to the west of the church, sloping up towards the Head Row, or High Row, which formed its western extent. Occupying a dominant position in the market place were the tollbooth and the market cross. An early mention of the market cross occurred in 1313 when the bishop issued a proclamation banning an unlicensed joust that had been arranged in the town. It was ordered that this be read out before the cross, in full market, on the following Monday.[198] The tollbooth, the focal point of the market place, was the principal administrative centre in the town. Here the bishop's officials and the burgesses met to convene the courts that controlled many aspects of social and economic life in Darlington. Here, too, all aspects of marketing and trade were supervised. The tollbooth was mentioned in Hatfield's survey of c. 1382 but it had probably long been in existence by that time. An account roll of 1459–60 noted how the old building had been completely demolished and rebuilt during the episcopate of Thomas Langley (1406–37).[199] The tollbooth was a large, two-storey structure measuring some 22 yards by eight yards.[200] The courthouse which occupied the upper part was reached via a row of external steps. The ground floor comprised a dozen or so shops or workshops, together with the town gaol and the granary. In Hatfield's survey, two men, John Teesdale and William Hutton, between them paid 10s. a year for the farm of four stalls under the tollbooth, whilst in 1434 a mercer, John Ashbey, was noted as holding a shop there.[201] In the stagnant economic climate of the later 15th century the building fell into disrepair. The borough bailiffs' accounts of that period indicate that it was in state of near dereliction, with its shops continually in and out of tenure and the granary unoccupied due to the poor repair of the building.[202] By the mid 16th century, however, there were signs of improvement. A bill of repairs from 1514 notes the employment for 20 days of a tiler and a mason, with further payment made to bring in two wagons of slate from Auckland to Darlington. An account of 1541 details payments to plumbers for repairs to the leads and porch, whilst another dated 1588 notes payments for the hewing and setting up of two pairs of spars for the gable end.[203] This evidence points to a building of stone and timber construction. The foundations and lower courses of substantial buildings were often made of stone, with the main structure of timber, a pattern common in Durham city and probably the case here.[204] The steps leading to the upper storey were probably also of stone. The employment of a tiler in 1514 indicates that the roof was tiled in slate. Tilers also worked with bricks, which became increasingly common as an infill for timber-framed houses in the 15th century. However, the mention of slates in the account, coupled with the lack of any reference to bricks, suggests that the tiler was engaged in roof tiling.[205]

Close by the tollbooth stood the pillory and stocks.[206] The borough bailiffs' accounts of the period refer to a shop situated 'under the pillory in the market place of Derlyngton'.[207] Malefactors were usually taken to Durham as the bishop had no right of gallows in Darlington, although executions were carried out in the town on occasion. Following the rebellion of the northern earls in 1569, 41 condemned rebels were executed at Darlington. These included 16 townsmen and 23 constables of Darlington ward.[208] Another execution took place in the town in 1594 when George Swalwell, a Catholic priest who had been born in the town, was hanged, drawn and quartered for high treason. The execution took place in the market place, and according to tradition his remains were buried in the 'baker's dunghill' on Bakehouse Hill.[209]

Later records note the existence of the shambles, the trading centre of the town's butchers, which was situated in the market place, at the southern end of the tollbooth.[210] There is no reference to this building in the medieval period, although the existence of rents in kind, called 'shamelhire', which were paid to the bishop by certain butchers, suggests that trading premises of this nature were probably in existence.[211] Also situated in the market place were the common forge and the bakehouse, on the site known as Bakehouse Hill.[212] This was indeed on an incline, although the area was levelled during alterations made around the beginning of the 20th century.[213] Early mention of the bakehouse comes in Boldon Book, with further reference in Hatfield's survey.[214] The bakehouse was leased with the borough by 1183 and remained part of the borough farm throughout the medieval period. As such, it appeared in the accounts of the borough bailiff, who was responsible for the collection of its annual farm.[215] By the early 16th century the building was unoccupied and in a state of disrepair, although by 1557 it was again in the hands of tenants.[216] One obligation of the tenants of Bondgate, Cockerton and Blackwell was to carry lead, wood, lime and stone for the repair of the bishop's palace, the tollbooth, the bakehouse and the mills [217] This custom seems from earliest times to have been a focus of continued dispute.[218] In later years, the tenurial status of Bakehouse Hill was also the subject of conflict between the bishop and his tenants. In 1382,

Hatfield's survey had noted the existence of a tenement there called Pennes Place, which lay adjacent to the bakehouse. This property was designated as exchequer land, suggesting that the bishop had retained immediate control of at least part of Bakehouse Hill at that time.[219] At some point, part of the site was granted as copyhold, which returned it to the direct control of the bishop and out of the hands of the borough freeholders, who remained insistent that the bishop was encroaching upon their freehold rights and privileges. The issue remained one of contention, to the extent that in 1741 the grand jury of the borough court was still declaring its displeasure at the encroachment upon the rights and liberties of borough freeholders.[220] The bishop retained his control, however, since Surtees, writing in the 1820s, mentioned the continued existence of copyhold houses on Bakehouse Hill.[221]

The market place was surrounded on three sides by the streets of the borough, with the church making the fourth

8. *Post House Wynd, the vennel connecting High Row with Skinnergate.*

side of the rectangle. High Row formed the western extent, with Skinnergate, as now, running behind and parallel; the two were connected by the vennel now called Post House Wynd but known in the medieval period, as 'Le Chares'. A demise of 1447 recorded the grant of a burgage and six acres of land lying adjacent to the vennel called 'Chare'. The meadow named in the accounts as Charegarth may have been associated with this locality.[222] Northgate adjoined the northern end of High Row, while to the south Blackwellgate ran downwards to the east and was connected to Feethams Field by Houndgate, which formed the southern row of the borough. This southern extent was the earliest area of settlement in the vicinity. It was probably in existence before the creation of the borough since an excavation in Houndgate unearthed pottery dating from the 11th century onwards. It has been suggested that this may have been the site of a seigneurial residence which pre-dated Bishop du Puiset's palace. The excavation, however, found no evidence on the south side of stratification or other features from the medieval period. It has been suggested that the south side of the street remained in the town fields, beyond the confines of the borough boundary, until the expansion of the town in the 19th century.[223] The earliest mention of Houndgate occurs in the charter of Bishop Bek dated *c.* 1297, which detailed the grant of land to the vicarage, and which included mention of the vennel leading from the gate of the bishop's palace to the well in 'Hundgate'.[224] The nine-acre meadow of 'Fycton' (Feethams), lying beyond the bounds of the borough, but adjacent to the market place, the palace and Houndgate, was first mentioned in 1312 and appeared thereafter in Bishop Hatfield's survey of *c.* 1382.[225] A medieval tithe barn once occupied part of this site.[226]

A 14th-century reference to a messuage in Houndgate appears in the Clervaux chartulary, a collection of 14th- and 15th-century charters relating to property in Darlington and elsewhere, which refers also to other streets within the borough.[227] The earliest reference to Blackwellgate dates from the early 14th century. Mention of 'Borowerawe', as High Row or the Head Row was originally known, appears in a late 14th-century charter, as does Northgate. Skinnergate, which may also have been the street referred to in early charters as 'Behindgarthes', dates from the same period.[228]

Tubwell Row, which was formerly known as 'Le Wellgate' or 'Briggate', formed the northern side of the market place and provided the access road to the bridge. This street was certainly in evidence by the mid 15th century. In 1444–5, the 2nd earl of Westmorland, who held three burgages there, granted one of these to Thomas Bichborne at an annual rent of 3s. 4d.[229] As its name suggests, Tubwell Row was the location of one of the two main wells of the town, the other being in Skinnergate. From the early 17th century and probably earlier, two overseers were appointed annually in the borough court to supervise the maintenance of each of these wells.[230] Prebend Row, leading into Northgate, together with Priestgate, running parallel with Tubwell Row, were so named as a result of their being included amongst the possessions of the prebend of Darlington. Prebend Row was leased along with the deanery, following the dissolution of the collegiate church.[231] Priestgate may have originated as a vennel connecting the properties of Prebend Row and Northgate, developing later into an access street for houses built behind the frontages of Prebend Row and Tubwell Row.[232]

Also on the east bank of the river lay Clay Row, the eastern part of which was at some early stage incorporated into the borough.[233] References in the halmote court records indicate that the remainder lay within the manor of Bondgate.[234] To the south end of Clay Row stood the property known as the Hermitage. Whether this was once the site of a hermitage is not known, although at one time the bishopric had a large number of such establishments.[235] By the mid 15th century, however, the property was being used for more practical purposes, with an account of 1459–60 noting its alternative name of 'Swynhirdesplace'.[236]

THE HOUSES OF THE TOWN

Within the borough, the burgages were probably grouped around the market place. Such properties were usually rectangular with the narrower side facing onto the street and of varying measurements. A study of burgages in Alnwick, for example, has shown that these were generally between 475 and 580 feet long, and between 14 and 64 feet wide.[237] The few details pertaining to Darlington burgage sizes surviving in the Clervaux chartulary suggest a variety of shapes and measurements. A burgage in 'Behindgarths' was square in shape, being 56 feet in both length and breadth. Another, in an unnamed street, was 31 feet long and 22 feet wide, whilst a third measured 152 feet in length and eight feet in breadth.[238] The small frontage of the latter suggests this may have been in the most commercially desirable part of the borough. This was the case in the city of Durham where long thin plots, arranged in a 'herringbone' pattern, were discernable in the outer boroughs. Nearer the commercial centre, however, plots were smaller. One central burgage, for example, measured 48 feet in length but only eight feet in width.[239]

The number of medieval burgage properties is difficult to estimate. Hatfield's survey, which does provide details of burgage tenures in the borough of Stockton, does not enumerate those of Darlington. What is clear from the evidence is that a substantial number of Darlington burgages were concentrated in the hands of a few prominent landed families.[240] In 1422, Ralph Eure, the head of a prominent Durham gentry family, died seized of an unspecified number of burgages in the town. One of these was situated on 'le bururawe'.[241] Ralph Neville, the 1st earl of Westmorland, who died in 1426, was seized of 24 burgages in Darlington.[242] A surviving 15th-century rental, of unknown origin, details another 14 burgage properties, although these may have been part of the Neville holding in the town.[243] The Clervaux family held a number of burgages in the 'Borowerawe', Houndgate, Blackwellgate and Skinnergate, although the precise number of these is difficult to ascertain from the evidence. These properties, most of which would have been leased to tenants, were probably divided up, although the 15th-century rental which enumerated such tenants made no mention of partial holdings. Nevertheless, the sub-division of such properties was commonplace. In the city of Durham at this time, changes of internal property boundaries were frequent. Some holdings were halved or even quartered whilst others were absorbed into adjacent properties.[244] A similar state of affairs existed in the town of Stockton, where in 1382 holdings of halves and quarter parts of burgages were in evidence.[245]

An even greater division of holdings may have occurred in the 16th century at a time of rising population. In 1563 an ecclesiastical census of households revealed that there were 366 households in the parish of Darlington.[246] Since the outlying vills of the parish – Archdeacon Newton, Blackwell and Cockerton – remained far less populous throughout the period and beyond, it seems likely that the bulk of the households enumerated were in Darlington, although the distribution of households between the borough and Bondgate is impossible to determine.[247]

The properties of the town varied in size and quality. One or two surviving examples of medieval buildings have been identified within the vicinity of Darlington. The west part of Butler House, Haughton-le-Skerne, is of an early to mid 15th-century construction. In its original form this would have been a substantial two-storey building of rendered stone. Surviving medieval features include a two-light stone traceried window, a lancet window and two further windows with cusped heads.[248] Buildings of this quality were not common; most houses would have been timber-framed infilled wattle and daub, and with thatched roofs.[249] Thatch seems to have been in use until well beyond the medieval period.[250] Two cruck-framed buildings have survived into modern times in the locality, indicating that this may have been a usual method of construction. One of these, Field House Farm, is situated in the Carmel Road area of Darlington.[251] A pair of two-storey cruck-framed cottages were also identified in Cockerton, although these have since been demolished.[252]

Layouts of properties varied according to the wealth and trading requirements of the occupier. In 1549 Ralph Colling, a tanner, occupied a house in Tubwell Row which adjoined the river and comprised, in addition to the house, a tan-house with an adjoining garden, a vault, a cellar or shop, a garth called Cherry Garth, and two lime pits.[253] The inn occupied by Christopher Dale, who died in 1570, was a two-storey building with a stable attached. On the ground floor there was a large hall, a buttery and a kitchen. The upper rooms were clearly furnished to accommodate a number of guests. Above the hall was a parlour, which boasted a 'litle iron chymnay', 'two standyng beddes and 'a trindell [truckle] bed furnished with a [feather] bed and bolster'. Another chamber, which held two more beds, also stood over the hall. The 'newe' chamber held a further four beds, all furnished. The 'littell chamber' held two beds for men servants while 'the lofte benethe the doores' accommodated two women servants.[254]

Evidence of a far wealthier establishment is drawn from the inventory of Henry Brickwell, who died in 1590. He was the nephew of Captain Thomas Brickwell, the farmer of the deanery.[255] It is not clear whether Henry Brickwell inherited the deanery lease from his uncle, but the description fits a property that was certainly grand enough to have been the deanery. It comprised, on the ground floor, a dining parlour that held numerous pieces of furniture as well as several carpets, fifteen cushions and 'painted clothes of anticke work'. This room, together with one of the bedchambers, also contained an iron chimney. On the ground floor also stood a hall, buttery, pantry, kitchen and brew house. On the first floor there were five chambers, one of which was the great chamber, containing mainly bedroom furniture and furnishings. A second floor garret served as the servants' quarters. Outside the building was a stable, which housed several horses and cows. A garth in the 'backsyde' held 'one pece of a haystack, together with some poultry, a peacock and peahen'. In the barn were quantities of grain, beans and peas as well as various farming implements and a little iron-bound cart.[256]

THE FIRE OF 1585

The deanery was one of the few buildings in the town to escape the great fire of 1585. A pamphlet published in 1585 entitled *Lamentable Newes from the Towne of Darnton* provides evidence concerning what proved to be a major disaster within the late 16th-century town. A 'most fierce and terrible fire' swept through the town on 7 May 1585. According to the pamphlet, some 273 houses were destroyed in the blaze, amongst them 'the most fairest houses in the Towne'.[257] It seems that the fire gutted the houses along High Row and Skinnergate, destroying the 'chiefe mercers houses' where highly combustible commodities such as pitch, tar, flax and gunpowder were stored. Its flames were fanned by the 'boisterous' wind and it spread a quarter of mile, firing other houses in its path. The houses were clearly crowded closely together since 'one house was fired by the heate of another' and all were beyond recovery within two hours. The speed with which these properties burned suggests that they were constructed primarily of wood. The house of the Eure family, noted as one of the fairest in the town, was completely destroyed, indicating that even the more substantial properties may have been constructed of timber. This was perhaps the same burgage on 'le bururawe' which was mentioned in the charter of 1417.[258] Other wealthy townsmen suffered considerable losses. The merchant Francis Oswell reputedly lost goods to the value of £1,000 in the blaze. The wives of Richard Stanton and John Johnson, both wealthy merchants, were lying in childbed and were carried from their burning houses 'otherwise they had beene both burned in their beds'. The situation was exacerbated by a drought which had depleted the town's wells so that the inhabitants were forced to run down to the river for water. Many tried to quench the blaze with the nearest liquids to hand, throwing beer, ale and milk on to the flames. Barns, stables, trees, hay, corn, wood and livestock were also destroyed in the fire, which caused damage reputed to be in the region of £20,000.

A memorandum in the State Papers confirming the devastation caused by the fire probably inspired the pamphlet and was based upon the suggestions of Captain Brickwell, the farmer of the Darlington deanery. [259] It outlines a series of measures to be taken for the relief of 'the poor distressed people of Darlington' and records that some 800 persons had been left without lodgings or maintenance. Many of these had been forced to take refuge in the barns of the outlying villages but would soon have to be removed since it was almost harvest time.[260] The measures suggested for the acquisition of building materials included the issuing of a warrant to the bishop of Durham for 1,000 trees out of his woods and parks, at the most reasonable price possible; a similar warrant to the dean of Durham for 500 trees; and a warrant for permission to obtain stones in the common quarries. The emphasis on timber suggests that this remained the most common building material.[261]

Undoubtedly the pamphlet exaggerated the scale and cost of the damage in order to generate the maximum support for the rebuilding programme. The 273 houses reputedly lost in the fire probably did bear some relation to the number of households enumerated in the 1563 census. The writer may well have been aware of the census figures and used these to emphasise the large-scale nature of the disaster. Yet the town's entire housing stock was not destroyed. Indeed, no mention of the disaster appears in the episcopal accounts or the halmote court records, suggesting that little damage may have been done beyond the confines of the borough. The borough records themselves, which presumably carried some account of the devastation, do not survive for this period. Nevertheless the extent of devastation was such that the majority of the town's medieval buildings were destroyed. The fate of the tollbooth and the market buildings is unknown, although the main public buildings – the church, the episcopal manor house and the deanery – clustered in the south-eastern corner of the market place, all survived.

The town had long functioned as a staging post for travellers passing to and from the north. Indeed, early mention of hostelry in Darlington occurred in a case brought before the Durham Court of Pleas, in 1390–1, by the prior of Brinkburn and John de Stockton, a fellow monk, who sued John de Acle for goods worth £10 which had been stolen from Stockton whilst he had been lodging with Acle in the town.[262] By the later 16th century, the town apparently boasted a considerable number of inns and hostelries and many of these were destroyed in the blaze. The 1585 pamphlet noted that, before the fire, Darlington was 'a towne of good harbour for all travellers to Barwicke or from thence to London'. Afterwards, the damage was so great that the town was, 'not able to receive or entertaine the twentieth part of the passengers which heretofore it hath received'.[263]

The great fire of Darlington was remembered long after the event. The cleric and astrologer, John Vaux, who had been born and raised in Great Burdon, considered it of sufficient importance to be included in the local chronology of momentous events that appeared in his almanac, published in 1628.[264] Although rebuilding took place within the ancient street plans, nevertheless the character of the medieval town had to a large extent been destroyed in the blaze.

2. THE GROWTH OF A MARKET TOWN, 1600–1800

EXTENT OF THE TOWN

Rebuilding started soon after the fire of 1585, and was carried out within the framework of the medieval street pattern. This is confirmed by the first surviving topographical survey of 17th-century Darlington, the schedule of St. Paul's Rents for 1630–2. Although these rents were payable to the churchwardens on only a handful of Darlington properties, the houses were scattered across the town and the locations which are given provide a strong indication of the extent of the town at that time. Houses mentioned were in Skinnergate, Bondgate, Northgate, Ratten Rawe (later Church Row, next to the Boot and Shoe), Borrow (at the foot of Prospect Place), Hungate or Houndgate, Lamb Flatt (later Larchfield), Head Rawe or High Row, as well as property behind Bennett Hall, and at Blackwellgate End. There are also references to Weand and Wend, which was known at other times as Chairgate,

9. Houses of 17th and 18th century date in Church Row, recorded as Rattan Row early in the 17th century.

Glover's Wynd or Post House Wynd.[1] The use of the term 'Wynd' without further qualification suggests that there was then only one such through passage between Skinnergate and High Row. There were also dwellings in Priestgate, Prebend Row and across the river in Clay Row.[2] A total of 273 households was counted in Darlington in the 1666 hearth tax. Approximate locations were given, in 'Brough-gate', 'Pribin' and Bondgate.[3] The 184 households noted in the town in 1674, adjusted for the level of under-recording found elsewhere in hearth tax returns, indicates a figure of about 250 households in all. Allowing for multiple occupation, the number of houses would have been rather lower, so that it appears the town had not been completely reconstructed after the great fire.[4]

A more comprehensive survey is available from the 1751 poor rate book. This provides assessments for 628 premises in the town, some of which would have been purely industrial or commercial. The figure also disguises buildings subdivided to accommodate more than one household. The actual number of houses is likely to have been less than 600, but nonetheless a considerable increase since 1674, more than double the number of dwellings suggested by the hearth tax 80 years earlier. The 1751 assessments are grouped by main streets, so that, for instance, the total for Horsemarket includes Houndgate and Blackwellgate, and 'Head Row' presumably incorporates Post House Wynd as well as industrial and residential properties on the increasingly developed burgage plots behind High Row. The total numbers of buildings are: Backhouse (Bakehouse) Hill, 23; Bondgate, 76; Church Row, 26; Head Row, 113; Horsemarket, 116; Northgate, 74; Over Bridge (Clay Row), 20; Prebend Row, 11; Priestgate, 24; Skinnergate, 79; Tubwell Row, 41. There were also 25 buildings listed under 'Tolls', the locations of which are unclear.[5]

A local census, carried out in 1767 for the purpose of investigating the poor law entitlements of a rapidly growing population, offers further insights into the development and layout of the town.[6] A total of 3,280 people lived in 885 households. The most detailed sections of the survey reveal that some houses contained several households. Deducting these additional families takes the number of houses to a maximum of 870. Yet this figure is still too high, when compared with the estimated total from the 1751 Poor Rate, and to the 864 inhabited and 45 uninhabited houses counted in Darlington township in the 1801 census, which itself may be a considerable overestimate. It is likely that many other houses had been subdivided, although not recorded as such, so that the actual total of houses in 1767 may have been between 700 and 800. On the distribution of households, there were a dozen in 'Conscliff Lane'; 50 on the High Row, still referred to as Head Row; 29 in Richardson's Yard, much of which was owned by Miss Grainger and Mr Wharton; and 18 in 'Wind'. Skinnergate had about 140, including four single-person households at the Friends' meeting-house, itself a building of the late 17th century, recorded first in 1678.[7] The four residents there may have occupied charity housing which preceded the present block of almshouses of 1869 behind the meeting-house. The next section of the survey, covering the west end of Darlington bridge, Bakehouse Hill, Horse Market, Houndgate, Black-wellgate and Blackwell Street to the corner of Coniscliffe Lane, lists 174 households without locating them precisely. The third area had 156 households in Priestgate (25), Prebend Row (12), Tubwell Row (78) and Clay Row (41). Numbers resident in Tubwell Row and Clay Row had risen significantly since 1751, although several shared houses were in evidence, suggesting that at least some of the increased accommodation had been achieved by subdividing existing houses rather than by new building. The final part of the census, which lacks much detail, records 160 households in Bondgate and 148 in Northgate.

Housing was very much concentrated in the central area. There were a few isolated farms, but the land surrounding the town was almost all given over to cultivation, pasture or commons. Lord Vane's glebe land on the west of the town, for instance, remained entirely in agricultural use, its 200 a. let to 15 tenants in 1767.[8]

BUILDINGS FROM c. 1600

Although the fire of 1585 had brought such destruction to the town, major buildings, including the church, deanery and bishop's palace, escaped apparently unscathed, as did a number of other houses.[9] James I stayed in Darlington when *en route* to Scotland in 1617, reputedly in the old Mudhouse in Tubwell Row. This edifice had its 'rough material . . . tastefully beautified with cows' horns intermixed here and there' and contained two wainscotted rooms. It survived long enough to be remembered in the mid 19th century. Other properties in the 'Well Rawe', including the Crown Inn, were remarked upon for their thatched roofs into the 19th century, and for the 'beautiful plaster ornaments on their ceilings', suggesting that these may have been the oldest surviving buildings in the town, dating perhaps from before the fire.[10] Yet it is known that thatch was still used on new buildings in the 17th century, as shown with Francis Forster's almshouses in Northgate, built in 1632.[11]

The Crown and the Bull, at the north-west corner of Bull Wynd, were supposedly the only inns in Darlington in 1600, though it is possible that one or both was then of recent building. Stone plaques set in the wall in Bull Wynd, one with a relief of a bull – the emblem of the Bulmer family – and the other showing the names of Anthony Bulmer and Mary Lasenbie, who married in 1665, appear to be all that remains of the Bulmers' inn, which was demolished probably in the mid 18th century.[12] The Bulmers are said to have owned other property nearby, possibly including the large house reached via Bull Wynd from Horsemarket, and now known as Pease House. This house, bought by John Pease in 1760 and re-fronted some time after that, contains an earlier core which may have been medieval.[13] In support of this early date, a survey in 1952 cited large random rubble stonework on the return; the shape of the back as seen from the alley; and the extreme irregularity of the three-storey, five-window frontage, which faces away from the town. However, no internal investigation was carried out, and since that date the house has been radically altered, with an extension added along the full length of the rear.[14]

A supposedly Elizabethan house, later the Nag's Head inn, was said to have been built for a parsonage, though it was more likely a private house before becoming the residence of one vicar, John Hall, between 1712 and 1727.[15] Parts of the old building survive as a wall in Church Lane behind the modern Nag's Head. Illustrations of the frontage suggest that the house was most likely of the late 17th

10. *The Nag's Head, dating from the late 17th century.*

century, comparable with Alderman Fenwick's house in Newcastle, built in the 1650s, and with Crowle House (1664) and Wilberforce House in Hull.[16] Similarly a 'cheefe house' in Priestgate, forming an angle with Prebend Row, inhabited in 1620 by Simon Gifford, may have been a new construction after the fire. Gifford set up a horse mill on his burgage in 1624, which Longstaffe thought was next to the Hermitage in Clay Row, although Longstaffe's own dates do not support this contention and it seems that the Hermitage mill was a different one. A horse walk survived as late as 1845 next to Kitching's foundry near the site of the 'cheefe house', and this may have been Gifford's mill, which he had built behind his new house.[17]

Other old cottages, possible survivals of the town fire, have been recorded on the north and west sides of the churchyard, some of them in a group behind the Hat and Feathers public house.[18] John Cowton paid rent in 1630–2 for his house 'at the church gaites', later occupied by parson Robert Hope, who died in 1640, and by George Bell, vicar from 1661 until his death in 1693.[19] This is likely to have been the vicarage house in the south-west angle of the churchyard, a recollection of which was noted in a glebe terrier of 1806, by which time all trace of the building had disappeared.[20] In 1630–2, Robert Ile also paid rent to the churchwardens for his door into the churchyard, and Mr Robson of the Flower Pot had the same liability but was unable to pay.[21] A house at the bottom of Tubwell Row, demolished in 1909, was found to be half-timbered, with lower courses of dressed stone.[22] Other apparently long-standing features in the area include the kiln at the bottom of Houndgate,[23] and the well-established 'incroachments' on Bakehouse Hill, formerly Smithy's Hill.[24] William Appleton's house by the market place was part timber built, although it should be noted that timber in conjunction with brick building was still in evidence during the 18th century on the High Row, in an area which seems to have been totally destroyed in 1585.[25] Timber construction is therefore no sure indication that a building pre-dated the fire.

While the exact age of many of buildings extant in the 17th and 18th centuries remains in question, it is notable that the oldest survivals discussed by Longstaffe and other

19th-century commentators were situated on the north, south and east of the market place, in Houndgate and Tubwell Row, or near to St Cuthbert's church, away from the most intensively developed areas behind High Row. This suggests possible limits of the 1585 fire, although it can be no more than a rough indication. Rebuilding was in progress soon after the fire: John Pape had a house in High Row before 1599, presumably the same well-appointed residence described in 1603, and later owned by William Plewes in 1725, then successively by William Wetherell, Ralph Chipchase, Thomas Pease and J. Brantingham.[26] William Barnes in 1606 had 'latelie builded' a number of 'free houses and burgages', probably in Skinnergate and High Row; Miles Guy owned a house and kiln in Skinnergate, another house at Bondgate end, and his own dwellinghouse on High Row, at the time of his death in 1607.[27] Some of the old houses described in the 19th century may therefore have been new in 1600.

ROADS AND WATERWAYS

Despite Darlington's position as principal post town, a centre of mail collection and distribution, complaints about the state of the roads recurred. Longstaffe claims that roads in the south of the county had been 'long famous for their miserable condition' with the road to Croft, 'through the marshy pastures of Oxenlefield', denounced in 1746 by the duke of Cumberland as the worst upon which he had travelled.[28] The township of Blackwell was liable for repairs for much of that road's length between Darlington and the Tees, including the maintenance of Nought, or Snipe, Bridge, which crossed the Skerne near Snipe House. This was rebuilt in 1696 from 'a construction of timber laid on stone piers' to become 'a stately erection of two brick arches', produced for £20 by local craftsmen with re-used timber and iron bolts from the old bridge.[29] Longstaffe defines 'nought' in this context as a general word for cattle, and the bridge provided a detour east of the main road, avoiding the mud of Oxneyfield.

The main road south from Darlington to Northallerton passed via Bank Top and across Brankin Moor, where responsibility for its upkeep proved a source of dispute between the moor's owners and inhabitants of the borough who were expected to 'afford one day in common days work towards the repairing of the common highways there' in the 17th century. Major improvements were carried out in 1777, with an easterly section of the road reduced in height.[30] The highway between Brankin Moor and the town was the responsibility of Darlington copyholders, who repaired the Hermitage causeway in 1667, and the following year mended the horse bridge in Brankin Moor lane.[31]

The major highways were turnpiked from the mid 18th century. An Act to repair the Northallerton – Croft – Darlington – Durham road passed in 1745, followed by the upgrading of the Stockton – Darlington – Winston – Barnard Castle road in 1746–7, and that from Darlington to West Auckland, known as the coal road, in 1750–1.[32] In 1755 the coal road trustees had made progress in repairing that highway, and had borrowed a further £3,200 to continue their work, but argued that higher tolls were needed. The 'many heavy carriages laden with coal and lime', running on narrow wheels, caused severe damage, and the roads were said to remain 'in many parts . . . in a ruinous condition'.[33]

In the town itself, some minor street improvements took place. A new road, called Windmill Lane and later Four Riggs Lane, was constructed in 1777 between properties on the north side of Bondgate, as a more direct route to the town's windmill.[34] The three-arch bridge noted by Leland in the 16th century had been replaced by one of nine arches by the 18th. This rebuilding may have resulted from an enquiry into the state of repair of the county's bridges in 1615, when Darlington and Northgate bridges, as well as Oxenfield bridge and the bridge which crossed the Skerne between Blackwell and Brankin moor, were described as ruinous and in need of repair.[35] The road on the north-east side of Darlington bridge was said by the justices in 1752 to need raising 'with a battlement or flank wall on the side thereof' so that it was 'fit for Carts and Carriages to pass along . . . with safety'.[36] It is not clear whether this work was carried out, for in 1767 a new bridge was constructed next to the old one, by R. and W. Nelson of Melsonby, at a total cost of £1,000. The original plan to build a brick parapet was changed in favour of Gatherley Moor stone, as the

11. *The three-arched bridge of 1767, with St Cuthbert's church beyond, seen from approximately the site of the pound, with Clay Row in the foreground.*

justices feared 'the insecurity of a 140 yards line of brick which would be a perpetual charge to the county' as it had apparently been with the old bridge 'where repaired with brick'.[37] The new bridge was soon considered too narrow, and was 'shamefully encroached upon by ugly sheds, &c., built upon the parapet walls'.[38] Other crossings used to pass the Skerne and mill race were less permanent, such as the 'planks which then served for bridges' connecting Priestgate with Clay Row by the end of the 18th century.[39]

Other improvements to the central area were long in coming. The town, despite its well-proportioned market place and a number of impressive buildings, wallowed in filth. Each house, including those around the market and on the main thoroughfares, had its own dunghill at the front door. An order in 1621 to clear these, and periodic requests thereafter until as late as 1710, to remove the dung before Whitsun, appear to have been largely ignored.[40] A dunghill was even included as an asset worth 5s. in a probate valuation of 1607.[41] The streets were said in 1749 to have been 'only lately paved' and in 1790 to be very dirty in winter, 'not being paved'.[42] Cobbling the market place was not completed until the 1790s or later.[43]

The Skerne, diverted to form a mill race which was usually referred to as the mill dam, was another continuing source of nuisance, despite John Bousfield (b. 1812) recalling 'a clear stream bounded by tall trees'.[44] This 'Ancient Dam mill race or Watercourse' started near Nicholson's Hill, running south through copyhold land in

Cockerill Holme and Mill Holme.[45] Copyholders in Bondgate, responsible for cleaning and maintaining individual lengths of the dam and its walls, each knew, it was said in 1677, 'their parts that they are to scour'.[46] The greeve's book records payment of 3s. 10d. to '6 men for clencsing the Scearne one day' in 1675.[47] More than 60 individuals were involved in repairing sections from four to 22 yards in length by 1726, when the bishop of Durham filed a bill in chancery to enforce the work. The copyholders resisted his claim, asserting that 'all the mill race is now in good repair & no way ruinous except only in one small part of . . . Widow Wright or J[ohn] Perkin', where 'firr deales or timber & other Materials' had been used by the miller to prevent a breach.[48] But in 1754 the Skerne along its full length was said to be 'choak'd and grown up with sand, weed, bushes and annoyances' causing 'much overflowing' of adjacent land. A public meeting was called to appoint commissioners of sewers to cleanse and open the river, although it appears that the landowners decided instead to avoid expense and clear up by voluntary agreement.[49] A proposal in 1763 that copyholders would pay 1s. 9d. a yard to Ralph Robinson, who would then assume permanent responsibility for repairs, was not enacted as Ralph Stamper, the miller, built a new leather mill next to the corn mill, altering the scale of liabilities for the mill dam.[50]

THE MARKET PLACE AND NEIGHBOURING HOUSES

The former grandeur of the bishop's palace suffered varying fortunes during the 17th and 18th centuries.[51] It was partly destroyed during the Civil War, and an indenture of 1652 valued it only for its materials, estimated to be worth £240.[52] Along with the tollbooth, the palace was restored from dilapidation by Bishop Cosin in 1668. The rebuilding used stones, slates brought via Ingleton which probably originated west of Barnard Castle, and brick from Brankin Moor.[53] Nathaniel Crew, Cosin's successor and bishop from 1674 to 1721, is said to have been the last prelate to live at the palace, but it had previously been in lay occupation.[54] Cosin's son-in-law, Charles Gerard, lived there from 1669.[55] Further repairs were carried out in 1679 and 1680.[56] By

1703, the palace had become the town's poorhouse, for Ralph Thoresby, the Leeds antiquary, commented on his concern when visiting St. Cuthbert's church to see 'the adjoining house of the bishop of Durham converted into a Quaker's workhouse'.[57] Enlargements to the building were made in 1808, and its use as a workhouse continued until 1870, when it was demolished by Richard Luck and the site filled with the cottage dwellings of Luck's Terrace.[58]

The deanery, which had ceased to be an ecclesiastical residence at the Reformation, stood on the corner of Horse Market and Feethams, its surrounding orchard reaching to Bull Wynd on the west, and with a semi-circular boundary to the south which cut across the bottom of Houndgate.[59] The property was tenanted by Richard Fletcher in 1634, when its address was given as South Row.[60] In 1735 it was described as the 'Mansion House or Dwelling House, Rectory or Deanery of Darlington', with no indication that it had then been divided.[61] By 1767, though, the town census shows it as occupied by five households, all of freeholders: Mrs Newby and a servant; Thomas Routledge and his wife; John Dixon and his wife; Thomas Feetham, his wife and five children; and John Wind, his wife and three children, making a total of 18 residents.[62] Further division seems to have taken place, with the 'Old Deanery houses' let to seven tenants in 1778,[63] although a 19th-century account speaks of four residences there, including a school and a shop.[64] A photograph taken just before its demolition c. 1901 shows the damage done by various alterations to accommodate these changing uses.[65]

Behind the deanery, at the bottom of Houndgate, a number of substantial brick-built residences had appeared by the end of the 18th century. The largest, now numbered 11, later became the town clerk's office. Below it was the residence of George Allan on the Kilngarth. This 'large commodious mansion house . . . substantially built of the best materials, and commanding extensive and beautiful views of the fine surrounding country to the south' had been divided into three smaller houses by 1833, and was later converted to offices as Houndgate chambers. A plan shows Allan's house, which faced away from the street and the town, with perhaps six or eight reception rooms and presumably a similar number of chambers above.[66] Its style suggests a date of the late 18th century. Allan paid duty on 38 windows in Darlington borough in 1790, and certainly had a house in Houndgate by 1796, when he published a notice warning trespassers against passing through his 'garden at the bottom of Hungate and also through the garth and gardens there called Kilngarth and breaking down the walls, rails, fences and plantation of trees'. A similar bill was circulated two years later, suggesting that Allan was trying to stop the use of an habitual short cut past his new house and garden.[67]

The house called Feethams, with a garden on the south side of the churchyard and the medieval tithe barn in front of the house, was leased from Lord Vane. There were said to be three houses there in 1694, which may have been apart from the main house, or could have been subdivisions of the larger property. The tithe barn seems to have been demolished by 1782, when the property was sold by the assignees of Francis Holmes to a creditor, Miss Lumley, who was resident there. Its site became another garden.[68] The house then passed to Joseph Pease, brother of Edward, usually called Joseph of Feethams to distinguish him from his more famous nephew.[69]

The hermitage formed a substantial portion of the detached part of the borough in Clay Row, lending its name to a length of road running east from Clay Row towards Yarm Lane and Neasham Road, the 'hermitage cawsay'.[70] There were two buildings on this land in the 17th century, the hermitage itself and an adjoining horse mill. They faced south over open land across Yarm Lane, with the hermitage the last building on the fringes of town.[71] The mill, sometimes said to be 'Ultra Skerne' was described in 1618 as 'a house called le Horsemill' and in 1713 'Darlington Horse Mill house'. Its early date seems to distinguish it from Simon Gifford's horse mill of 1624, which was probably behind Prebend Row.[72] Longstaffe is clear that the hermitage mill had been demolished before 1760 and a shop erected on its site; a plan dated 1776, though, shows the 'Old Horse Mill', which suggests a conversion rather than demolition of the building.[73] Furthermore two houses offered for sale in 1772 were said to have been 'in Clay-Row, near the horse-mill'.[74] The burial record of Edward Robinson of Hermitage in 1712 confirms that the area was then commonly known also as Bank Top.[75] The hermitage was rebuilt and converted to dwelling houses soon before 1731; it was again referred to in 1746–7 as 'a parcel whereon a horse-mill lately stood, containing 12 yards in length by 8 yards in breadth at a place called Hermitage'. A freehold house and garth called the Hermitage, elsewhere called Bank Top House, at the foot of Hermitage Bank, was sold with other property of Francis Holmes in 1782.[76]

A visitor to Darlington in 1749 noted with approval the 'spacious market-place upwards of 200 yards long, and 130 broad, well filled on Mondays, its market-days; and a much greater every other Monday from the first of March to Christmas for cattle and sheep'.[77] The market and the passing trade of travellers on the Great North Road stimulated development around the square, and within it. There were several inns by 1700, for instance the Fleece on the corner of the market place and Blackwellgate, in business from at least 1688.[78] The King's Head inn, said to have been established in 1661, had acquired considerable stabling by the 1720s.[79] The Cross Keys opened before 1731.[80] A new market cross was erected on the Tubwell Row side of the tollbooth in 1727 by Dame Dorothy Brown,

12. *The King's Head inn, c. 1880, and Northgate.*

mother of two bailiffs of Darlington, Daniel and Charles
Moore. This cross was taken down in 1862 and moved to
Park Street, then into the covered market, before being
taken back to the market place, where it stands in the north-
west corner. [81] The assets of the bailiff were recorded in 1762
as including 13 messuages, a market house, a bakehouse,
a toll booth, 12 shops and 12 shambles, indicating
considerable development in the market area.[82] Plans to
replace the toll booth with a new Town House, drawn up in
1770 by Samuel Wilkinson of the King's Head, 'a clever
artist' responsible for a number of drawings of the town,
were not taken further until 1806, and then in a much
reduced form. Wilkinson had proposed a building with
'small cupolas at the corners, the north and south fronts to
extend eighty-four feet, and the east and west seventy-two
feet. In the centre from west to east the shambles were to
extend, and to have a pump, the dungeon was to occupy the
north-east corner, while in the upper storey of the west
front was to be a large room, forty-eight by twenty-one feet,
lighted by five windows. Style, Italian of course.'[83]

Recent archaeological investigation has suggested a redevelopment of the market place during the early 18th
century, involving a reduction of its gradient and some
demolition and rebuilding on the eastern side.[84] This report
also indicates that there was no formal boundary between
churchyard and market place before the building of a new
wall in 1791, but this is contradicted by Wilkinson's drawing
of the town from the south east in 1760, clearly showing a
wall around the churchyard.[85] The wall built in 1791 at a cost
of £51 9s. appears to have been a replacement, or may have
marked the date of an extension to the burial ground.[86]

NUMBERS AND SIZES OF HOUSES

Early 17th-century inventories indicate a general pattern for
the more substantial housing in Darlington, much of it then
of recent construction. Although precise locations are not
given, most of the inventories apparently relate to town
centre properties. At the centre of dwellings was the hall, or
'hawle house', or forehouse, which was sometimes equipped
with beds. Mary Throckmorton, who died in 1620, had such
an arrangement, along with kitchen, green chamber, a

chamber over the hall and a 'street chamber'.[87] The name of this last room suggests that Throckmorton's hall was not directly on the street frontage. It was quite common to have beds in one or more parlours. The tanner Thomas Johnson had beds in two parlours.[88] Michael Jeffreyson, also a tanner, kept a stand bed with feather mattress in the parlour, as well as four beds in each of two other chambers.[89] John Fawcett, cordwainer, had a truckle bed in his low parlour while a chamber over the buttery was used for storing oil, tallow and other household items rather than for sleeping.[90]

Chambers were usually on the first floor, and some houses also had lofts over workshops, or possibly on a second storey. Thomas Pape, who died in 1603, had three beds in the loft over his shop on the High Row, and more in his parlours 'on the back side' and 'beneath the doores'.[91] Miles Guy, a cordwainer, also of High Row, had a far loft with five beds, as well as a 'lawe house' with two.[92] It is possible that he, and also Robert Loryman, a smith, of Northgate, with three lofts fitted out with beds, and Robert Dent, who had seven guest beds in a loft, accommodated travellers. The three owned disproportionate quantities of trenchers, spoons and other dining equipment, an indication that their houses may have been hostelries.[93]

Most of the inventories mention a kitchen, and in many cases there were also specialist storage or working areas for food and drink and other household goods: commonly butteries, sometimes brewhouses, a 'naperye' or linen store, vaults, oil and tallow houses, a malt loft.[94] Workshops or warehouses were often an integral feature of the house, with stables and sometimes substantial agricultural buildings at the back. Lawrence Catherick, described as yeoman on his death in 1623, had a milk house, 'barne on the backside', a stable with loft over, a malt loft over the kitchen and other agricultural equipment and stock 'on the backside of the house'.[95] While the inventories do not necessarily supply a comprehensive list of all rooms, in some instances there was clearly more working than living space. The well-to-do mercer Anthony Dennis left £177 worth of wares in his shop on his death in 1610, but only a few domestic rooms were listed: a buttery, parlour, kitchen and stable, and loft above the hall.[96]

Access to workshops and other developments behind was

gained via passages, sometimes with rooms above. The inventories of Margery Lasselles and Michael Jeffreyson both mention chambers over the entry.[97] The apparently smaller house of George Marshall had lofts rather than chambers, one of which was over the entry.[98]

The largest house recorded in the early-17th century inventories occurs twice. It was the residence of William Barnes, gentleman, of Bedburn Park, Hamsterley, and Darlington, who died in 1606. He leased the borough bakehouse and tolls, and held much other freehold and, through his wife Barbara, copyhold property in the town.[99] Later it was home to John Lisle, who had married Barbara Barnes, succeeded William Barnes as borough bailiff, and died in 1623.[100] On the death of Barnes, the inventory records a hall house, buttery with little parlour adjoining, a kitchen, milk-house, larder and brewhouse, little low parlour with a number of beds, chamber over the parlour, great chamber over the hall, chamber over the buttery parlour, maid's chamber, and highest chamber. There were 'iron chimneys' in the hall and chamber over. Lisle's inventory is less detailed but the house is recognisably the same. Its identity remains a matter for speculation. The deanery was then in other occupation, and Lisle's residence does not obviously match the layout of the bishop's palace.

Of the 273 households recorded in the 1666 hearth tax returns in Darlington, there were 36 with three hearths, 18 with four, and four with six, as well as one each with five, seven, nine and 10 hearths. As each hearth equates only to a heated room, so that unheated rooms should be added to the total, some of these dwellings were of substantial size. Yet of all the households, almost four out of five had only one or two hearths – 152 and 59 households respectively.[101] An analysis of the 1674 hearth tax indicates that Darlington, with a mean of 1.87 hearths per household, had an average well below that of Durham city (2.73), Gateshead (2.23) and Sunderland (2.12), and below the average for all towns in the county.[102] This suggests that dwellings in the town were smaller and more modest than was generally the case in the north-east.

Darlington's central yards were intensively developed during the 18th century. Houses, some with shops, fronted directly on to the street, with access through a passage to long and narrow rear gardens and orchards which were increasingly built over with stables, workshops, privies and cottages to sublet. Basements were rare in the central area.[103] As pressure for accommodation increased, there was further subdivision of some larger houses. The dimensions of burgage and copyhold plots, and of the buildings within them, showed considerable variation. A 'little cottage house' in Northgate, sold in 1751, measured eight yards by five in breadth. Its orchard or garden was 19 yards long by 10 yards wide, with one and a quarter yards of ground forming a passage from the street to the orchard.[104] In Bondgate, a cottage and garden measuring 11½ yards by six was sold in 1767; a similar property in 1783 was said to measure exactly half that, 5¾ yards by six, indicating that subdivision of plots may have been in progress.[105] A newly built house in 1775 'at the high end of Stephen Robson's garden' adjoining his warehouse in Northgate, was 12½ yards long and six and a half wide. The house had two ground floor rooms, two chambers, and 'a teafall or shade used as a coal house'. It was sold on in 1781 'with free passage through the yard or garth adjoining', a right of way to the well and river, and liberty to bleach one web of cloth each year in the garth, or garden.[106]

Property deeds illustrate a gradual change in the nature of central holdings. The original pattern was of a house and shop, with garth and stables behind. Examples of this are a burgage [house], shops and rooms, with a little close or

13. *Clark's Yard , a central garth intensively infilled during the 18th century.*

orchard at the back of two acres 'abutting the King's Street to Piercebridge on the south and west' in Blackwellgate in 1678;[107] a burgage, garden, orchard and shop in 'Norgate Street' on the north side of Currier's or Cobbler's Garth in 1713;[108] two burgages 'with a plot of ground on the backside in a street called Badellgate or Blackwellgate' in 1725;[109] another two burgages on the north side of Bondgate, with garths, orchards and stables behind, in 1730;[110] a 'messuage with garth' in Bondgate in 1739;[111] a house in Northgate with adjoining garth in 1743;[112] and two other houses 'with garth or yard behind' in Northgate in 1754.[113] This was gradually giving way to a more concentrated use of the central gardens and orchards, with property converted and subdivided and its use generally intensified. A house and garth in Northgate had acquired a 'dyehouse with appurtenances' in 1722.[114] In 1734, another burgage in Northgate had, in addition to its garden, orchard and garth or little close, a dyehouse, stable and 'other edifices and outbuildings'.[115] In 1746, a similar or perhaps the same property had been further divided and developed, for there was sold 'the north end of a house or tenement, garden or garth, on Northgate, Darlington; and messuage lately erected on the same, and shop or workhouse, which was formerly only a barn, and a dyehouse built at the east end of the said garden, and the messuages built at the west end of the garden or garth'.[116] A deed of 1757 hints at the division of a larger house, with mention of 'part of a forehouse facing Northgate . . . on the north side of the entry or passage therein'.[117] The one-acre North or Cobbler's Garth, off Northgate, had been built up with houses and other buildings, and there had been housing development on part of Thornbeck Hills.[118] The sale of a burgage and garth in Bondgate in 1770 refers to 'dwelling houses lately erected on the backside of the above premises'.[119] The result of such developments is starkly illustrated by later plans of town centre plots, where a maze of yards and passages gave access to cottages, ash-pits and dung heaps, wash-houses, privies and stables as well as various industrial workshops and warehouses behind shops and large houses fronting the street.[120] Some of the burgage plots disposed of in 1833 by the Allan family's successors had been split up for sale, with more than one tenant even within the subdivided portions.

Lot 5, the Talbot Inn, for instance, included a brewhouse and stables next to Post House Wynd, with the remainder of the burgage plot sold as lot 6, a shop and house fronting High Row, occupied by a linen draper and others. Lots 11, 12 and 13, apparently carved out of one plot on the corner of Priestgate and Prebend Row, contained four houses and front shops, a public house and front shop, with yard and out offices, six stables and a garden.[121]

While the general picture towards the end of the 18th century is one of pressure by a growing and increasingly overcrowded population upon the central plots, Darlington had also acquired some sizeable properties with fine frontages in the town centre. A 'large and convenient' well-heated seven-bedroomed house in Tubwell Row formerly occupied by a saddler, Robert Dobson, boasted a large shop with 'outshot glass windows'.[122] In 1790, 18 individuals in the borough paid duty on more than six windows each; in total, 2,189 windows were taxed in the town.[123] It is probable that a number of the larger houses were inns, as with the 57-windowed property, attracting by far the largest liability, owned by Richard Thompson. This was presumably the Talbot inn, in Post House Wynd, of which Thompson was landlord in the 1770s.[124] The identities and location of other premises listed are likewise a matter for conjecture. George Allan had 38 windows, presumably in his Houndgate house. The bailiff of Darlington, Henry Ornsby, paid duty on 18 windows, for a house probably in Houndgate or Horsemarket.[125] Edward Pease's eleven windows may also have been in Houndgate, at the property now called Pease House; there were a further four Pease residences on the list, including Joseph Pease with 18 windows, possibly at Feethams. Two Iansons had 13 windows each, perhaps in Northgate. William Kitching's eight windows were almost certainly in his Prebend Row house. The Backhouse family had three of the largest properties, with 23, 17 and 14 windows, one of which was presumably West Lodge, built by James Backhouse.[126]

As late as 1800, the town's development, apart from the built area around Bondgate itself, was still almost exclusively limited to freehold land within the borough bounds. Constraints imposed by the surrounding undeveloped copyhold estate were most vividly illustrated at the

bottom of Houndgate, where the road and all buildings ceased abruptly on the borough boundary. In Northgate, similarly, the town had grown little beyond the borough limits.[127] The number of houses, which was no higher in the mid 17th century than it had been before the fire of 1585, thereafter doubled in the century to 1750, and maintained the high level of growth to 1800, largely through intensive building in existing back yards and gardens. Within the narrow confines of the borough, there was considerable overcrowding. Yet the attraction of Darlington's market and associated commerce which had brought about this problem, also supplied the means through which it was alleviated. Building barely encroached upon the market place itself, and it was this extensive and pleasing central space, surrounded by good quality housing and inns, which gave the town its main redeeming feature.

14. *South-east aspect of Darlington, 1760, from the bishop's Low Park.*

3. URBAN AND SUBURBAN DARLINGTON, 1800–1914

DARLINGTON IN *c.* 1800

Although closely associated with early railways, Darlington was a well-developed and busy market centre long before their advent. The trade associated with its extensive rural hinterland, and resulting from its location on the main road north to Scotland,[1] helped support a population of 4,670 in 1801.[2]

Wilkinson's view of Darlington from the south east in 1760 confirms that though a prosperous settlement, with the main market place surrounded by substantial buildings, the town had barely extended beyond its medieval bounds, and retained a rural aspect.[3] The diarist Francis Mewburn, resident from 1809, noted that into the 1780s there had been 'a great many thatched houses in the town'.[4] Others remembered a prominent corner house, thatched and panelled, on the market place, and thatched cottages with mud floors in Clay Row.[5] According to the local historian Longstaffe, as late as 1790 Darlington was very dirty in winter, 'not being paved'.[6] Into the 19th century, Tubwell Row, where the Great North Road passed the market place, retained a boggy patch where cattle stuck fast.[7] Compared with those of other well-populated towns, though, Darlington's streets were of 'princely width', and trees and gardens in the town centre added to generally spacious and pleasant surroundings. A property as central as the Bull, in Bull Wynd, was known in the early 19th century as the Grove in recognition of the 'numerous lilac and other trees with which the large garden in the rear of the buildings was stocked'.[8]

Above the new Darlington bridge of 1767, the mill race re-joined the Skerne at a point where the river was at its widest. Rushes growing 'luxuriantly' in the water were harvested 'for conversion into matting and chair seats' and dried on a hedgerow near the road to Cockerton.[9] East of the bridge a row of houses fronted Clay Row and Yarm Lane

15. *Darlington in c. 1830, by Richardson.*

end. The hermitage and old horse mill were demolished or radically altered around this time. Otherwise the area over the Skerne was barely developed in 1800. South of Yarm Lane, the bishop's Low and High parks remained agricultural in character, except for Kendrew's mill buildings.[10] On the town side of the river, to the south, Feethams was also open land.[11]

In the town centre, some change was in progress. Certain industrial activities, including a saw mill on High Row, and unsavoury premises such as the 'miserable' shambles, came to be viewed as inappropriate to the thriving market town and were gradually removed.[12] Commercial trades – banks, inns and retailers – colonised market place frontages, although there remained many industrial workshops, facing the streets or in yards and wynds behind. Skinnergate, the back lane of the medieval borough, was a thriving mix of residential and industrial activity.

Darlington began to develop more rapidly during the opening decades of the 19th century. A committee formed in 1806 designed the layout of new public buildings: 'the West Front of the Town House shall be parallel with Prebend Row, the Shambles to stand on the East, and the South front of which to be in a line with Bakehouse Hill.' Shares were sold, and Jonathan Backhouse and John Atkinson deputed to negotiate the demolition and re-building with representatives of the bishop. The estimated cost of the new town house was £985, and of the shambles, eventually reduced to 35 in number, £558.[13] The old town house, considered by Mewburn to have been as miserable as the shambles, was replaced in 1808, and a dispensary for the relief of the sick poor added to the new building in 1809.[14] The new town hall incorporated a 'dismal and noisome little room' called the kitty, or lock-up, in service until 1846 when a new police station opened in Grange Road.[15] The new shambles, in 'a neat building' on the west side of the market place, and 'well supplied with butcher's meat', were erected in 1815.[16] They had 'wide interstices between the roof ridges which allowed the rain to enter, and open railed sides which permitted the wind to pass freely through, to the sore discomfort of the stall keepers and their customers', faults which were remedied by additional building in 1851.[17] To the south of the church, the bishop's manor house, long in use as the poor-house, was bought by the town in 1808 and much extended to the south, work financed partly through the bequest of a Quaker, Gideon Gravett Phillips.[18] The Friends' meeting-house in Skinner-gate, a building of c. 1760, was also substantially altered in the early years of the century, to provide two halls separated by a partition; the forebuilding on the street frontage with its Doric porch came rather later, in 1839.[19] The Bondgate Methodist Church was built in Saltyard in 1812, on a corner of the glebe land bought from the earl of Darlington.[20] In 1813 the original thatched building of the Free Grammar School, standing east of St Cuthbert's church on the bank of the Skerne, was demolished and its land taken into the burial ground. A new grammar school was built beyond the southern boundary of the churchyard, and subsequently enlarged by the addition of a second floor in 1846.[21] A national school, also later extended and improved, appeared in 1824 next to the grammar school.[22]

A scavenger had been appointed to the town in 1783, paying £8 a year for the privilege of collecting manure.[23] Street lighting was considered by a vestry meeting as early as 1788, although no progress in that direction appears to have been made until the passing of a local Act of Parliament in 1823, after which paving, cleansing and lighting in the central area began to improve.[24] The streets were 'tolerably lighted with oil-fed lamps', well enough for the constables to deal with the 'Black Troop', described as 'an organised gang of desperados who annoyed, terrified and robbed

16. THE FRIENDS' MEETING-HOUSE, SKINNERGATE

(a). *The meeting-house from Skinnergate c. 1838.*

The building, purchased and repaired for the Friends' use in 1687, is presumably that shown (left) in this lithograph. It stood immediately south of the present meeting-house. In 1768, it had two windows on the west side and a stable at the south end. In either 1760 or 1768, premises north of it were conveyed to the Friends. They included three tenement houses (right) and land to their west, on which the much larger and taller meeting-house (background) was built. The houses, shown here with mid 18th-century fronts, were occupied by Friends as almshouses. Between them and the old meeting house a gated passageway gave access to both old and new meeting-houses. The new meeting-house contained a men's meeting room and another for women, each under a pitched roof. The women's room was smaller until extended east in 1796.

(b). *The façade, as rebuilt in 1837–40*

In 1839–40, the old meeting-house and almshouses were replaced by a brick, two-storeyed range with a sober neoclassical façade, containing lobbies, cloakrooms and committee rooms.

(c). *Interior of the south room in 2002.*

In 1846 the meeting rooms were replaced, excluding a section of the north wall, by one big square meeting room with an east gallery, which could be divided by sliding shutters (right) into rooms of equal size for men's and women's business meetings. The ministers' stand, with later coved sounding board, and long benches, originally filled both rooms. The area between the new meeting-house and the fore-building became a high passage housing a double-flight of gallery stairs, which were rearranged when a floor and first-floor rooms were inserted in 1960.

(Sources: D. M. Butler, The Quaker meeting houses of Britain, *ii.* 1999, 157–160; C. Stell, An inventory of nonconformist chapels and meeting-houses in the north of England, *1994, 61–2*)

every person walking alone after nightfall'.[25] The Darlington Gas Light Company was established as a co-partnership in 1830, and supplied street lighting until new arrangements for gas supply were made in 1846.[26] The 1830s also saw street and pavement improvements in Tubwell Row, where the slope between footpath and carriage road was reduced. The borough overseer of highways, John Chisman, was much criticised for the cost of this work but later the changes met general approval. The overseer also bought out rights to sheep pens, which had been situated in Prebend Row since the opening of the 19th century, in an attempt to eliminate an unhygienic obstruction.[27] The erector of the market sheep pens, Thomas Reed, a Quaker who 'had no great love of water as a beverage, and was a narrow economist in its use for personal ablutions', had also been responsible for driving the flocks down Tubwell Row into the Skerne to be washed. This practice appears to have ceased after Reed's death in 1828, aged 80.[28] The sheep market was moved to Bondgate, which proved to be unsatisfactory, and the pens eventually found a more convenient location on the slope of Tubwell Row.[29]

On the outskirts of town, a few larger residences started to appear from the late 18th century.[30] Among the first was Polam Hall, off Grange Road, built in c. 1780 by a linen draper, Harrington Lee, as a modest dwelling with a four-room plan, on land which he leased from the Lambton family. The 'Powlam' property, including more than 50 a. of land, was let by the Lambtons in 1818 to Edward Backhouse, and subsequently the house reconstructed on a grand scale by his brother Jonathan, its owner from c. 1825.[31] West Lodge, described as the first suburban villa, had been built for the Backhouse family in the late 18th century on the outskirts of town at the end of Bondgate and was re-fronted by Thomas Backhouse in 1803.[32] Elmfield, off Northgate, the home of William Backhouse, dated from the early 19th century, as did Greenbank,[33] near to West Lodge, and Southend, formerly known as Borrowses, which was on Coniscliffe Lane.[34] Larchfield, first called Lamb Flatt, then Paradise, where Mewburn spent the majority of his life in Darlington, had been built in 1811 for the Backhouse family.[35] Beech Villa, later called Beechwood, with grounds adjoining those of Polam Hall, was built c. 1825 by John

Botcherby, who lived there before building Pierremont.[36] Woodlands is said to have been built in the late 1820s by another Botcherby, Robert, on the Staindrop lane, later Woodland Road.[37] North Lodge estate was carved out of Elmfield's grounds some time after 1832 for John Beaumont Pease.[38] East Mount, another Pease residence, appeared at about the same time, above Freeman's Place and the only one of these properties on the east side of the Skerne.[39]

Mewburn said of Darlington in 1825 that he knew no town where greater improvements had been made.[40] A plan by John Wood made in the following year[41] shows recent development of two areas on the fringes of the town centre. New commercial streets were being constructed between Northgate and Bondgate, while a small residential area, Wellington Place, extended south from Blackwellgate. The first of these developments was Wellington Place, at the start of Grange Road, said to have preceded the slightly later building of Commercial Street, Freeman's Place, West and North Terraces and Harewood Hill and Grove. It was constructed by George Spencer on a half-acre plot which he bought from Samuel Booth's executors in 1818.[42] Various gentlemen and private individuals occupied the houses from about 1820, and Grange House was built soon afterwards.[43] A plan to develop this area further in 1823 by running a new street of large properties south-east from the end of Wellington Place, to turn at right angles back into Houndgate, was not pursued.[44]

The Commercial Street district was developed on a former market garden owned by John Kendrew.[45] It had a mixture of business and residential properties – some of each, and many in combined use – although their character was rather different from the older shops and houses on the market place and main road. Several public buildings were constructed in the new streets: an Independent chapel in Union Street, built as early as 1812 by James Ianson of London and enlarged in 1824; a Baptist chapel in Albion Row; the Queen Street Primitive Methodist chapel in 1821–2; the Mechanics Institute library in 1825; a National School in Commercial Street, joined by another in Union Street during the 1850s.[46] Premises in Union and Commercial Streets were recorded in a directory of 1820, and the names

17. *Commercial Street, one of Darlington's earliest streets.*

of King, Queen and Regent streets imply that the district was laid out before 1820.[47] But as the number of houses in Darlington barely increased between 1801 and 1821, it cannot have been much developed until the 1820s.[48] By 1827 the streets were host to a range of industrial activity, both new and traditional. The new quarter's proximity to the railway depots was fortuitous for the trades located there, as its development had been in progress some time before the Stockton and Darlington's decision in 1823 to route the railway nearby. Some of the newer businesses in and around Commercial Street grew in conjunction with the railway, for example the several insurance agents, and two transport companies located in warehouses, contrasting with the inn-based carriers in the older part of town.[49] It is unclear who instigated the development of these streets. Several local owners held blocks of property there in 1826, including a timber merchant who was also treasurer of the local mutual insurance company; two carriers; a surgeon; a bookseller-stationer who was also involved in insurance; a partner in a firm of flax and tow spinners; and a brazier and plumber.[50] Houses were a mixture of sizes and styles, from impressive town houses to modest cottages. A later resident of the district noted that the drains and sewers had not been well planned: 'Between King Street and Queen Street, where the houses stood back-to-back, were open middens which served the houses on either side; into these middens went everything that wasn't wanted.'[51]

THE RAILWAYS AND URBAN DEVELOPMENT, 1825–1840S

The Stockton and Darlington line opened in September 1825. Because its destination was Witton Park, three miles east of Bishop Auckland, rather than Darlington itself, it skirted the town about a mile to the north. [52] Initially most traction was by horse, although soon locomotive steam engines came to predominate, transporting coal, lime, lead and manufactured goods.[53] Despite its rapid expansion – it was described in 1834 as 'of vast importance to this town'[54] – and the introduction of steam power, the railway's immediate impact upon the local environment was limited. It was only one of several large-scale industries, alongside textile factories, breweries, foundries and brick, tile and tan yards, most of which were centrally located and near the river. There were also private schools, including boarding schools, as well as wealthy private residents in the town centre, suggesting that Darlington's industries were not exceptionally unpleasant.

A cluster of activity grew around the Stockton and Darlington station near the Durham road. A short branch line, running south-east from the station, connected the main railway with coal depots by the Northgate bridge over Cocker beck.[55] The coal depots were brick-arched cells 30 feet long, 18 feet wide and 13 feet high.[56] Adjoining them, in the Cocker valley, Henry Pease laid out Westbrook gardens, 'large and beautiful' with intersecting walks, a pond and temple, before 1835. Edward Pease called his son's work 'Henry's folly'.[57] By 1829 a very early railway hotel had appeared in the vicinity.[58] The first local engineering concern dedicated to railway work was that founded in 1831 by Alfred Kitching, a Quaker and early subscriber to the Stockton and Darlington Railway, who left his brother's town centre foundry[59] in order to establish his own works. Kitching's Railway Foundry was built next to the station, in a triangle of land between the main and branch lines. In 1859, Kitching sold these works to the Stockton and Darlington Railway Company and acquired a new foundry nearby to make structural products for the railway.[60] Until the 1850s, though, his was the only major engineering works in the town.

The railway attracted other industry to the area between the station, which was rebuilt *c.* 1842, and the River Skerne.[61] There were a lime depot and goods station, a worsted factory and gasworks. The railway company itself built roads, houses and cottages with gardens. The beginnings of an industrial settlement at Hope Town were discernible by 1840: a few terraced houses, and later another railway hotel and a sawmill.[62] This remained, for a time, physically separate from the town centre. Edward Pease, who lived near the great Bulmer's stone and opposite old cottages known as 'Darlington House' which marked the northern edge of town,[63] commissioned a map of his considerable property along Northgate in 1843 which shows little development between town and railway.[64]

More significant for Darlington's landscape was the new north-south main railway line which skirted the town on the higher ground of Bank Top, following in part the route of the 1829 Croft branch of the Stockton and Darlington railway. In 1841 the Darlington to York section of the Great North of England Railway opened for mineral traffic. It amalgamated with Hudson's 1842 Newcastle and Darlington Junction Railway line in 1846, to become the York and

18. *Darlington from the road to Yarm, by T. Allom, c. 1830. Taken from the place where the main railway later crossed the Yarm Road, this shows some new development of terraced housing.*

Newcastle Railway.[65] By 1842 there were extensive buildings on the site of the present Bank Top station, designed by John Green jun., with coal depots and a large railway shed nearby.[66] Streets of houses were soon in evidence all around.[67] Longstaffe saw Bank Top in 1854 as a new town 'gradually arising on the east of the Skerne'. It was initially a railway colony, its church first established in a converted railway warehouse.[68] The Bank Top settlement was the first and most obvious manifestation of the way in which the GNER line would re-order Darlington's industry and transform its landscape. Other development followed the railway's lead. A branch of St Cuthbert's Sunday school opened at Bank Top in 1842; a permanent church, St John the Evangelist, seating 650, was consecrated in 1848.[69] Nearby, Edward Pease in 1856 built eight cottages for use as almshouses, to replace Forster's early 17th-century alms-houses in Russell Street, Northgate, and Bellassis's alms-houses at the south end of the east side of Skinnergate, the sites of which he had taken in exchange.[70]

Darlington during the second quarter of the 19th century was growing rapidly, quite apart from the effects of the railway. The census enumerator in 1831, explaining a 50 per cent increase in the population and an almost 40 per cent rise in the number of houses over the previous decade, gave some credit to the railway but suggested a more general prosperity: 'This increase I attribute to a Railway from the Coal Mines to nearly the mouth of the River Tees and to the Steadiness of the Linen and Woollen Manufactures.' Railways were neither a major employer of labour, nor a provider of large-scale housing.[71] A diverse range of industry, along with the continuing importance of weekly and seasonal markets and fairs,[72] contributed to the town's expansion. In the 20 years to 1821, while Darlington's population had risen by almost a quarter, the number of houses had, if anything, fallen, although the figure given by census enumerators in 1801 is suspect. They counted 864 houses, accommodating 1,111 families, in 1801, with a further 45 properties empty. The equivalent numbers for 1811 were 818 houses for 1,205 families, 18 empty houses and three being built; in 1821 there were said to be 876 properties housing 1,213 families. The town's prosperity and pressure of overcrowding appear to have stimulated house building before the railway was established. In addition to the Commercial Street district, other new streets and rows date from the early 1820s. Park Street and Freeman's Place had developed to the east of the Skerne by 1826, with a Wesleyan chapel built in Park Street in 1831.[73] The area between Park Street and the river on the bishop's Low Park was soon built over with other terraced housing, reached from the town by a cast iron footbridge erected at the lower end of the Leadyard in 1833.[74] North of Bondgate, Archer Street and Temperance Place were laid out by 1837.[75]

A major sale in 1833 of freehold town centre property and land on the outskirts of town released further sites for development. The Allan estate included land north of Bondgate, fields around the Northgate railway development, and property in Clay Row, as well as town centre premises.[76] While some lots were laid out and offered explicitly as building sites, and some were bought by builders, demand outside the town centre was limited, with much of the land going for agricultural use, and not all lots

19. *Bridge Street, an early development east of the Skerne in the 1820s, pictured on the eve of its demolition a century later.*

20. *Blackwellgate, c. 1848, with fashionable new shop frontages.*

sold.[77] The main consequences of the Allan sale were to be seen in the town itself, where several burgage plots on the High Row and Prebend Row were offered, with mixed residential and commercial accommodation and with narrow but long gardens. Following the auction, Mewburn noted that all the houses sold were undergoing repair and alteration, and land was still selling for building. There had been another visible effect of the sale: 'In this summer [of 1834] a great change took place in the shops in Darlington. Large windows became all the fashion. A number of new shops were opened out this year in consequence of the sale of Allan's houses; and no sooner had one shopkeeper put out a large and elegant window than his neighbour did likewise'.[78] By 1860, every one of the shop fronts on the High Row had adopted the fashion for plate glass. The redesigned shops, rather than sell wares made on the premises in the manner of previous generations, instead displayed 'fashionable attire for gentlemen, and millinery fripperies for ladies'.[79]

MID-CENTURY SUBURBAN GROWTH

The mid-century Ordnance Survey of Darlington shows a town only modestly extended from its earlier bounds, although the railways were then of considerable size and significance. They did not encroach physically into the medieval core of Darlington as, unlike many other towns where different companies' routes eventually converged upon a central point, stations and lines remained outside the town.[80] Longstaffe at this time described a fine market place with good buildings, though still a few incongruous constructions marring 'the noble square'.[81] The Central Hall, in Bull Wynd, designed by John Middleton in the Italian style and opened in 1847, offered a range of facilities and more extensive accommodation than the assembly room, or 'long room', at the Sun Inn in Prospect Place, previously the main venue for social activities.[82] Bondgate, though relatively unimproved, was considered far from disagreeable. In all directions extended 'handsome villas and spreading gardens'. Harewood Hill, opposite Polam Hall, had been developed from about 1830 with 'pleasant houses', as had Coniscliffe Lane as far as Southend.[83] The elegant brick houses of West Terrace on Coniscliffe Road, and those at Mount Pleasant, where Coniscliffe Road now meets Cleveland Terrace, date from this period.[84]

In comparison with neighbouring towns Darlington was relatively attractive and healthy, despite the confinement of its steeply rising population to a barely changing town plan, and the continuing practice of infill in the narrow central yards.[85] Epidemics such as the cholera of 1832 and smallpox in 1846 did reach Darlington but the town escaped lightly. It had the advantage over other Tees valley towns of being at a distance from the main river, although this was not a complete guarantee against Tees pollution as water backed up the Skerne during floods.[86] When disease did occur, the newer streets were no better placed than older property in escaping it. Longstaffe wrote that depressions in the bishop's Low Park had been filled with bark and rubbish – waste from nearby tanneries – and that 'on this decaying substructure streets have been built, the perpetual abode of fever and disease'.[87] The town's medical officer followed the course of epidemics during the 1840s, street by street. Blackwellgate and Houndgate were 'the principal seats of disease', and the Skinnergate and Bondgate yards featured, along with the notorious Catterick's yard, other yards around Priestgate to the Skerne, and Clay Row. But he also listed many new streets where disease had taken hold: Union Street, Brunswick Street, the Park Street and Church Street areas, and Bank Top.[88] Streets on the flood plain east

21. *Local Board of Health plan of Darlington, c.1850–2.*

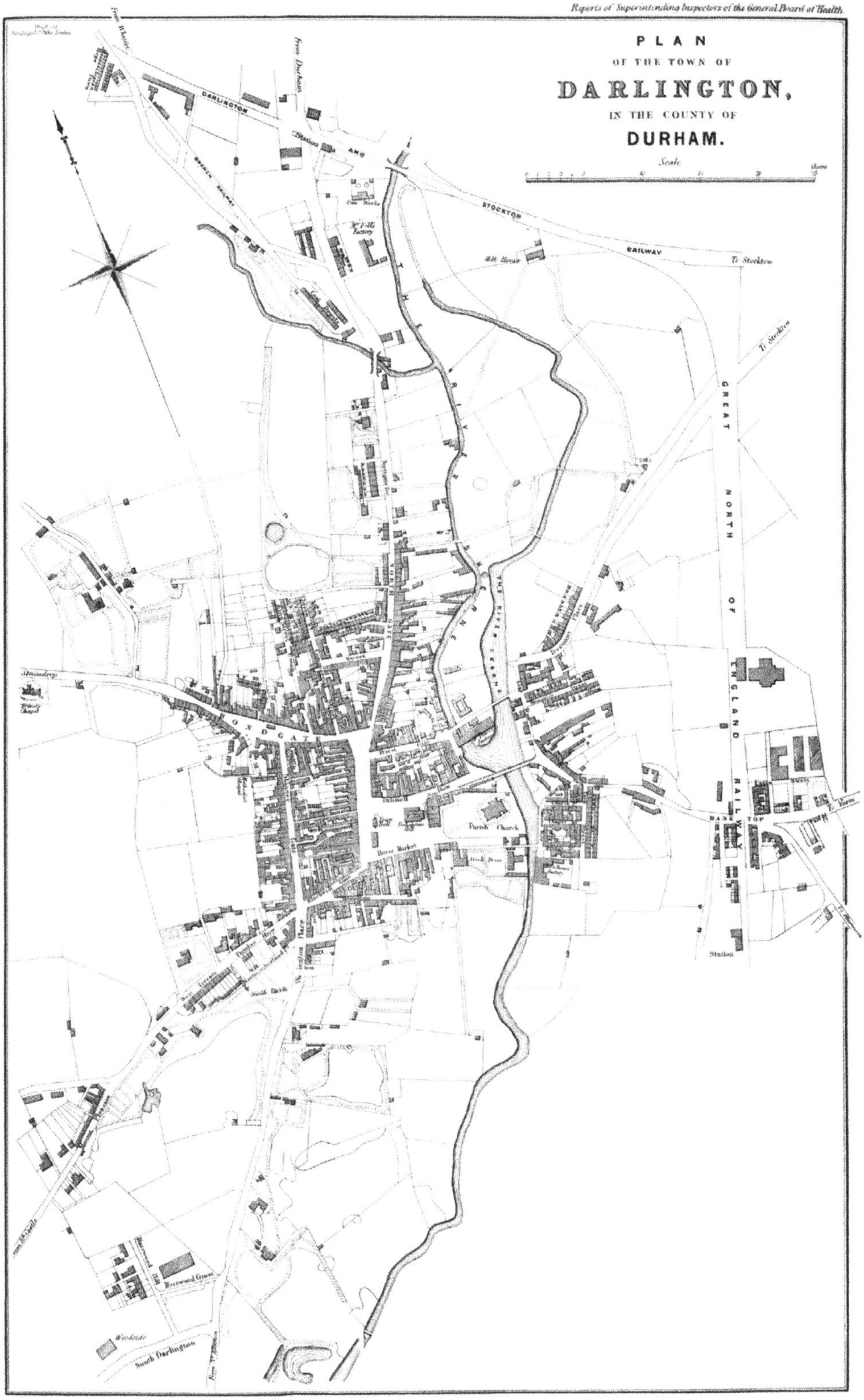

PLAN

OF THE TOWN OF

DARLINGTON,

IN THE COUNTY OF

DURHAM.

Scale

STOCKTON

RAILWAY

To Stockton

To Stockton

GREAT NORTH OF ENGLAND RAILWAY

DARLINGTON

Station

Parish Church

South Darlington

of the Skerne were soon as infamously insanitary as the riverside yards. Residents there had a poor life expectancy, although the lowest average age at death, 11 months, was to be found in Catterick's Yard, between Northgate and the Skerne, 'showing', said the medical officer, 'that the infantile population cannot be reared in such a place'.[89] Although there was little back-to-back housing in Darlington, in streets such as Brunswick Street, off Clay Row, accommodation was let room by room. The medical officer in 1851 described an Irish family of 10 suffering smallpox in one such lodging.[90]

The number of houses in Darlington had more than doubled between 1821 and 1841, from 876 to 1,783. In the less prosperous 1840s this rate of growth fell sharply, to under 11 per cent for the decade.[91] Mewburn, attuned to fluctuations in the property market through his work as a solicitor, thought it less buoyant. He gave the example of Pierremont, built in the early 1830s by John Botcherby in 22 a. of land at a total cost of £10,300, and sold for only £3,800 in 1844 when Botcherby ran into financial difficulties.[92] Mewburn took this as a symptom of 'the great depreciation of houses in Darlington'. But Pierremont, with its ornate Gothic style, windows stained with the initial of Botcherby and other decorations,[93] was exceptionally large and splendid, and there were few who could afford such a property and even fewer who would wish to live there. Many of the town's richest individuals were Quakers and there were still, in the 1840s, strong reservations among their number about flaunting wealth. In fact Pierremont was sold on two years later for £5,000 to become a Pease residence.[94] Mewburn also remarked that 'builders go on buying land at an enormous rate of 16s. per square yard and building houses thereon', suggesting no longstanding failure in demand for property.[95]

While change had been slow in the centre, dramatic growth was about to transform Darlington's suburbs. In the 20 years after 1851, Darlington's population, which had expanded little during the 1840s, increased almost two and a half times, from 11,582 to 27,729.[96] In 1851 the railways employed directly only about five per cent of the total male population, rising a little, to perhaps six per cent, by 1861.[97] After the discovery of new mineral deposits in Cleveland in

1851 came a major expansion of the Stockton and Darlington railway. A decision was taken to enlarge and relocate the railway's locomotive works, from Shildon, where they had been established in 1826, to Darlington, with the advantage of proximity to the GNER line. This new works, north of the old station and opened in 1862, employed 391 workers by 1865.[98]

Yet the railway workshops were only a minor cause of the town's exceptional growth. Much more important was the iron industry. The 1871 census report attributed the increase in population to 'the introduction of the manufacture of iron, to the erection of blast furnaces, rolling mills, forge works, engine building works and other smaller manufactories'. The engineering industry, with about four per cent of male employees in 1851, employed c. 14 per cent a decade later, a change largely explained by the establishment of the Darlington Forge.[99] The Forge was the first of four firms, together representing all stages of iron manufacture, to locate at Albert Hill between 1854 and 1864.[100] By 1875, 3,500 out of a total male population of 15,300 worked in the local iron industry, and a further 1,000 in the railway workshops. A great explosion of house building, and the creation of industrial suburbs in Darlington's rural surroundings, was triggered by this inward migration.

The new industrial settlement of Albert Hill was built on a green field site north east of the town, more striking than Bank Top or Hopetown in its 'uncompromising isolation'.[101] In 1853 Robert Henry Allen had agreed to sell 52 a. of land – the remaining portion of his Hill Top Farm estate, along with two acres which had been detached from the main Nestfield estate by the York to Newcastle railway line – for £10,000, to the proprietors of the Darlington Land Company, a group almost identical with the partnership of the South Durham Iron Company.[102] Industrial development of the site, on the north-west side of the junction of the North Eastern and Stockton and Darlington railways, began with the Darlington Forge Company early in 1854.[103] Allan himself laid the foundation stone of the South Durham Iron Company's works later that year.[104] The Darlington Iron Company set up alongside it in 1858.[105] Its owner, William Barningham, bought the Springfield farm,

an adjoining estate of 85 a. to the north, in 1859 for
£11,000, planning a further works even before his first was
completed.[106] The last of the four ironworks, the Skerne, was
established in 1864, but across the North Eastern Railway
from the other three, and bounded to the north by the river
Skerne. The plot of 22 a. had been bought from Allan in
1863.[107]

The construction of houses started with 11 'model
dwellings' by the South Durham Iron Company in 1854,
west of the NER line on a short track which would later
become Cleveland Street.[108] It is significant that when Henry
Pease and his associates sold the property to Barningham
for his works, house building was specifically prohibited. In
this way, the surrounding acres maintained a high value as
housing land for the thousands of ironworkers whose
arrival was anticipated. This was made explicit by Allan in
his calculations. Barningham had bought 13 a. for £2,733.
In agricultural use, the land would have been worth £1,674.
But Barningham's works would increase the population by
3,000, requiring 750 houses over the following decade.
With each house occupying 150 square yards, and the price
of a plot £30, 23 a. of residential land would make, with
interest, £23,625 over 10 years.[109]

In 1854 and 1857, Allan sold a total of eight acres of land
on the Haughton Road side of Albert Hill, part of his
Nestfield estate, to the developers Robert and William
Thompson, who had links with the Darlington and Albert
Hill Land Companies as well as the South Durham Iron
Co.[110] For the remainder of Nestfield, afterwards renamed
Albert Hill, a different approach was taken. Street plans
were drawn, and Allan's agent, George Dickinson,
advertised the sale of numbered plots, in groups or singly.
The first plans were laid in 1858, although it took some time
for the scheme to proceed.[111] A number of new streets were
approved by the local board of health in 1864.[112] It has been
calculated from the local board's building registers that
Albert Hill acquired 291 houses in five years from 1862, the
vast majority (207) during 1864. Development was mainly
piecemeal, with 29 different builders responsible for up to
20 houses each; two larger developers erected 35 and 57
dwellings over the period.[113] Some uniformity in the size,
quality and use of buildings was enforced by covenant; for

instance, roofs had to be of Westmorland slate.[114] The houses spread between Nestfield Street to the north, Allan Street on the south, and to the east, Barton Street; all street names in the triangle have Allan family connections. Albert Hill was surrounded on three sides by railway lines and sidings, and though apart from the town was soon densely populated. Development of streets on Haughton Lane soon followed, and continued after 1900.[115]

Proximity to industry was presented as an advantage, as in 1873 when building ground and new housing east of the railway in Killinghall Street was advertised as 'situate in the best part of Albert Hill Estate being near a great range of iron works there existing . . .'.[116] Part of the Darlington Land Company's property south of Cleveland Street and immediately west of the main railway line was developed by 1869 with small terraced houses bounded on all sides by foundries and engineering works.[117] Further streets, including Westgarth and Alexander, were built on the opposite side of Haughton Lane during the 1870s.[118] By the early 1900s, Albert Hill had nine pubs and four 'selling out shops', or off-licences.[119] An Anglican chapel of ease had been built in the 1860s, and there were also schools and Methodist and Roman Catholic churches.[120]

It is said that the Albert Hill site was selected after John Pease declined to sell land nearer the centre 'on the ground that there was a feeling in Darlington against having the atmosphere vitiated by manufactures and he would not be the first to introduce such a nuisance into his native town'.[121] Whether or not this was the case, Pease did soon allow land from his Hill House estate, south-west of the Stockton and Darlington line and a short distance from the Albert Hill industrial sites, to be developed with railway sidings and coal depots.[122] Not until the 1870s did housing development encroach on Pease's East Mount estate, between Upper John Street (now East Mount Road) and the railway, and it was after the turn of the century that the area became thoroughly built over.[123]

The other area of rapid expansion was around the original railway station, where Hopetown and Rise Carr were also transformed into engineering colonies. Whessoe Lane was diverted from its existing route in 1858. The old road, which had left North Road just past the coal depot and then crossed the rail spur on the level behind Westbrook gardens before traversing the main Stockton and Darlington railway by means of a long and narrow tunnel, was re-named Hopetown Lane. The new Whessoe Road avoided this series of obstacles by joining the main road north of the station and main line.[124] The 1871 census shows new streets in this area populated almost entirely with railway- and iron-workers.[125] Hopetown started with Foundry Street and Alliance Street, bordering the rail line on its western side by the mid 1850s,[126] and grew south across open fields towards the town.[127] The area north of the station, on either side of the Durham road, developed more intensively still. Whessoe Lane was laid out with new streets from the early 1860s.[128] Robert Thompson, of Honeypot House, in Honeypot Lane (now Longfield Road), launched an ambitious plan to develop his land in 1859.[129] He built Thompson Street, running from near his house, across North Road, and as far as the North Eastern Railway line. Farmland in the angle between Thompson Street and Honeypot Lane was proposed as the site of new streets with 182 houses.[130] Thompson was also responsible for building many streets in Neasham Road in the 1870s. Development around Thompson Street took longer than anticipated but several dozens of houses were in place by the century's end, and building continued thereafter.[131] To accommodate the increase in traffic, Northgate was widened in 1899.[132] Housing also grew up around Robert Stephenson's works, south of Thompson Street, after the Peases' enforced sale of 1902.[133] The level of development was such that in February 1908 Stephenson's was ordered to start work within three months on a new bridge over the railway, to eliminate the increasingly dangerous Thompson Street level crossing.[134]

Terrace housing also colonised open land along North Road, mainly in streets set at right angles to the main road. On the east, on W. A. Backhouse's land and designed by George Dickinson, came Aldam, Charles, Alfred, Gurney, and Katherine Streets, named after Backhouse's family; then Havelock, Shildon, Henry, Grass, Close and Field Streets.[135] West of the main road, between the locomotive works and the North Cemetery, a group of parallel streets was laid out. One of these, Westmoreland, linked into Whessoe Lane via Jane Street.[136] Some at least of the properties built here in the 1870s were back-to-back.[137] Shorter roads between the cemetery access and Thompson Street were culs-de-sac ending at the cemetery boundary wall.[138] North Road acquired a mission church in 1861, seating 400, and provided by the local developers Robert and William Thompson; it was replaced by the permanent building of St Paul's in 1872.[139] South of the Stockton and Darlington station, McNay and Stephenson Streets were fitted into a confined site along with several other working-class terraces.[140] The nearby Westbrook Villas, overlooking the gardens laid out by Henry Pease and the Cocker Beck, were built mainly after 1855. Plots for one or two houses were sold gradually by Pease,[141] and by 1871 there were 14 occupied dwellings, of a distinctly middle-class type. Other than living-in servants, few of its inhabitants were natives of the town. Heads of household included the secretary of the South Durham Iron Company, managers of the railway and of the wagon works, and a colliery agent. One house there was a school with 18 resident pupils.[142]

In contrast with Darlington's industrial settlements, a very different scheme was taking shape near the town's eastern boundary on Yarm Road. The Freeholders' Home Estate, soon re-named Eastbourne, was initiated in 1849 as the Darlington and South Durham Freehold Land Society, registered as a building society.[143] Emulating similar schemes elsewhere, the stated objective was to sell plots cheaply so that industrious working-class men could become 40s. freeholders and qualify for the county vote.[144] It was also intended 'to lay the foundation of an honourable independence and to elevate the social and moral condition of the people', and included the provision of 'gardens for the industrious'. Through buying wholesale and dividing among members at cost price, plots with a market value of £50 could be offered for £18 to £20. It was calculated that members contributing 1s. 6d. a week could pay for a plot in five years. The prospectus stated that applicants of any age, sex or party, and from within the town or outside, were acceptable, although the fact that streets were named after Cobden and Bright suggests the trustees' political preference.[145] Other streets were called after some of the Liberal Quaker promoters, who included Henry Pease, John Harris and Alfred Kitching, all of them also proprietors of the Albert Hill Land Company.[146] By 1855, roads had been laid out and the land apportioned into 144 plots, ready to be allocated by lot to members who were allowed to buy up to six each. After some argument about street widths, the local board of health declared itself satisfied with the plan in 1858.[147] Although 91 shareholders had paid a deposit before the prospectus was published, only a scattered handful of houses was built in the 1850s.[148] The varied style of housing at Eastbourne is witness to its gradual and piecemeal development.[149] However laudable the aims – ' a stepping stone to an honorable independence – as offering the means for a noble resistance to the invitation of the workhouse – and as a machine to effect man's political redemption . . .'[150] – there were disadvantages in Eastbourne's situation away from major workplaces. The trustees had been influenced by the cheapness of land on the outskirts of town, and by chance selected a position away from the districts where industry was to flourish during the following decades. The inconvenience of Eastbourne is one possible cause of its slow growth. In addition, although the scheme represented good value and was flexible in the case of a member's inability to pay subscriptions, home ownership was simply

22. *Cobden Street, part of the Freeholders' Home, or Eastbourne, Estate.*

beyond the means of most. The low cost of land in Yarm Road was presumably a factor which also influenced the poor law guardians in choosing a site next to Eastbourne for the town's new workhouse, designed by Charles J. Adams of Stockton-on-Tees to accommodate 250 inmates and 50 vagrants, and opened in 1870.[151]

A MEETING OF TOWN AND SUBURBS

In the town centre, pressure for cheap working-class housing was greatest. Despite its concerns about health in the central yards, the local board approved plans for further dwellings in Catterick's Yard in 1857 after a scheme incorporating schools and cottages was apparently revised. Behind three shops fronting on to Northgate, Catterick's was a narrow yard with 18 houses, the end of the row hanging over the mill race. It was proposed to add 11 new cottages of single room plan, with an improved access street. In the yard would then be 29 houses and three shops with living accommodation, served by 11 privies.[152] The land-owner was the same John Pease who was said to have opposed industrial development because of its impact on the town's environment.[153] After abandoning his plan for Catterick's Yard, he laid out Russell Street to the south, in place of the access road of the earlier scheme. Other property of his nearby, between Half Moon Yard and Tyson's Yard, was offered for sale as building ground in 12 lots, each of about 200 square yards.[154] In 1860, with Russell Street almost complete between Northgate and the Skerne, Pease proposed to extend it further by moving slightly the site of an existing bridge; the present bridge there was built by John Dunning in 1881.[155] In conjunction with new bridges crossing the mill race and river in East Street built in about 1870, this gave access to the new terraced housing in the area behind Freeman's Place.[156] Pease laid out Chesnut Street in 1868 in 36 plots, including sites on either side of the street in Northgate for a police court and Presbyterian chapel.[157]

Except for North Terrace and a few villas, Northgate had been little developed between Bulmer's stone and the coal depots. From the 1860s the town began to grow north-wards, with streets of houses encroaching on any vacant site.

Buck's Charity obtained permission in 1864 to dispose of Buck's Close, on the east side of Northgate; the site was sold in 24 lots, development proceeding after drainage problems had been solved.[158] Leadenhall Street and the area around Chesnut Street began to be built up soon afterwards, mainly with housing.[159] Livingstone Buildings replaced the redundant coal depots in Northgate in about 1870.[160] Edward Lyall, on behalf of the Peases, laid out new streets between Russell Street and Chesnut Street in 1885, although some of the sites there were still vacant and available for building at the time of the Pease liquidation sale in 1902.[161] After the family's failure, their various Skerne bridges – Russell Street, the very similar one in Chesnut Street, and East Street – were transferred to the corporation of Darlington.[162]

To the east also, the town met its suburbs as the bishop's Low and High parks were further developed. The bishop's palace or manor house, no longer used as the poor-house, was bought in 1870 by Richard Luck and demolished to make room for a terrace which took his name.[163] Beyond Park Street, home of unskilled, mainly textile, workers at the time of the 1871 census, the quality of housing improved as the land rose towards Bank Top. Park Place, Model Place and Swan Street had residents of a rather higher class, skilled manual workers such as textile factory mechanics, a master builder and a railway inspector. Hargreave Terrace, running along the boundary between the High and Low parks, was still under development, with only six inhabited houses, where could be found a railway clerk, a master stonemason and master hatter. Pensbury Street, completed in 1874, occupied the last open ground before the station.[164]

TOWN CENTRE DEVELOPMENT, 1860s–1900s

Despite the intensive development in and around the centre, by 1879 the architect G. G. Hoskins was able to write that 'our town is a pleasant town, a clean town, with picturesque surroundings, and on the whole a healthy town'.[165] Environmental improvements had followed the establishment of the local board of health in 1850, including clearance of a group of old cottages – 'that vile eyesore' – which stood in the middle of Bondgate; the moving of

23. Model Place, a second phase of development on the bishop's Low Park beyond Park and Bridge Streets.

pumps to more convenient locations; and a programme of street repair and re-paving.[166] Removing the cattle market to the outside of town was first suggested in 1859.[167] There was also concern about the old butter market, a gift of the late Edward Pease 'for the protection of the market women' which had been superseded by a covered building. The old market, an open shed at the north end of the town hall, had become 'a place for play on the Sabbath, and is otherwise objectionable'. Demolition was recommended.[168] By the following year, 1860, it had been decided that Darlington should have a new covered corn market and an architects' competition was advertised.[169] Joseph Pease, on behalf of the board, enquired of fellow Quakers around the country for ideas about essential design features.[170] The board's surveyor, George Dickinson, and the Middlesbrough civil engineer, John Dunning, who also acted as surveyor to the Owners of the Middlesbrough Estate and had other connections with the Pease family, continued the investigations and a visit was made by board members to see the market in Blackburn, resulting in a change of policy against an open-sided building.[171] The scheme when it finally came to pass included a new town hall as well as a market building, both designed by Waterhouse in 1861–4.[172]

Spencer in 1862 looked back to a time 40 years earlier when 'the mill at the foot of Priestgate was considered a huge building', but times had changed and 'its dimensions are remembered now as insignificant when contrasted with the magnitude of the successive erections'.[173] Many new public and commercial buildings appeared in the town after 1850. The Mechanics' Institute moved to impressive new premises in Skinnergate in 1854, which had been designed by Joseph Sparkes (1817–55), a minor architect and member of a local Quaker family.[174] A police station designed by William Crozier was built in Northgate in 1866–7, and the county court building in Coniscliffe Road dates from the same time.[175] Waterhouse built a new bank on High Row for Backhouses. His clerk of works on Backhouses' bank, George Gordon Hoskins, settled in Darlington and built up his own business designing some of the finest new constructions, including Crown Street Chambers (1879–86) and the *North Star* newspaper office in Crown Street (1882); the Edward Pease Free Library (1884); rebuilding the King's Head Hotel (1890–93); the technical college in Northgate (1894); shops and offices on the corner of Skinnergate and Coniscliffe Road (1895–7); rebuilding the Red Lion Hotel, Priestgate (1903); and the Hippodrome theatre, Clay Row (1904).[176] Darlington bridge, called St Cuthbert's bridge to distinguish it from the series of new bridges along the Skerne, was rebuilt in 1895 under the supervision of the county engineer, William Crozier, funded jointly by the Durham county council and the corporation of Darlington, with steelwork by Teasdale Brothers of Darlington.[177]

With the town hall barely 30 years old, a scheme was proposed for new municipal buildings. In 1893, rules were published for an architectural competition, to which 84 plans were submitted. The winning entry, selected by the president of the Royal Institute of British Architects, was that of Clark and Moscrop; Hoskins trailed in third.[178] It proposed a building with frontages to Horse market and to Feethams, incorporating a public hall at the corner of Feethams and Houndgate, and with a large court for light on the west side.[179] Though the cost of £27,622 was within the £30,000 budget, it nonetheless raised great contro-versy.[180] Cllr. Edward Wooler took a leading role in opposing the development. Shortly after the new town hall was proposed, a syndicate headed by Wooler bought the Central Hall from the National Provincial Bank of England with a view to modernising and extending it.[181] The town, it was said, 'lacks a comfortable and commodious hall'. The Central Hall, with its 'want of warmth and erratic ventilation' was known as 'Darlington's death trap'.[182] Wooler and his associates proposed increasing the capacity from 1,200 to 1,450, and installing heating. They argued that these improvements to the Central Hall made the municipal scheme unnecessary, and were successful in preventing it from proceeding.[183]

To accommodate new developments in the town came additional central streets, some instigated by Pease family members. One such was John Pease's Russell Street, at the Northgate junction of which he erected new buildings in 1864.[184] The local board of health bought up premises in Tubwell Row in about 1862, with the idea of driving a new street through to Priestgate. This involved the demolition of several properties, including a lodging house registered for 25 residents, formerly run by Billy Mead, 'an extensive dealer in mutton pies' and the first Irishman to gain a settlement in Darlington. Despite its clientele of vagrants and tramps, the house was considered very clean compared with those of other towns.[185] A more ambitious scheme followed in 1869, to form Crown, Quebec and East Streets, run the latter through to Freeman's Place, and culvert the mill race.[186] Drawn in more detail in 1871, it proposed considerable demolition alongside the water channel.[187] Various permissions were obtained from 1872, and streets subsequently laid on other parts of the Pease's Mill Dam property, north of Russell Street.[188] Further construction of streets and the culverting of the mill dam prompted the demolition of an old warehouse at Crown Point, and other buildings connected to the Pease textile factory in Priestgate.[189]

At the end of the 19th century came renewed debate about extending Darlington's market facilities. The civil engineer and surveyor E. W. Lyall, apparently acting on behalf of the Pease family, offered a site in Mill Street (the re-named East Street) for covered and uncovered markets, with a fish market next to the Poor Law Guardian offices, in

1896.[190] A new road would extend, parallel with Quebec Street, to Russell Street, and the market would occupy land between this and the River Skerne. Lyall told the council that there would be 'no objection to your covering in the river with steel joists and brick arching . . . thus adding a further 1572 sq. yards to the area . . .'[191] The scheme came to nothing, and soon afterwards the Mill Dam holdings had to be sold along with other Pease properties in the family's financial catastrophe of 1902. [192] Another former Pease possession in Crown Street, sold in 1909, became the site of the offices and printing works of the North of England Newspaper Company Ltd.[193]

On the other side of town, John Beaumont Pease was responsible for further significant road-building. Victoria Road and Beaumont Street, to the east of Grange Road, were started in 1867.[194] Victoria Road, crossing the old cricket ground which had been on the bishop's Low Park, was later extended to Bank Top, to the new station which opened in 1887.[195] The road became the main approach to Bank Top station after the corporation, which had bought Feethams Lane and opened out the road to the west entrance of the 'New Central Station', petitioned the directors of the North Eastern Railway Company.[196] The west entrance to the station was shortly afterwards re-opened and the station approach completed. A hotel had opened there by the century's end.[197] The old way to Bank Top, now called Parkgate, about which there had been many complaints, was widened in 1899.[198]

QUAKER ESTATES AND THEIR REDEVELOPMENT

There were several very wealthy families in Darlington by the middle of the 19th century, yet few ostentatious properties in the town. Many of the most prosperous individuals, as members of the Society of Friends, still adhered to a code of relative modesty in worldly goods. Edward Pease retained some influence over his family's business ethics and lifestyles, although after 1850 this was weakening. Pease himself lived in a plain three-storied 18th-century house in Northgate, his garden running down to the Skerne where it adjoined the grounds of East Mount, home of his eldest son John from 1838.[199] When Pease moved into Northgate House in 1798, it was the last building on the right on the route out of town, and had a library and drawing room opening on to a back lawn, and a rustic bridge leading over the stream to an orchard.[200] Other Quakers remained in similarly substantial and comfortable though unpretentious houses: Jonathan and Hannah Chapman Backhouse at Polam Hall; Joseph Pease (d. 1846) at Feethams, close to the Market Place; his son John Beaumont Pease at North Lodge until 1873, although by then the town was growing all around.[201]

Around the mid century, there was much activity extending and improving Quaker houses, and especially a fashion for conservatories and vineries from 1851, reflecting a love of gardening among members of the sect, and also a general enthusiasm for glasshouses after the Great Exhibition. The architects and builders Richardson and Ross were responsible for many of these, and also designed new windows for North Lodge and Southend, and extensions to Woodlands, as well as a lodge for Pierremont.[202] To Woodside, built for John C. Hopkins by Thomas Robson jun. in 1842 and bought by the Quaker civil engineer John Harris c. 1848, Richardson and Ross

24. *North Lodge, built in the mid 1830s for John Beaumont Pease.*

added a vast conservatory and a tower and wing. By 1860 Joseph Pease, second son of Edward, had filled the 27 a. grounds of his Darlington house, Southend, acquired from the Backhouses in 1826, with 'summer houses, temples and ponds', as well as building a seaside home at Marske during the 1840s.[203] His brother Henry offended their father even more when in 1845 he bought Pierremont, described as the Buckingham Palace of Darlington, and by Edward Pease as 'this showy mansion'; some of its 22 a. were laid out as South Park Garden in 1873.[204] Edward Pease was similarly displeased by extensive alterations to John Pease's East Mount in 1845.[205] Woodside became another Pease residence after Harris's death in 1869.[206] Part of the grounds was sold off for housing, but the mansion retained a park and gardens of more than 17 a.[207]

Before 1860 the extensive Pease clan tended to buy existing properties and build little. After that date, several new Pease residences appeared on the outskirts of town. For Henry Fell Pease on his marriage in 1862, Brinkburn was built of the Peases' own buff-coloured brick as an adjoining estate to that of his father at Pierremont. The local firm of Richardson and Ross consulted Alfred Waterhouse about their plans for Brinkburn.[208] John Pease of East Mount built Woodburn for his daughter Sophia Fry, and Elm Ridge for

25. *Woodside, greatly extended by John Harris between 1848 and 1869, was demolished in the 1930s and its park sold for building.*

another daughter, Mary Anna Hodgkin, both designed by G. G. Hoskins in 1865–7.[209] Hummersknott, designed by Alfred Waterhouse, along with Uplands and Wilton House, all for Pease family members, were built west of Carmel Road, beyond the developing west end.[210] Mowden Hall, by Richardson and Ross in 1862 and with alterations in 1881–5 and 1899 by Waterhouse, replaced an older house called Bushel Hill off the Staindrop road.[211] The new hall was of a style and on a scale which would not have found favour with an early generation of Quakers, and its first owner, Edwin Lucas Pease, was killed in 1889 while following the un-Quakerly pursuit of hunting.[212]

The town's growth on its northern and western fringes was dependent upon a handful of landowners. The tithe map of 1847 shows three principal estates to the north and north-west – those of John Beaumont Pease of North Lodge, Ann Pease of West Lodge and William Backhouse of Elmfield – while there were two estates to the south-west, belonging to Joseph Pease of Southend and Edmund Backhouse of Polam Hall.[213] The land was occupied primarily by large houses and their grounds, the remainder leased as pasture and market gardens. In 1855, with Elmfield, there began a trend of dividing these land-holdings. The mansions more centrally located, having been embellished and extended, were abandoned as an older generation died out and their heirs preferred to live out of the town. Sometimes the building survived intact, sometimes it was sub-divided or demolished. The parkland was set out for new housing. According to Mewburn, Back-house's gardens at Elmfield had been 'laid out and beautified with great taste. Now he has left the town, and those charming grounds are to be divided into building lots!'[214] Elmfield itself was bought by Alfred Kitching, and the estate developed, with a swimming bath and a new street, Kendrew Street, and later with Elmfield Terrace and Gladstone Street.[215] The rest became North Lodge Park.[216]

The building up with terrace housing of the grounds of Greenbank began in 1875, when the villa, latterly the home of Henry King Spark, was demolished.[217] Francis Parr, a local architect and surveyor, acted for the Greenbank Estate in drawing street plans.[218] A style of terraced house believed unique to Darlington appeared on part of the Greenbank property, in Wycombe Street and on the north side of Dodds Street. Known as 'back and front houses', they differed from back-to-backs in having both back and front doors, linked by a long passage.[219] From 1881, Greenbank's development was taken over by a new company, the Darlington Estate Co. Ltd., in existence until 1890, whose directors included a Pease son-in-law, Theodore Fry M. P., and the newspaper proprietor Hugh Gilzean Reid.[220] E. W. Lyall was appointed agent.[221] The estate was offered in lots to suit purchasers in 1881, with a block sold for the new hospital.[222] An area beyond Greenbank was opened for development when bridges were built over the Cocker beck, linking Salisbury Terrace to Surtees Street in 1893, and Easson Road (the extension of Four Riggs Lane) to Brook Terrace in 1897.[223]

The home of John Beaumont Pease, North Lodge, was let for a time after the deaths of Pease and his wife in the 1870s.[224] In 1892 his executors began to develop the estate, including the area north of Corporation Road, using the architects Clark and Moscrop as agents.[225] By 1914, the houses of the Greenbank and North Lodge estates had met Hope Town's southward development, with only the small valley and allotments around the Cocker Beck, and the retained open space of North Lodge Park, providing relief among the terraces.[226] Most of the new housing was designed for the working class, though of a better standard than that, for example, on the Cleveland estate behind Skinnergate. Middle-class terraces lined Greenbank Road and the sides of North Lodge Park.

Southend was redeveloped at about the same time. There were plans to break up the estate in 1872 after the death of Joseph Pease. His eldest son, Joseph Whitwell Pease, who had lived in Woodlands from the time of his marriage in 1854, moved away from Darlington in 1867 to enjoy the lifestyle of a landed magnate.[227] Initially Southend passed to various members of the Pease family, and some peripheral land appears to have been sold for building.[228] The property was eventually disposed of in c. 1897 to the Darlington Southend Estate Company Ltd., established specifically to develop it.[229] The villa survived to become a school, surrounded by streets of houses designed by Hoskins.[230] Pierremont lasted a little longer as a private house, until the death of Henry Pease's widow, Mary, in 1909. Its division into three dwellings was completed in 1913, and the grounds laid out with roads of good quality housing.[231]

MIDDLE-CLASS HOUSING AND THE CLEVELAND ESTATE

Before 1850, there had been only limited building on the west side of Darlington. The 'commodious and substantial' nine-bedroomed mansion called Field House, beyond the coal road a mile to the west of town, stood alone but for a few agricultural cottages. The mansion may have resulted from a rebuilding of Field House Farm after the farm's tenant, Francis Holmes, was bankrupted in 1782.[232] John Wetherell lived there in 1783, and the property was sold in 1818 after the failure of the bank in which he was a partner.[233] It was divided for sale, the lots including Pease Porridge Farm.[234] The mansion was still isolated enough at that time to attract a religious community, becoming the Mount Carmel convent in 1830, with St Clare's Abbey built in the grounds in 1855–8.[235] Some other small projects took shape in the west end before the mid century, but a restricted demand for high quality housing meant that schemes could take years to complete. In *c.* 1838 'very grand arrangements' for a development to be called South Darlington, which included 'imposing' houses with front gardens, on land owned by William Falkous at Bank Close in the junction of Blackwell Lane and Grange Road, came to nothing.[236] A plan for 'genteel houses'[237] at Harewood Grove in 1845 had not started 10 years later.[238]

From the 1860s, there was a much more sustained demand for houses suitable for the growing managerial and professional sector. Mewburn identified 1864 as the year when houses and land in Darlington rose greatly in price,[239] and his view is supported by the rate at which building plans were deposited with the local authority. Applications peaked in 1864, with 398 houses, and again in 1876, when 435 were proposed. The figure for 1864 was somewhat inflated by the extraordinary rate of development at Albert Hill, which contributed more than half the total.[240] The peak in 1876, coinciding with a boom in house building across the north-east region, included many more homes for the professional classes, and in particular the development of the Cleveland estate.[241]

Before the Cleveland scheme, there had been other attempts to provide housing for the middle class in the 1860s. Freehold building land divided into 37 lots, in the triangle between Coniscliffe Road and Cleveland Terrace, was offered in 1863, though only half was sold.[242] Between six and seven acres around Pierremont Crescent and Woodland Terrace were divided for auction in 1864 following the death of the owner, James Barlow. Of the 45 plots, several were quickly taken before the sale date.[243] The Backhouses themselves instigated plans to develop housing around West Lodge in 1865, although the scheme fell into abeyance until 1909.[244] Polam Lane was laid out in 1873 to open up the extensive grounds of Polam Hall for building; the hall itself had long been converted to a school.[245] Another group of executors offered plots in the Linden Avenue area between Coniscliffe Road and Carmel Road in 1874, but the land remained undeveloped more than 20 years later.[246] Small scale building continued in Grange Road, Coniscliffe Road and Woodland Terrace over the following decades.[247]

But it was building on the duke of Cleveland's estate from 1870 which transformed Darlington's west end. The houses there accounted for much of the building activity of the 1870s, and about half of the houses that were approved during the boom year of 1876.[248] As lay rector, the duke held the parochial glebe, a wedge of land running out of town from Skinnergate to Carmel Road, bounded on the north by Woodland Road and a lane later called Milbank Road, and to the south by Coniscliffe Lane and Cleveland Terrace. The glebe land was almost entirely given over to agriculture. There were few buildings: the parsonage stood isolated in fields until later approached by Uplands Road; Cleveland dairy lay between the parsonage and Cleveland Terrace; the Glebe farm was situated on the northern boundary lane;[249] Holy Trinity church had been built by the architect Anthony Salvin on Woodland Road in 1836–8.[250] The first encroachment on the Green Tree Fields, that part of the glebe adjacent to Skinnergate, was the Drill Shed, joined by Edwards' wooden theatre which was near the Friends' wall, and which moved to a permanent building near the Bridge inn, Northgate, in 1867.[251] In 1857 the duke sold small plots from the Green Tree Field, adjoining the Friends' burying ground behind Skinnergate, which enabled gardens of two private houses, and the precincts of St Augustine's church, to be extended.[252] For the glebe to be developed further, a private Act of Parliament was obtained in 1867, authorising leases and sales. [253] The first plan to build on the Cleveland estate was submitted to the council in 1868 by John Ross, whose firm, Ross and Lamb, handled most such applications on the duke's behalf until the end of the 1870s.[254]

Although the Cleveland estate appears a pleasant and leafy middle-class enclave, most of the early development was of working-class housing. Of houses approved by 1876, it has been calculated that 157 were in working-class streets, and only 48 in middle-class areas.[255] Roads were laid out and named by the duke's agent, and plots or whole streets then sold for building. Working-class dwellings, which were all sited in streets nearest the town, were mainly rented out by small-scale owners. Beyond Stanhope Road, houses were exclusively middle-class, and almost entirely owner-occupied, either built speculatively for sale, or designed specifically for their owners.[256] It was envisaged at the outset that Duke Street, breaking out of Skinnergate as the new route into the west end, would have streets of small terraced houses on either side. From its junction with Stanhope Road there were to be larger houses. The area around Holy Trinity church, the north side of Cleveland Terrace, and Langholm Terrace (now Crescent) would be developed with terraces of middle-class housing, obliterating the Cleveland dairy. Far to the west, in Carmel Road, facing the abbey, convent and some of the Pease houses, plots were offered for eight very substantial villas.[257] By 1881, there had been adjustment to this plan. The area between Skinnergate and Stanhope Road was indeed almost filled with small terraced houses, including some in a separate scheme off Bondgate, where proposals made in 1875 for Granville Terrace, Corporation Road and Portland Place were carried out with some amendment.[258] Duke Street was only half complete, and its houses and shops more substantial than originally proposed, serving to conceal the back streets behind.[259] The construction of villas there was still in progress at the end of the century.[260] Building on the west of Stanhope Road had

only recently started, and with a significant change from the original scheme. The grammar school and ladies' training college filled one side of Vane Terrace,[261] so that the projected development of the field in front was abandoned, leaving Stanhope Green as a pleasant public space.[262]

It has been argued that the duke's plan to develop the west end as far as Cleveland Avenue, submitted to the local authority in 1874, proved to be over optimistic as it was still incomplete 20 years later.[263] But the estate did not approach the development of the area west of Stanhope Road with the same urgency it had applied to the working-class streets nearer the town centre. That the duke held a long view of the development of his land is shown by the tight control exercised over the size, style and quality of housing erected, ensuring that the estate's residual holding maintained its value, to be realised in due course as further plots were disposed of. The duke continued to invest heavily in extending roads and other infrastructure, and sales of land were steady if unspectacular.

26. *Middle-class housing in the west end, Stanhope Road.*

Between 1881 and 1896, the Cleveland estate's agent in Darlington, J. P. Pritchett, made one to three sales a year of property on the west end development, with the exception of 1885, when six were sold. Some of these transactions included land for more than one house. In 1897, when there were eight sales, and 1898, with nine, building activity started to increase. The value of sales from 1881 to 1898 amounted to £12,823. Between January 1898 and May 1904, Pritchett sold 75,600 square yards of land for a total of £15,504, and leased a further 19,360 square yards to the trustees of the grammar school. During this period £4,700 had been spent on roads, opening up land with a possible market value of £11,000. Pritchett argued in 1904 for further investment in road-building in Abbey Road, Cross Street and Uplands Road, which would cost £3,755 while making available building land worth over £30,000 and giving access to future roads and sites.[264] Considerable street-building activity took place in the first decade of the 20th century. Langholm Crescent was completed in 1901, Vane Terrace extended, and the area around Swinburne and Uplands Roads developed, along with numerous rear access streets.[265]

Pritchett received a small commission on each sale negotiated, and retained a right to specify a minimum value and approve the design of each house. In practice this meant that he was often employed as architect, leading to possible conflicts of interest when he was not, as a dissatisfied client complained in 1903.[266] The superior plots on Carmel Road were still little taken up by 1902, when a resident wrote to Lord Barnard complaining of trees being felled. 'One of the most beautiful roads in Darlington' had been 'disfigured', and the sale of land there may be prejudiced.[267] Buildings started to extend west of Cleveland Avenue shortly before the First World War, with a new girls' high school, on land bought and leased by the Durham county council, and several detached villas adjoining.[268]

WORKING-CLASS HOUSING, 1890S–1914

There was concern, if not agreement, about the standard and quantity of working-class housing in the borough. A serious epidemic of enteric fever in 1890–1 caused sufficient anxiety to trigger an enquiry, and for the outbreak to be charted on to a street list.[269] This shows eastern and central areas, including Albert Hill, as worst affected; the crowded streets of North Ward escaped lightly. In 1902 a councillor described housing in the town as 'a pinching and pressing question', although he was much in a minority. Others argued that Darlington was a healthy and sanitary town, and that it was a mistake to exaggerate the overcrowding. The issue arose at this time because of a scheme to lend money for house purchases at rates lower than building societies, which the council declined to join, on the grounds that this would help only those who could already help themselves.[270] The local authority set up a limited enquiry in 1903 into working-class housing, at which witnesses argued that there was a scarcity of good quality accommodation, especially in the north of the town, where an influx of workers to the Stephenson factory had exacerbated the shortage.[271]

On the eve of war the council, still reluctant to become involved in house-building, tried to identify sites suitable for working-class, as distinct from 'better class', homes.[272] A list was produced of houses built in each ward between 1873 and 1913, showing the North-West Ward with the highest rate of house-building after 1895. Growth in the East-bourne area was much faster after 1900 than before; but slowing in the Albert Hill district of East Ward, despite a single year's upsurge in new houses in 1903.[273] Building during the first decade of the 20th century was mapped by the council's surveyor, who pointed to major growth between Pierremont, the hospital and Bell Lane (now Brinkburn Road) in the north west of the town, and also between Hope Town and the technical college in Northgate. There were also high rates of development in the west end around Linden Avenue and Elton Parade, and in the area between Cleveland Terrace and the ladies' training college; Grange House to Harewood Grove, in Grange Road; in the Victoria Embankment and cattle market areas between the town centre and main station; further out of town, south of Bank Top and west of Eastbourne; and in the Haughton Road area, between Upper John Street and the wagon works, and between the brewery and brick works.[274] The cattle market had been relocated to Park Lane, and the

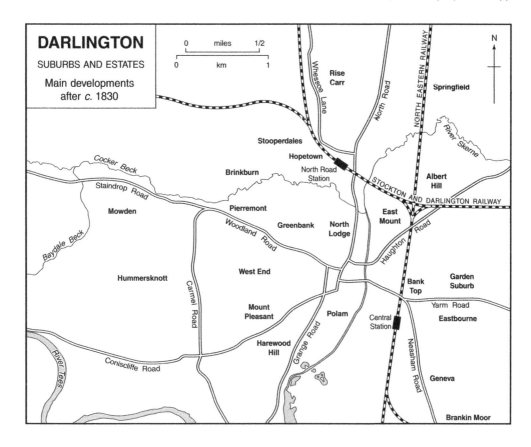

DARLINGTON

SUBURBS AND ESTATES

Main developments
after *c.* 1830

0   miles   1/2

0   km   1

27. *Darlington suburbs and estates developed after 1850.*

surrounding area was built up, extending along the Victoria Embankment, from the 1860s.[275] East of Bank Top station, a network of streets grew up along Neasham and Yarm Roads.[276] New streets off Borough Road, between Clay Row and Freeman's Place,[277] were packed around the town's power station, built 1900–01.[278] This last development brought a wider benefit to the town as a whole, in making possible electric street lighting from 1901.[279]

The intensive building in some districts was to a degree relieved by new public open spaces. Darlington had a public park as early as 1853, and one which acquired a reputation for its botanical specimens, appropriate in a town with a long tradition of Quaker horticulturalists. South Park was originally laid out in 1853, incorporating a 20 a. farm, the Poor Howdens, which was part of the Bellasis charity, and situated on the southern boundary of Darlington township, immediately east of the Skerne.[280] Joseph Pease arranged its lease from the vestry, contributed to the cost of making the park, and donated 100 tons of furnace slag to surface the footpaths. The name changed from Bellasis Park to People's, New, Victoria and finally South Park, and it was bought by the corporation in 1877. After four extensions it came to cover 91 a.[281] Its buildings and facilities were also augmented. The butter market shed was moved there from the town centre in 1859.[282] Tennis courts appeared in the park in 1885.[283] A new bridge was built at the Grange Road entrance in 1887.[284] Out of fees paid by skaters in the 1890s, a bandstand was bought for £250; it opened in 1893.[285] Later, in 1901, came the tower, with a clock by Potts of Leeds, and a tea pavilion which opened in 1908.[286]

In general, Darlington's existing parks, those private ones belonging to Quaker mansions, did not become public, although several escaped the immediate pressure of housing development and found a new life in commercial horticulture. After Henry Pease's death in 1881, his seven-acre botanical garden, called South Pierremont Park, was let to Kent and Brydon, seed merchants and nurserymen.[287] John Brydon also rented four acres and a greenhouse at Hummersknott from Arthur Pease in 1902.[288] North Lodge Park was exceptional in having been formed from the grounds of two Quaker residences, North Lodge and Elmfield, for a public park in 1903. It acquired a bowling green and pavilion shortly afterwards.[289] Darlington's second public park was also unusual in having been part of a private estate. Stanhope Green, originally intended as a site of housing in the duke of Cleveland's west end, was instead re-designated as open space when the grammar school and ladies' training college were built opposite. It was bought by the council in 1878 and laid out in 1879.[290] After arguments over its name – College Green was suggested – it was soon provoking further controversy amidst claims that it was a 'neglected park'.[291]

Other new parks followed in the most intensively populated areas of town. North Park, 15½ a. adjacent to the North Cemetery on the Honeypot estate, was bought by the council in 1894, opened in 1896 and had a bowling green laid out in 1903.[292] Albert Hill recreation ground was opened in 1901,[293] and East Park the following year, acquiring a bowling green in 1908.[294] Eastbourne Park was counted the town's seventh, opening in 1902.[295] Almost 24 a. in the Cocker beck valley was acquired by the council in 1912 for use as allotments.[296] Other land was secured as open space through the establishment of cemeteries on the periphery of town. St Cuthbert's churchyard was full by the mid 19th century, its condition described to Ranger's health enquiry as 'disgraceful'. Further interments there were prohibited in 1856, and its place was taken by Holy Trinity, the burial ground of which also rapidly filled.[297] The West Cemetery opened, on the west side of Carmel Road, in 1857.[298] It covered 12 a., of which half was Anglican, consecrated in 1858. Further extensions were made to it in 1872 and 1878. The North Cemetery, of 14 a., was laid out near the North Road in 1874. Divided into sections for dissenters, Roman Catholics and the established church, it opened in 1877.[299] Evidence of a growing interest in more informal open space – the surrounding countryside as a leisure facility and escape from the developed and polluted town – can be seen in the foundation of the Darlington Footpaths Preservation Society in 1875. The society quickly became embroiled in a dispute with members of the Pease family over the blockage of ways around Mowden Lane and Coniscliffe Grange farm.[300]

A departure from the ubiquitous streets of terrace housing came in 1912, when the Darlington Garden Suburb Company Ltd.[301] bought the White House Farm estate on Yarm Road for a model housing scheme.[302] This was the first development to the north of Yarm Road beyond Hundens Lane, other than two isolation hospitals: the fever hospital at Hundens, started in 1872, opened two years later, and extended in 1911;[303] and the smallpox hospital, established in 1903.[304] The White House estate was promoted as 'Darlington's Garden Suburb' and 'an Eastbourne Utopia'. Its architect, G. Walesby Davis of High Row, was also at work on plans and drawings of villas for the west end beyond Cleveland Avenue.[305] For the garden suburb, he proposed 115 semi-detached cottages at a density of about 11 an acre, although the longer term plan was for 400 to 500 houses, 'of a type ... readily purchased by the better class artisan', along with communal facilities such as an institute and places of worship.[306] Some of the new houses were to front Yarm Road, which was widened, and

others would be built along new roads called the Mead and
the Fairway.[307] By October 1912, the first houses were ready
and open to view by the public. They were semi-detached,
well-spaced, with gardens front and back and no 'unsightly
outbuildings', 'germ-fostering ashpit privies', back streets
or brick boundary walls. The intention was to produce
model cottages of 'picturesque appearance' which sold for
between £250 and £450 each. The estate's gently curving
roads were to be tarmacced, and trees planted on the grass
verges. The promoters had identified a need in Darlington
for working-class housing with gardens. Apart from
Eastbourne, the utopian scheme of 60 years earlier on the
opposite side of Yarm Road, which had become old-
fashioned in its layout and which was 'spoiled by the long
and narrow streets', there was little available.

> In other parts of the town the long straight lines of
> workmen's houses are characterised by dull monot-
> ony, the aim of the builders apparently having been
> to crowd as many houses on a given space as they
> could possibly do without contravening the bye-laws
> of the local authority, and instead of pleasant gardens
> in the rear most of them have dull and dismal back
> yards surrounded by high brick walls and opening
> into back streets on which abut the sanitary
> conveniences.[308]

The garden suburb provided houses with mains electricity,
each one of which had a living room with kitchen range, a
sitting room, scullery with gas cooker and boiler, pantry,
store, coalhouse, three bedrooms, a bathroom 'splendidly
fitted with heated linen cupboard' and indoor W. C. The
main contractor on the project was T. Robinson and Son of
Victoria Road, and all other work was carried out by local
craftsmen.[309] But despite its apparent attractions, like
Eastbourne before it, the scheme proceeded slowly, being
beyond the means of most even at its relatively modest
price. It also resembled Eastbourne in being removed from
most employment in the town. The housing plan was never
fully realised, the communal facilities did not materialise,
and of the 37 a. of the White House estate, only that third
within the borough boundary came to be developed by the
company.[310]

Much more numerically significant was a housing scheme at Brinkburn after the deaths of Henry Fell Pease and his widow. The council's surveyor produced a plan in 1910 of proposed new streets between Brinkburn and Woodland Roads.[311] Brinkburn Road, the former Bell Lane, was widened, the mansion partly demolished – demolition was completed during the 1990s, although the stables survive – Pierremont Road extended over Cocker beck, and Cockerton Bridge enlarged. The first streets were built from 1912,[312] although most would appear after 1920.[313] The supposed developer of part of the Brinkburn estate, also said to have been in negotiation for land in Stooperdale Avenue in 1926, was Durham County Garden Villages Ltd., but no other record of this company has been found.[314] Plans by the British Land Company during the 1890s to develop some of the Stooperdale estate, north of Brinkburn Road, for housing had been delayed by uncertainties over access and the company did not pursue its option to purchase. Two of the partners in the Whessoe Foundry Company bought the whole estate of Stooperdales, a sizeable farmhouse with 41 a., in 1898.[315] During the following decade, the railway company had stopped off Honeypot Lane west of the line and constructed a new

28. *Subway beneath the Stockton and Darlington railway connecting Rise Carr to Hopetown, with terraced housing dating in part from the 1850s.*

Hopetown subway, which was opened in 1911.[316] By 1919 the house at Stooperdale had been demolished and part of the site used for the North East Railway's Locomotive Works Boiler Shop and its extensive general offices, but the long awaited house-building had not taken place.[317]

THE MAKING OF A MODERN TOWN

Darlington was reborn as a centre of heavy industry during the 1860s. In the 20 years to 1881, the population more than doubled, and the townscape was spectacularly transformed by new industrial suburbs and by the development of the west end as a residential district. Yet change was not confined to that period. Overall, the 19th century was a time of steady increase, so that by 1901 there were more than 42,000 people living in the town, nine times the number of a century earlier. The blooming of the outer areas after 1850 as land was released for building, was followed by coalescence of town and suburbs, as Darlington became a modern town.

4. THE ARCHITECTS OF 19TH-CENTURY DARLINGTON

Darlington's enduring Victorian landmark – its market hall and offices – was designed early in his career by one of England's most famous 19th-century architects, Alfred Waterhouse. The patronage of Waterhouse by Darlington's Quaker families proved important to the architect's success and to the visual character of the town but it forms only one aspect of architectural developments in which little known and entirely provincial figures played a vital role. Their careers are also worthy of record and their contribution to the design and construction of Darlington's stock of interesting and effective buildings, including the handsome suburban villas of the wealthy, deserve examination.

ARCHITECTS IN DARLINGTON BEFORE 1840

Names of architects cannot be securely attached to any of Darlington's buildings before 1800. Throughout the 18th century, in Darlington as in all small provincial towns, masons and builders constructed buildings according to the practices they had learned as apprentices, using pattern books for the fashionable details. As long as the buildings were of small scale this procedure worked well. Architects were usually brought in only for prestigious houses or important public commissions and Darlington at this time was not large or nationally important enough to create such opportunities. Neither the leading architects active in the region, such as Daniel Garrett, James Paine of London and John Carr of York, nor any of the designers then emerging in Newcastle, such as William Newton and David Stephenson, received commissions in Darlington or its immediate environs. Indeed Colvin in his *Biographical Dictionary of British Architects, 1600–1840* lists only five buildings in the town in his index and the earliest of those is dated 1812. In comparison, for Sunderland Colvin has 13 buildings, for Durham 17, and for Newcastle 120.[1] While in

29. *Darlington market place c. 1830 by W. Westall, with market cross, town hall of 1808, and shambles beyond.*

Sunderland two new churches were built in the 18th century, Darlington's population did not grow sufficiently to require a church in addition to the parish church of St Cuthbert until 1836. The houses, business premises and meeting houses needed in the town before 1800 were well within the competence of local building firms. The major exception to this statement was the town hall, a lumpy Italian construction of 1808, said to have been based on drawings produced in 1770 by a local artist, Samuel Wilkinson, although the building as erected did not wholly follow Wilkinson's design.[2] It is likely that the committee set up in 1806 to oversee the new scheme for the market place employed a master builder and used Wilkinson's ideas for the town hall, but there is no clear evidence about the involvement of a recognised architect.

Two of the earliest buildings in Darlington known to have been designed by architects were nonconformist chapels – the Wesleyan Methodist Chapel in Bondgate and the Bethel Independent Chapel in Union Street. Both architects came from London, perhaps a reflection of the limited opportunities to establish a practice within Darlington or its locality at that time. The Bondgate chapel was built in 1812–13. Its designer was Revd. William Jenkins, who had trained as an architect before becoming an itinerant Wesleyan preacher for about 20 years. In his retirement he returned to architecture, specializing in Wesleyan chapels. He had no local connexions and was chosen by the building committee because of his reputation in the field; they may have known his chapel at Carver Street, Sheffield (1804), the finest example of his unostentatious classical style. Jenkins's Darlington chapel, built in brick, has a simple five-bay façade of round-headed windows under a three bay pediment, a form used by the Methodists until the mid 19th century. Despite later additions and alterations it still makes a dignified contribution to the townscape.[3] The small Bethel Independent in Union Street (1812) was designed by James Ianson, and was replaced in 1862 by the Bicentenary Memorial Chapel.[4]

Another architect-designed building of the first decades of the 19th century – the new Free Grammar School of 1813, to which an upper storey was added in 1846 – was the work of Ignatius Bonomi (c. 1787–1870), who, it has been argued, was then the only architect in County Durham.[5] As well as his official position as county surveyor of bridges based in Durham, he had an extensive private practice. His other work in Darlington included St Augustine's Roman Catholic church in Coniscliffe Road, which, as built in 1825–7, was an early example of the Gothic style in the town.[6] At that time he also designed major extensions to Polam Hill for Jonathan Backhouse, transforming the simple villa which had been built in 1794.[7] But his most important contribution to the town and to the development of railway architecture was the Skerne Bridge, for which he either produced a design or acted as advisor to the engineers of the Stockton and Darlington railway in 1824–5. He thereby became the first architect in the world to work on a railway structure, all others having been designed by engineers responsible for the line.[8]

Two other respected regional figures made brief forays into Darlington in 1832, in this case from Newcastle: John Dobson designed a house for a Mr J. Wilson;[9] more importantly John Green, an ingenious bridge builder responsible for the suspension bridge at Whorlton and two railway bridges in Newcastle using a laminated timber construction which won the admiration of the Institution of Civil Engineers, built Blackwell Bridge on the edge of the town.[10] Otherwise the leading regional architects were not given commissions. Even the first new Anglican church, Holy Trinity, built in 1836–7 to provide accommodation in addition to the parish church and to serve the newly growing residential district to the west of the town, was

30. *Holy Trinity Church, built 1836–7, with the unmade Woodland Road in the foreground, pictured in 1839.*

designed by a London-based architect, Anthony Salvin, who had Durham family connections. These contacts brought him commissions for five churches in the north-east, of which Holy Trinity, designed like many cheap town churches in a spare Early English Gothic style, was the best.[11]

THE FIRST DARLINGTON ARCHITECTS, 1840–60

Industrialization and, from the second quarter of the 19th century, the rapid rise in population, brought a demand not only for more buildings, but also for different types of building adapted to the new needs of the urban economy. As in other English towns, factories using new technologies, specialist offices and shops, public buildings such as libraries and schools, as well as new services such as municipal cemeteries, and sewage and water supply systems with their associated buildings, began to appear. In Darlington, in particular, railway companies required facilities. Coupled with this growth in demand came an increasingly professional approach in the trades which dealt with planning, design and construction. Mechanical and civil engineers created professional bodies, land agents and surveyors formed their own institutes, and architects sought to define their role as the designers of buildings separate from the building industry, with a code of conduct and a system of payments that reflected a fully professional approach. The founding of the Institute of British Architects in 1834 (it was granted royal status in 1837) was the public symbol of a change which would not have been possible without a substantial increase in the demand for such professional services. This did not mean that the old ways died out. The building trade continued – as it still does – to build according to accustomed practice, even after 1862 when the local board of health in Darlington began to require plans of buildings to be submitted in advance of construction.[12]

It has generally been accepted that the first qualified architect to practise in Darlington was John Middleton.[13] In fact John Green (1807–1868) was established there before him. Green was the nephew of a more famous John Green (1787–1852) who worked in Newcastle in partnership with his son, Benjamin (c. 1811–1858), and whose practice was the major rival to that of John Dobson. Green used the title 'junior' until his uncle died, and may have come to Darlington specifically to avoid confusion with the other firm. Green jun. had practised in Newcastle from 1832 and always considered himself a Newcastle architect. Though he was in Darlington from 1839 until 1844, with offices in Bondgate and later in Northgate, most of his known buildings in this period are not in the town.[14] One important building for which he was responsible was Paradise Chapel, Coniscliffe Road, demolished in 1972 to make way for an office block. Designed in 1840–1 for the Wesleyan Methodist Association, which had broken away from the Wesleyans, its façade followed in plainer fashion the formula Jenkins had used for the Bondgate Wesleyan chapel, but was only four bays wide with a door in each of the end bays.[15] Green also carried out projects for the North of England Railway company including, in 1840–1, work-shops, coal depots and warehouses and a coach station and repair shop at Bank Top.[16] As North Road station was built on its present site in 1842 it raises the possibility that Green was the architect of that too, though no firm evidence has been found.

John Middleton (1820–1885) came to practise in Darlington in 1844, just as John Green jun. was returning to Newcastle, and Middleton's firm was continued by his successors until late into the 20th century. Indeed he may have moved precisely because a vacancy was created by Green's departure. Though he spent only 10 years in the town, he seems to have made more impact on it, mainly because his major buildings are still well known. Middleton was born in York and was trained by J. P. Pritchett sen., whose daughter he married in the year he came to Darlington. Middleton may have been made aware of Green's departure through his brother-in-law, Revd. Richard Pritchett, who had preceded him as minister at Bethel Chapel in 1840.[17] Almost as soon as he arrived in Darlington, Middleton was appointed architect to the Stockton and Darlington railway on an annual retainer, and received additional fees as the company expanded in the 1840s. This gave him a secure financial base while he established his practice, and the company procured designs at a lower cost than it could by employing him on a commission basis. The work he did for the company was outside Darlington and involved stations, houses and workshops in Cleveland and County Durham.[18] Within the town he was responsible for two important buildings, Central Hall and St John's church, Neasham Road. Central Hall, a plain brick classical building with a giant arcade, now incorporated into the modern Dolphin Centre, was designed as a public meeting place in 1846–7.[19] St John's, the 'Railwayman's Church', was a consolatory commission obtained through George Hudson in 1847 after his contract as architect to the Great North of England railway had been terminated. Although lacking the spire that was originally intended, it is an imposing church that makes good use of its elevated site. Like Holy Trinity it is Early English in style, with a west tower as part of a symmetrical plan, which by then was old-fashioned.[20] His other work in the town included a National Provincial Bank in High Row and, further out, alterations at Neasham Hall.[21]

In the early 1850s Middleton was joined by another brother-in-law, James Pigott Pritchett jun. (1830–1911), whom he made a partner in 1854. They worked together briefly before Middleton left the firm and the town to travel in Europe. After five years he returned to settle in Cheltenham and, though he had no intention of practising as an architect, by doing work for his local church he resumed practice, becoming well known in Cheltenham and in Wales where he did much church restoration.[22] Middleton's move left Pritchett in control of the practice and he continued in Darlington until his retirement in 1910, when his son Herbert Dewes Pritchett (1859–1945) took over until about 1939.

J. P. Pritchett had been trained by his father in York and worked in the family firm of J. P. Pritchett & Son for a short time before establishing a substantial practice in Darlington. He became the first Darlington architect to establish professional credentials as a founder member of the Northern Architectural Association in 1859 and by election in 1863 as Fellow of the Royal Institute of British Architects (FRIBA).[23] Although his father worked extensively in the classical style (for example at Huddersfield Railway Station, 1846–7),[24] Pritchett designed almost exclusively in the Gothic style, perhaps not surprising as in his lifetime his reputation was founded on his church architecture. At the beginning of his career he used competitions as a means to obtain commissions and to make his name known, winning the important commission to replace in 1854–8 the church of St Nicholas in the market place at Durham.[25] He did 25 new churches and 20 restorations or extensions for the Church of England, but he also used his connections with Congregationalism to gain commissions for 28 nonconformist chapels, as well as several Sunday schools.[26] Many of his chapels were built in Yorkshire, tending to follow a fairly standard pattern of a gable end facing the street with a central doorway under a large Decorated window and a spire at an outer angle.[27] The Darlington Bicentenary Memorial Congregational Chapel, 1861–2, in Union Street, which is now in commercial use, is typical of his style, despite having more doors than usual in its façade.[28] Pritchett added a Sunday school to it in 1875.[29] That he was capable of more interesting designs is proved by the Grange Congregational chapel, Sunderland, of 1881–2, where a splendid semi-circular Sunday school wraps around the chapel's apsidal end.[30] Pritchett was particularly successful in winning competitions for cemeteries, and his 17 cemetery designs include Darlington West Cemetery of 1856.[31]

Surprisingly, this busy and successful practice produced only a minority of its designs for Pritchett's home town. Of the 150 commissions already identified, only 35 were for buildings in and around Darlington, and most of the houses date from late in his career when his son had taken control of the practice.[32] His most important commission was the Training College for Women, built for the British and Foreign School Society in Vane Terrace to train teachers for nonconformist schools in the region,[33] a commission he may well have gained because of his 'uncompromising Protestant attitude'.[34] Started in 1873, the college was built in a smooth red brick in a simple version of the then fashionable Italian Gothic inspired by John Ruskin. Extensions in a similar style, including Practice Schools in 1886–9, continued into the 1890s, creating a rather complex building which since 1979 has been used as the town's arts centre. Pritchett did little domestic work apart from alterations to the Tudor Gothic Pierremont in 1860,[35] though his work for the Cleveland interest on the estate laid out between Woodland Road and Coniscliffe Road from 1881–96 involved the design of some 100 houses as well as the road layout. The designs varied in style as fashions changed.[36] Nor did he design many churches in Darlington. Three of the churches for which he was responsible have been demolished: St Paul in North Road, 1870;[37] St Luke, Leadenhall Street, 1883;[38] and the Northlands Wesleyan chapel, North Road, 1871–2.[39] He was however involved with the restoration of the chancel of the parish church of St Cuthbert in the mid 1860s after G. G. Scott had worked on the building, and he wrote about the church, as did his son.[40] He also undertook commissions for commercial and philanthropic buildings, including the offices of the Stockton and Darlington Railway in Northgate which he enlarged in 1856 and 1863,[41] the Savings Bank of 1869 in Tubwell Row,[42] the rebuilding of Thomas Pease's grocery shop, Market Place, in 1900,[43] and the supervision of the construction of the Mary Pease Almshouses on behalf of Paul Waterhouse in 1896,[44] though he never established a leading reputation for such buildings. In fact by the end of his long career in Darlington, Pritchett had managed to create a greater impression outside the town than he had within it.

Someone who practised only briefly in the 1850s was Joseph Sparkes (1817–1855). He came from a local Quaker

31. *Mechanics' Institution, Skinnergate, by Joseph Sparkes, 1853.*

family, was related to J. M. Sparkes, secretary to the GNER, and is worth mentioning because he designed in 1853 the impressive Mechanics Institution in Skinnergate,[45] classical with heavy details that betray its Victorian date. Sparkes was also architect to the NER and designed the extensions to North Road station and carriage repair shops in 1853.[46]

ALFRED WATERHOUSE AND HIS QUAKER PATRONS

Darlington has the distinction of having several buildings by the eminent Victorian architect Alfred Waterhouse, FRIBA (1830–1905), whose practice, based in Manchester and by 1864 also in London, was national in scope. Waterhouse was recognised in his lifetime as a distinguished practitioner by being elected president of the RIBA and as a Royal Academician. His Manchester Town Hall, the Natural History Museum in London and his Prudential Insurance buildings stand, on account of their architect's firm but imaginative control of plan, style, silhouette and materials, including terracotta, iron and steel, among the key buildings of the century. It was Waterhouse's connections in Darlington, based on the Quaker beliefs he shared with many influential local families, which enabled him to establish a reputation. The style of building he adopted then remained influential in the town long after he had moved on to more prestigious commissions elsewhere in the country.

After a pupilage with the Quaker Richard Lane in Manchester and a tour on the continent, Waterhouse established an independent practice in Manchester in 1854. An obvious way to find work was to design for his immediate family and to use the closeness of the Quaker community who preferred to work with fellow religionists whenever possible. Amongst his fellow Quakers were the Peases, whom he had met at Grove House school, and the Backhouses, to whom he was related through marriage into the Hodgkin family.[47] He was prepared to undertake small commissions to get himself known, and quickly established a reputation for being businesslike in completing work within budget and on time. The first commissions for his Darlington contacts were for a porter's lodge which was not built, and for which he was not paid, and in 1858 and 1860 alterations to two Backhouse mansions, Blackwell House, Darlington, and Shull at Hamsterley.[48] He was probably also responsible for alterations to Beechwood, on behalf of J. C. Backhouse in 1861.[49] Further small works followed in 1861 for the Peases at Brinkburn and Woodlands, both Darlington houses.[50] These jobs led to more significant opportunities in designing mansions, especially for J. W. Pease, as well as to public commissions placed by his Quaker contacts on behalf of the public bodies they served.

In Darlington, his public commission was for the market hall and public offices designed to stand prominently in the market place. This ensemble remains the most distinctive of Victorian Darlington. The commissioning body in 1861 was the local board of health, which was dominated by Quakers, with J. W. Pease as chairman: Pease himself paid for the clock tower, a feature borrowed from northern French or Flemish town halls. It is the key element in the design and shows that Waterhouse already had mastery of composition in the northern European Gothic style with which he is predominantly associated. The completed building was less grand than the original design, which had larger offices with more elaborate detail and a more finely

32. *Waterhouse's market hall and public offices, 1861–3.*

proportioned tower.[51] Perhaps Waterhouse hoped to be asked eventually to design a full-scale town hall. The market hall, which forms the main element of the building, is one of Waterhouse's few essays almost entirely in iron and glass. As the site sloped markedly a basement was necessary, its vaults and the floor above supported on iron brackets. At the opening of the market in 1863, there was a collapse of part of this flooring, in which a man was killed.[52] The accident was attributed to faulty castings for which Waterhouse was found not to blame. All of the cast and wrought ironwork, including railings, had been supplied by the Quaker firm Charles Ianson and Co. of the Whessoe Foundry.[53] Waterhouse made the necessary repairs, and his reputation in the town was not damaged as he received several more commissions from his friends. Subsequently he was cautious in his use of iron, and meticulous about ensuring its quality.[54]

In 1864 he was asked to design a bank for Backhouse and Co. in High Row. As the main office of the company, it provided a house style for branches in other towns. At a time when bank design was nearly always based on the Renaissance town palace, symbolizing elegance and security through its connexion with the heyday of Italian banking, the French Gothic style of the Darlington bank was unusual. Built on a larger budget than the town hall and market, it was faced in stone rather than the local Pease-manufactured bricks and was more sumptuously detailed.[55]

The Darlington families with whom Waterhouse had contact were particularly interested in building new houses or improving their existing homes and, from this early start, Waterhouse built up a large practice in this field, designing some 90 mansions throughout the country. He made additions or alterations for the Pease family at Uplands, 1862–4, Pierremont, 1873–6, and Mowden Hall, originally Bushell Hill, 1881–5 and 1899.[56] Some of these additions amounted almost to complete rebuilding, but the only new house was Hummersknott, 1863–4, which followed his normal pattern of a solid and comfortable house with attention paid to convenient planning rather than showy detail. Following a familiar 19th-century arrangement, a central hall gave access to the main rooms, with service facilities placed in a wing. The asymmetrical, gabled elevations were rather harshly detailed in brick with sparse Gothic detail.[57] Waterhouse was also active in building mansions for established branches of these families wishing to move into the country. Hugely expensive houses, such as Hutton Hall near Guisborough for J. W. Pease, which cost over £30,000 in the extended period of building 1864–71; Dryderdale near Hamsterley for Alfred Back-house, 1871–2; and Hurworth Grange, 1873–5 and 1886–7 for J. E. Backhouse, were constructed in splendid garden settings.[58] The first of these country houses, Pilmore Hall in Hurworth, was completely rebuilt in 1861–4 and was further extended in 1876–9, again at a total cost of £30,000.[59] This project brought G. G. Hoskins to Darlington as Waterhouse's not always satisfactory clerk of works, who also worked on the Backhouse Bank. The experience led Hoskins to establish his own practice in the town, where he was to become not only one of the leading architects in Darlington but a significant local figure until 1900.[60]

DARLINGTON ARCHITECTS, 1865–1900

George Gordon Hoskins JP, FRIBA, (1837–1911) was born in the Midlands and trained in London where he stayed to gain experience in building firms and with several architects before coming to Pilmore Hall with Waterhouse. What made him decide to establish his own practice in the town is not clear, but he may have felt that he had made useful contacts with the Quaker families that would stand him in good stead. Certainly his early commissions included work for Darlington Quaker residences, such as Woodburn and Elm Ridge for John Pease in 1867,[61] as well as projects sponsored by the extended Quaker network. His first job, the Temperance Hall at Hurworth, 1864,[62] and the Victoria Hall in Sunderland, 1870, were largely paid for by the Backhouses.[63] But his most important commission turned out to be his addition of a manager's house to the Backhouse bank in 1867,[64] as through this he became architect to the banking house. He subsequently designed branches in Sunderland (1868), Bishop Auckland (1870), Middlesbrough (1875), Thirsk (1877) and Barnard Castle (1878),[65] all of which were variations on the theme of Waterhouse's original design. It appears that, because of his association with Waterhouse, the staunchly Anglican Hoskins was more to the taste of the Quakers than the nonconformist Pritchett. This association proved even more important when Hoskins entered – and won – the competition for Middlesbrough Town Hall in 1882. This, in a Gothic style clearly influenced by Waterhouse who was the adjudicator, remains his major work.[66]

Hoskins focussed on Darlington and, in contrast to Pritchett, about two thirds of his traced work is in the town. It includes several important public projects, notably the North Cemetery with its Pease memorial,[67] Queen Elizabeth Grammar School (1875–6),[68] the Pease Library (1884),[69] Greenbank Hospital (1885),[70] the Poor Law Offices (1896)[71] and the Technical College (1896–7).[72] Hoskins's early Gothic work in the style of Waterhouse is very different from that of his main competitor in Darlington, J. P. Pritchett. A comparison of their styles can most easily be made in Vane Terrace where Hoskins's grammar school

33. *Design by Hoskins for Elm Ridge, c. 1867.*

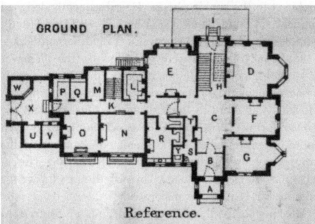

GROUND PLAN.

Reference.

A. *Porch.* B. *Vestibule.* C. *Hall.* D. *Drawing R^m*
E. *Dining R^m* F. *Library.* G. *Study.* H. *Princ^l*
Stairs. I. *Prop^d Conservatory.* K. *Corridor.*
L. *Store R^m* M. *Waiting R^m* N. *Kitchen.*
O *Scullery.* P. *Larder.* Q. *Pantry.* R. *Butler's*
Pantry. S. *Lavatory.* T. *Hats & Coats.* U. *Coals*
V. *Knives & Boots.* W. *Ashes.* X *Court Y^d* Y. *W.C.*

SCALE.
10   0   10   20   30   40   50 FT

stands next to Pritchett's slightly earlier but more austere training college. His late buildings have an easily recognizable manner, with an intricacy of surface detail and bold silhouette whether the style was late Gothic (the technical college) or Queen Anne (the public library), and they still make an impact on modern Darlington. Indeed with his board schools at Bank Top (1882) and Rise Carr (1902),[73] prominent commercial works such as the North of England School Furnishing Company, Blackwellgate (1897)[74] and the King's Head hotel (rebuilt 1890–3),[75] in addition to his public buildings, Hoskins almost came to be the man who designed late Victorian Darlington. He also became an important public figure, representing the Conservative interest on the town council and working hard as a magistrate in both the borough and Durham county. When he died in 1911, his funeral was a civic event of some importance, his public role rather overshadowing his architectural work.[76] On his death the practice was continued by his brother, Walter Hamlet Hoskins ARIBA (1845–1921), who had come to Darlington with his mother and another brother to join G. G. Hoskins and to run a painting contracting business which did some work on buildings designed by G. G. Hoskins.

34. *Technical College, Northgate, by Hoskins, 1896–7.*

Although Pritchett and Hoskins were the best known and most professional architects in Darlington before 1914, they were not the only ones. John Ross FRIBA (1836–1895) was already in practice when Hoskins came to the town. Indeed he may have been the first architect who was actually born in Darlington, though nothing is known of his background or training. Initially, from 1855–62, he was in partnership with William Richardson in a practice that included building and cabinet-making,[77] but when that ended Richardson took on the building side of the business and developed it into a horticultural engineering concern which specialised in conservatories. This allowed Ross to join the RIBA, which did not permit members to engage in building as well as design, and he worked alone until joined in 1869 by Robert Lamb FRIBA, who had come as an assistant after a period as the partner of Thomas Oliver in Newcastle. This partnership lasted until 1879 when Lamb emigrated to New Zealand for health reasons. Ross's main area of work was domestic design. He had worked for dominant Darlington families on several of their early mansions before Water-house appeared on the scene, and continued to do so throughout his career.[78] The work mainly involved alterations and additions, particularly conservatories, but he also produced new designs such as Brinkburn near Cockerton and Mowden Hall, both of 1862, and Blackwell Hill (undated).[79] Ross later developed a more general practice, but still with domestic architecture as the main element. Not one of his buildings was especially note-worthy, his only major public project being St George's Presbyterian chapel, Northgate (1867–9), built to a standard design of the period; this commission was gained because Lamb was an elder of the church.[80] Ross's major work, like that of Pritchett, lies outside the town, with two Yorkshire commissions – Grey Towers, a vast house of 1865–7 for W.R.I. Hopkins at Nunthorpe,[81] and North-allerton Town Hall of 1873[82] – being his most prestigious. Otherwise the practice was busy doing small jobs until Ross retired to Whitley Bay in 1882 and sold the practice to Clark & Moscrop.

The careers of Frederick Clark FRIBA (1854–1944) and William Jobson Moscrop FRIBA (1858–1929) demonstrate well the fully professional approach to architecture that was gaining strength in the latter years of the 19th century. Both men had been articled to Oliver and Leeson in Newcastle and both stayed on as assistants before seeking wide experience elsewhere, Clark in Birmingham and London and Moscrop in Stockton with Alexander and Henman. Clark came to Darlington first and was joined by Moscrop to create a partnership that lasted until Moscrop retired in 1924, when Clark was joined by his son. Clark and Moscrop were elected FRIBA on the same day in 1891.[83] Much of their work was in the district around Darlington. In the town it was mainly routine, with a large number of small commissions to design terraced houses and to alter business premises, public buildings and larger houses – over 150 such plans were submitted by them for local authority approval between 1882 and 1910[84] – so they were never able to put their mark on the town in the way that Hoskins and Pritchett had done. What would have been their most important commission was not built, for though they won the competition for new municipal buildings in 1893–4 to replace Waterhouse's public offices, the scheme was scrapped for financial reasons and a town hall was not built until 1967–70.[85] Their best-known work dates from the early years of the 20th century: the Co-op in Victoria Street (1901–3); the North Eastern Bank on High Row (1902–3); the Temperance Institute, Gladstone Street (1902–3); and the Union Children's Homes, Eastbourne Park (1903–4).

35. *Houses in Ashcroft Road by Clark and Moscrop, c. 1900.*

SURVEYORS, ENGINEERS AND
SALARIED ARCHITECTS, 1850–1900[86]

Of the other firms active in Darlington, some of their principals were trained as civil engineers and were mainly engaged in estate development. Most important of these was George Dickinson, surveyor to the board of health, whose practice ran from the 1850s to 1920 when his son, J. H. Dickinson, retired. Dickinson was responsible for many street plans in Darlington, as well as the original layout of Saltburn, on the Cleveland coast, for the Pease family.[87] Lesser figures, such as E. W. Lyall, William Hodgson and William Sowerby, produced plans for the expansion of the town without designing any notable buildings.

Amongst those who were more obviously architects, but about whom little is known, were William J. Agutter, who designed St James's church hall in Allan Street (1893) and the Baptist chapel in Corporation Road (1904–5);[88] W. H. Bourne, who trained with Clark and Moscrop and practised until he emigrated in 1912;[89] George Walesby Davis who designed the garden suburb in Yarm Road (1912);[90] Neil Macara who designed hardly anything in Darlington but who was responsible for some uninspiring Presbyterian churches in the region and in Scotland;[91] and Richard Robinson who worked for some 20 years and had a number of commissions from the Roman Catholic church and for schools.

The North Eastern Railway Company, an amalgamation of companies including the GNER which absorbed the Stockton and Darlington railway in 1863, was the first railway company in the world to appoint a full-time salaried architect to work with its chief engineer in the construction of railway facilities. Some of its architects were based in or were active in Darlington. Thomas Prosser, who held the position 1854–74, worked from Newcastle, assisted on the design of Newcastle central station, but built nothing in Darlington. His successor, Benjamin Burleigh, died after only two years in post, but the next incumbent, William Peachey, was based in Darlington for his equally brief period of office. Peachey had been architect to the Stockton and Darlington railway and when this merged into the NER he was made Darlington section architect. Most of his work was devoted to extending and improving railway buildings, though he did build the Zetland Hotel at Saltburn (1861–3) and the Royal Station Hotel at York (1877–82).[92] He was also allowed to practise privately and designed a few nonconformist chapels, including Darlington's Grange Road Baptist Chapel (1870–1).[93] William Bell, who worked for the NER for fifty years and was chief architect 1877–1914, made the biggest impact on the town. Though he designed a few buildings in the town as a private practitioner, especially for the Methodists, his major contribution was as NER Architect. Bank Top Station (1884–7) is one of the best examples of his designs for stations, for which he developed a standard system of roof construction.[94] He also added various elements to the North Road engineering works between 1884 and 1910, and designed the offices of the mechanical engineers' department in Brinkburn Road in 1912. While not quite as splendid as the NER headquarters offices in York, which he designed with Horace Field in 1904, it shows that Bell could adapt his usual style to accommodate the new influences of the Queen Anne Revival.[95] Arthur Pollard and Stephen Wilkinson filled the position of chief architect briefly before merger with the LNER in 1923 led to the abolition of the department.

The 19th century also saw the emergence of local authority surveyors and architects. The local board of health had used surveyors to advise them on sanitary work, but they had always been men in private practice employed with a retainer to the board. Darlington's municipal authority made provision for a full-time surveyor to work exclusively for the corporation in 1867, and Hudson Reah, an associate member of the Institution of Civil Engineers who came from the assistant's post in Sunderland, was the first of these.[96] He and his successors were mainly concerned with approving the sanitary provisions of new buildings, and extending and improving the water and sewage facilities, along with street improvements, but they also designed small projects paid for by the council. In Darlington the convention of opening large projects to competition continued until county borough status was achieved in 1915. After that, under the borough surveyor,

George Winter, the office designed several council schools as well as extensive housing schemes.[97] In the 20th century the role of the official architect grew extensively as authorities took greater responsibility for services within their boundaries; in Darlington, the first qualified architect was appointed to the Borough Surveyor's department in 1920.[98]

ARCHITECTS FROM ELSEWHERE, 1880–1900

Although not all buildings in Darlington were designed by Darlington architects, few of the leading firms in the north-east did much work there late in the century. C. Hodgson Fowler of Durham, the county's leading ecclesiastical architect, made only a few small alterations to churches. Hicks and Charlewood of Newcastle did much the same and Oliver and Leeson, who had the largest general practice in the region, appear to have built nothing at all. Of the few buildings designed by those with a national reputation, most important was St Hilda's church, Parkgate, designed in 1886 by John Loughborough Pearson when he was at the peak of his powers as an ecclesiastical architect and just as the first phase of his Truro Cathedral was being finished. Born in Durham and trained by Bonomi, he did surprisingly little work in the north-east apart from the sumptuously vaulted St George, Cullercoats (Northumbs.), of 1884. St Hilda's, at a cost of £4,500 for 520 sittings, was a cheap church and so Pearson's favoured stone vaulting could not be attempted. Despite its local red brick, lancet windows and lack of ornament, its dramatic massing makes it one of the most effective of Pearson's simple churches. Now used as a religious centre, it remains an interesting local example of the work of a major architect.[99]

Specialists in particular building types were brought in from time to time. The nonconformists employed specialists in chapel architecture: A. H. Goodall of Nottingham designed the red brick Love Memorial Chapel for the Methodist New Connexion in Victoria Road in 1883–4,[100] and W. J. Morley & Son of Bradford the Gothic Wesleyan chapel in Corporation Road in 1904.[101] The Roman Catholics also preferred certain architects, and both George Goldie and J. & C. Hansom were respectively involved in the Carmel Convent and St Clare's Abbey.[102] One of the London-based specialist firms, that of C. J. Phipps, was called in when the Theatre Royal in Northgate was rebuilt in 1885–7,[103] but Darlington's other theatre, the Hippodrome, Parkgate, of 1905–7, now the Darlington Civic Theatre, had a more complicated history. According to local papers Hoskins was the architect[104] but he seems to have collaborated with two theatre specialists, William Hope, who was based in Newcastle,[105] and on the interior with G. F. Ward of Birmingham.[106] More essential to the success of the growing city were the waterworks and supply system, masterminded by the leading water engineer of the century, Thomas Hawksley of Nottingham.[107]

CONCLUSION

In their skills, tastes and pattern of employment Darlington's architects were typical of those who worked in small English towns that suddenly expanded because of industrial growth. Although many of them simply followed the fashions of their age without much originality, the work of Middleton, Hoskins and Pritchett made a significant contribution. Together with some of their less prominent fellow designers and nationally recognized architects such as Waterhouse and Pearson who were recruited from metropolitan centres, they not only produced interesting and effective individual buildings but also provided Darlington with a built heritage which enriches its townscape and its history.

5. BUILDING MATERIALS AND THE BUILDING INDUSTRY

BUILDING MATERIALS

Clay Row, east of Darlington bridge, was known as such by the 15th century, which suggests that bricks may then have been manufactured in the town.[1] Yet there is no clear evidence of any medieval building having been constructed of brick. Plans to carry materials for the rebuilding of Darlington after the fire of 1585 mention timber and stone, but not brick,[2] although this may indicate only that local supplies of bricks were readily available, so there was no need for exceptional transport arrangements.

Bricks were certainly in use in Darlington by the 17th century. Nicholson in 1949 noted the presence of thin, two-inch bricks in Bondgate cottages then reputedly over 400 years old.[3] When in 1636 James Bellassis left directions to build several houses, he had 'made good provision of timber bricke and stone'.[4] The bishop's palace was restored from dilapidation in 1668 with slates and stone, but also, significantly, with bricks made at Brankin Moor;[5] walls of the upper chamber of the palace were said to have been made not of lath and plaster, but of rush and plaster.[6] In 1675 the Greeve's book for Bondgate recorded a payment to Matthew Taylorson of 5s. 3d. for '21 cart load of brick'.[7] The first known gentry residence to have been built of brick was the so-called Elizabethan house, later the Nag's Head, actually dating from the latter part of the 17th century. The bricks used there measured five inches by two, and varied in length from about 10 to 12 inches.[8]

While brick was used increasingly over the following century, stone continued to be the principal material for public buildings and gentry houses.[9] Hill Top House was said to be a stone building of the Tudor period, the only one surviving into Longstaffe's time.[10] Carriage of wood, lime and stone to repair the tollbooth, mills and bakehouse was a recurring item in manorial records.[11] Lime-burning and the pollution associated with it had disappeared from the town

by 1600, concentrating where supplies of coal and lime-
stone were more easily accessible, such as in the Denton and
High Coniscliffe areas to the west.[12] The mill dam, or mill
race, was reconstructed from stone in 1736; an estimate
includes 560 feet of 'hewen stone worck' for £16 6s. 8d. and
'60 rode of Ruf wall' costing £21 10s.[13] The stone bridge was
considered a feature of note – as far as Daniel Defoe was
concerned in 1724, the only feature worthy of comment
other than the mud: 'Darlington, a post town, has nothing
remarkable but dirt and a high stone bridge over little or no
water'.[14] The old, nine-arched, bridge had been repaired
with brick, and when a new bridge was commissioned in
1767 it was intended to build the parapets of brick, but for
reasons of strength stone was substituted.[15]

Late 18th-century insurance policies for Darlington
houses and workshops refer almost entirely to brick and
tile construction. The timber merchant Caleb Healey's
house, stable and adjoining tenements in Northgate; John
Gray's house in Blackwellgate, with bakehouse and tenanted
buildings in the yard behind; Michael Heavisides' book and
stationery shop, with its printing office behind, and Edward
Robson's woollen drapery, premises shared with a cabinet
maker, all on High Row; John Bailey's drapery shop and
house adjoining the tollbooth, were all brick-built and

36. *High Row, including brick
buildings of the 18th century.*

tiled.[16] Modest tenements on Priestgate and a widow's house and brewhouse in Northgate were brick.[17] The material was used also for industrial premises, such as John and William Ianson's new linen works adjoining the Skerne below Northgate, and the more traditional flax-dressing shops of Jonathan Hedley in Blackwell Lane, and of James Backhouse & Sons.[18] Many inns and their brewhouses were also constructed of brick and tile: Ralph Chipchase's Golden Lion, on the south end of the High Row; the Black Bull, kept by Ralph Taylor on the corner of Blackwellgate and Blackwell Lane; Christopher Hird's old Fleece inn and the neighbouring new Fleece and Marquis of Granby, in Blackwellgate.[19] There were still signs of older methods of construction in the town centre, however. While John Walker's Dolphin inn and adjoining buildings in the Horse Market were of brick, a malthouse, cinder house and stable which he occupied in a yard behind John Pease's old house on the High Row, were 'brick timber and plaister built'.[20] Anthony Dunn's grocery at the entrance to Richardson's yard on the High Row was brick and timber and tiled.[21] William Appleton, bookseller, stationer and printer, lived in a house at the side of the market place which, with adjoining property, was still part timber-built in 1787.[22]

Bricks were made on a considerable scale in Darlington by the 1760s. Robert Richardson produced them on contract to Francis Holmes from various sites in the town. In 1763 he was paid for 'making, setting and burning' 33,370 bricks in an unspecified place, followed by 17,360 in Short's Garth, and 21,789 in 'Park'.[23] This is likely to refer to the bishop's Low Park, for it was there and on Clay Row that much brick-making was located. Holmes, or more likely his son of the same name, later leased fields in the Low Park called Fenwick's Folly, Horse Close, Butts Park, Spenham's Rings, Trod Close, Snipes and Springs, in 1776 and 1781.[24] Richardson moulded 20,000 bricks at Cockerton in 1764, and dug clay for a further 160,000 bricks, presumably in Darlington, receiving payment through that year from Holmes for turning clay, and for drink. The elder Holmes, variously described as a grocer, merchant and gentleman, as well as being a soap-boiler and property owner, who lived adjacent to the market place in 1719, became insolvent in

1749 and died during the 1760s.[25] It may therefore have been his son who organised brick production. Holmes had bought 15 fields in Darlington township, in Townend Close, Dickonist or Dickonkists, Middlefield, Thornbeck Hill, North Garth or Cobler Garth, and Glover Pasture, a total of over 100 acres, in 1763, and it could have been on this estate that Richardson was working.[26] His bricks were sold to various individuals, apparently for their own use: 'Mr Hodgson Thornill Darlington' took 6,700 in 1763, James Backhouse 1,500, and John Pease various quantities during 1764.[27] Backhouse appears to have been engaged upon improvements to the Northgate premises recently inherited from his father-in-law.[28] The 'Brick Kiln Field' noted on the tithe map, south of Staindrop Road and behind the Carmel convent, may also have been a site of 18th-century brick-making.[29] The younger Francis Holmes's activities ceased with his own bankruptcy in 1782, and he later moved to Barnard Castle.[30]

Tiles were also manufactured in Darlington, in 'tyle kilns' on land owned in 1751 by John Wetheral at Brankin Moor.[31] A noted stone cutter named John Hodgson, or Hudson, worked in the town until his death in 1761.[32] On the east side of Darlington bridge, facing St Cuthbert's church, was the stonemason's yard of Andrew Lockie, or Lockey, accused in 1795 of encroaching upon the river with

37. Elegant brick houses of the 1830s on West Terrace, Coniscliffe Road.

his stone-cutting.[33] Stone remained the preserve of high-status housing such as Pierremont, built by John Botcherby in the early 1830s, and prestigious commercial premises such as the 'handsome stone-fronted' National Provincial Bank in High Row.[34] But bricks predominated for new building, and Darlington in 1800 was described as 'a town built of brick'.[35]

Brick-makers, absent from a directory of 1791 when the activity was small-scale and largely sub-contracted, began to feature in 1820, when Thomas Chilton and William Stamper were recorded in Clay Row.[36] Chilton and Stamper were still in business in 1827, listed as brick-makers along with William Allan, who was in fact owner of land at Bank Top where a brickworks was situated.[37] Stamper, described as brickmaker in 1832, and later as a gentleman, lived away from the works, at West Cottage in Coniscliffe Road.[38] Chilton's address, probably residential as well as business, was in East Street, between Clay Row and Freeman's Place.[39] By that time much of the area between Clay Row and the new branch railway line of 1829 at Bank Top was occupied by Chilton and by Ralph Smith, apparently Stamper's successor. Allan's property on Clay Row was then let to Smith, and that beyond the railway to John Crawford.[40] Allan's Clay Row lands, containing 'valuable beds of clay and sand and . . . very eligibly situated for building purposes' were sold in 1833. Smith's premises, described as 'two freehold buildings, formerly cottages, with two closes of grassland in one of which is an extensive and valuable manufactory of bricks', were bought by Thomas Robson for £1,340. Other Allan lots, occupied by Smith on the west side of the railway and by Crawford on the east, were purchased by Robert Thompson for £1,000 and £1,070 respectively. Ralph Smith apparently also worked as a builder, for he was described as such when buying a vacant plot in Northgate, beyond the Whessoe Lane junction, in the same sale.[41] Chilton and Crawford, both tile- as well as brick-makers, were listed at Freeman's Place in 1834, while Smith was based in Tubwell Row.[42] The Smith brickyard, just east of the bridge, had descended to Thomas Smith by 1847. A further brickyard immediately to the north, between the Stockton and Yarm roads, was owned by Thomas Robson and Thomas Oxendale. East of the railway and behind St

John's church was the brickworks of John Sugget sen. and Thomas Oxendale, rented from Robert Thompson & Co. Finally, William Walters had a brickyard north of Yarm Road and west of Bank Top station.[43] By the mid 1850s, the whole area between East Street and the North Eastern Railway, opposite Freeman's Place and behind the buildings on Clay Row and Brunswick Street, was filled with brick and tile yards and sheds, with a clay pit next to the railway. Off Neasham Road at Bank Top were kilns and a 'drying patent brick manufactory kiln' with engine house.[44]

Industrial development and associated demand for housing from 1854 brought new pressures to find sites for brickworks. Albert Hill, the site of much of Darlington's expansion in the 1860s, also proved a convenient location for brick-making. Thomas Robson rented from R. H. Allan the four and a half acre North Corn Field, near Haughton Road, for a brick yard in 1859. One square yard was calculated to produce 1,000 bricks, if excavated to a depth of nine feet, although it was planned to go deeper. Extra payment was made to the landowner for every additional foot in depth. Part of the site was set aside for a drying ground. In 1866, J. Burney & Co., architects and surveyors in Horsemarket, tried to acquire further land for brick-making from Allan. They wrote that 'having sold our Brickyard at Albert Hill and being desirous of having another in that Neighbourhood' they wished to buy or rent a field north of Nest Field Farm with a 'splendid seam of blue clay'.[45] By the 1860s, many brick-makers in the region settled into more permanent sites as steam-powered brick-making machinery was introduced, and also to take advantage of distribution of their products by rail.[46] At this time, the Pease buff-coloured brick, a by-product of their mining activities elsewhere in the county, became popular in Darlington for public buildings including the new town hall, and for villas such as Hummersknott, Uplands and Wilton House, where it was combined with red or brown sandstones.[47] For most local uses, though, bricks were home-produced. The engineers C. E. Lister & Co. of Hopetown Foundry found local customers for their machine which could make 15,000 bricks in 10 hours. There were about 10 brick- and tile-makers in the 1870s, supplying industrial needs as well as housing developments.

In addition, the Tees Scoria Brick Co. Ltd. dealt from their office in Station Street at Bank Top in distinctive blue-grey scoriae bricks made from slag in Middlesbrough, which were used as paving in drainage gutters and back-streets.[48]

Brick manufacture, visually intrusive for decades in the Bank Top, Whessoe Lane and Albert Hill areas, was contracting by the early 20th century to concentrate on a few large brickworks. Clay Row had been exhausted, its brick-making sites built over by housing as far as Borough Road by 1898, and the one remaining works, nearest the railway, closed by 1920. The last proprietor there, R. Blackett and Son Ltd., moved to a yard in Haughton Road, where common bricks, facing bricks, tiles and terra cotta were made until about 1958, employing 35 people.[49] The Bank Top brickworks left the scars of two large clay pits immediately next to the main railway station, before moving further out on the Neasham Road by 1915. William Burnip had re-opened an old brickworks at Firth Moor Farm, on the Yarm road, by 1914; after closure during the Second World War, one of its two clay pits was brought back to use in the late 1940s and early 1950s.[50] The works established behind Victoria Embankment in about 1890 had been replaced by 1915 with new housing, from Rockingham Street to Leafield Road, the bricks for which had presumably been made on site. The Drinkfield area of Whessoe Lane also showed signs of exhaustion, marked by old clay workings, while a newer brickworks stood east of the reservoir at Harrowgate Hill.[51] By the middle of the 20th century, only three brickworks were still in production locally: Blackett in Haughton Road, Burnip at Firth Moor, and Dunwell Brothers, or Dunn and Dunwell, at Whessoe and Harrowgate.[52] All had been closed during the Second World War when they were requisitioned by the army. They reopened in 1946 to serve a large demand for bricks in the town; millions were needed for the new Patons and Baldwins' factory, and Darlington corporation had embarked upon an ambitious housing programme. Together the three yards had the potential to make 370,000 bricks a week, enough for 20 average houses.[53]

The 20th century saw the rise of a new kind of building materials and construction industry in Darlington. The town developed a reputation for structural steelwork and bridge building. In addition, the Rise Carr mills, taken over in 1927 by the Crittall Manufacturing Co. Ltd., turned to steel window manufacture in 1930. By the middle of that decade the Darlington works was supplying 90 per cent of steel window sections for the U.K. market, many of which were installed in new council houses.[54]

CRAFTSMEN AND THE BUILDING INDUSTRY

Before the middle of the 19th century, construction in Darlington was carried out by specialist tradesmen working independently. Galleries added in 1700 and 1705 to St Cuthbert's church were built by a joiner, John Nesham.[55] Larger houses were usually erected under the supervision of masons or of their owner, as shown by the sales of bricks by Francis Holmes in the 1760s. Earliest directories list separate building trades, but no contractors in the modern sense. In 1791, there was only a handful of building craftsmen – a painter, a joiner and ironmonger, a cabinet

38. *Laying the foundations of Waterhouse's market hall, c. 1861.*

maker, and a glazier and tinner – substantial enough to be included.[56]

The bricklayers Samuel Adams and Edward Petty, partners who both lived in the deanery, were perhaps the first to organise building operations on a larger scale. In the early 1820s they built Beechwood for John Botcherby, and carried out extensive repairs to St. Cuthbert's church.[57] In Darlington at that time were other bricklayers, as well as joiners, plumbers, a stone-mason named John Duck in Clay Row, and a land agent called Jervis Robinson in Black-wellgate.[58] Robinson, who was also turnpike surveyor and magistrates' clerk, shared a house at the junction of Paradise Row and Blackwellgate with Robert Botcherby, who had succeeded to his father's timber business in Bondgate, later transferred to Union Row.[59] The Botcherbys have some-times been described as builders, although their main activity was probably timber supply. The building with which they were associated may have amounted to no more than overseeing the constuction of their own houses, including Woodlands, where the younger Robert Botcherby died in 1838,[60] and Pierremont, the first Gothic villa, known as the Buckingham Palace of Darlington. While John Botcherby is said to have built Pierremont, it is more likely that he contracted the work to others, as he had with Beechwood.[61] Robert Botcherby may have built a few smaller properties; he had, for instance, agreed in 1829 to buy a site for a cottage near the Cockerton Road from the duke of Cleveland.[62] Unlike his father, a joiner and cabinet maker, Robert Botcherby was invariably described as a timber merchant, and John Botcherby, originally an iron merchant with many financial and industrial interests, came to be called gentleman.[63] John Botcherby sold considerable property in Darlington in the early 1840s and moved to Hartlepool.[64] The Union Row timber yard, along with John Botcherby's iron business, was taken over by Thomas Laidler. Laidler had started as a maker of clogs, pattens, and rush-seated chairs – using rushes from the Skerne – then becoming a timber merchant in Clay Row and Grange Road before succeeding Botcherby.[65] Bright Wass, a former apprentice of Robert Botcherby senior, also became a timber and iron merchant, owning a large enclosure where Grange Road and Paradise Row meet Blackwellgate. Wass was also a builder, although on a small scale, responsible for demolishing 'two or three wretched cottages' and building the first houses of West Terrace on Coniscliffe Road.[66]

Thomas Todhunter, a joiner with a timber yard at the west end of Union Street,[67] developed an extensive contract business, though exclusively in woodwork. According to Spencer in 1862, 'he was such a master of his craft as we have not seen in Darlington before or since'. Todhunter employed only the best workmen, and his reputation brought commissions to fit out aristocratic mansions across the region. 'For sticking a moulding, framing a sash, panelling a door, or doing anything to be done in wood, from the ridge of the roof to the nethermost sleepers above the foundations, Mr Todhunter's hands were the men to be trusted . . .'.[68] The business passed to his son on Todhunter's death in 1834, but appears to have closed before the younger Thomas died in 1857.[69]

Edward Todhunter, who was possibly the elder Thomas's brother, and a plumber, glazier and tinplate worker in Tubwell Row, is noted for having introduced gas lighting to the town. In 1817 or 1818, his shop was lit by gas which he made himself, 'the novel brilliant flame in the window . . . the object of many curious remarks by the crowds that nightly flocked to gaze on the wonder'.[70] It was not until after the formation of the Darlington Gas Light Company in 1830 that this facility became more widely available.[71] The only record of Todhunter's direct involvement in building was the construction of 'a commodious residence' at Harewood Hill in about 1830, to which he retired, and where he died in 1832.[72]

A number of builders had, like Ralph Smith, links with brick manufacture. Thomas Robson, who in 1833 bought Smith's brickyard, adjacent to his own, was later, like the developer and brickyard owner Robert Thompson, involved in the building of Albert Hill.[73] A Richard Robson had been recorded as a bricklayer in Darlington in 1763,[74] and Thomas Robson and his son of the same name continued to be described as bricklayers. One of them developed a related interest in housing finance, as a director of the Darlington Working Men's Equitable Permanent Building Society, established in 1856, and a trustee of the Onward Benefit Building Society.[75] The Simpsons of Hope

Town, who started out as bricklayers, were responsible for much of the new terraced housing in that district during the 1840s and 1850s, and by the 1870s had their own brick works in Whessoe Lane.[76]

Some larger and more enduring construction companies appeared after the mid century. The most unusual was W. Richardson & Co. Ltd. in Neasham Road, which had developed out of the craze for greenhouses in the wake of the Great Exhibition of 1851.[77] Darlington Quakers were especially enthusiastic about conservatories, vineries and glass porches, and William Richardson was involved in constructing many such through the 1850s.[78] Richardson, originally a joiner, based in Northgate, was variously also described as architect and builder. The North of England Horticultural Works at Bank Top was built at the time Richardson's became a limited company in 1872, and the company then advertised itself as horticultural builders and hot water engineers.[79] Conservatories remained a significant part of the business through the company's life, but the heating and ventilation activity was developed considerably, and later other types of pre-fabricated buildings as well as air conditioning for industry.[80] In the 1960s the company also made boats.[81] The works, which had been extended in 1894, boasted a large illuminated temperature indicator facing passengers on the main railway line south of Bank Top station.[82] There were 225 employees in 1915.[83] The business and works were sold in 1924 to Reginald Pease, who was eventually succeeded as chairman and managing director by his son Maurice. Following a serious fire in 1960, the premises were rebuilt with steelwork fabricated by the firm.[84] After being taken over by Hillcrest Investments Ltd. in 1970, Richardson's survived for only 10 years before the receiver was called in.[85] The site was cleared in 1986 amidst fears of asbestos contamination.[86]

Another substantial joinery business, that of William Brown, had its origins in the same decade as Richardson's. Brown, a joiner, started in two converted cottages at Albert Hill in 1856, moving to Wooler Street and finally to a four-acre site in John Street. From about 20 employees in 1875–6, the firm had expanded to 100 by the time of its jubilee in 1906.[87] The sawmills produced a range of goods, notably 20,000 mineral water cases every year, for which they had the 'finest and most up-to-date plant in their industry in the north of England'. A 300 feet-long grandstand was constructed for Darlington Football Club within five days of the order being received. The firm also made coffins, and occasionally acted as undertakers during the 1890s. William Brown retired in 1897, to be succeeded by his son, Thomas, and died in 1908.[88] The sawmills underwent a large expansion in 1945, doubling their capacity, to accommodate a large new demand for window frames for houses. There were then 250 employees, compared with the 75 before the war.[89]

There were other sizeable joinery businesses in Darlington. The North of England School Furnishing Co. Ltd., established in 1876, had among its directors the architect W. H. Hoskins and the Darlington councillor G. Marshall, a builder. The company, based in Russell Street, made fittings and furniture as well as selling educational materials.[90] Its factory in East Mount Road had 300 workers in 1915, and 250 after the Second World War.[91] R. T. Snaith's steam joinery in Bondgate also underwent rapid expansion from the 1870s. Besides fitting out the new town hall and other public buildings in Middlesbrough, Snaith was responsible for all the woodwork in some of Hoskins' main commissions in Darlington: the new King's Head hotel, the hospital and the Queen Elizabeth Grammar School, as well as that in the Edward Pease Public Library. His firm also worked on renovations of old churches and stately homes, such as Raby Castle.[92]

The builder and contractor R. Blackett & Son Ltd. was established in 1896 by Ralph Blackett and his son John Joseph Blackett (d. 1931). When the clay ran out at Borough Road brickworks, they moved their brickyard and joinery works to Haughton Road. Blacketts built and commissioned Darlington's first power station in 1900, constructed the Thompson Street road bridge over the railway in 1906, and in 1910 built Darlington High School for Girls.[93] They built back streets on the site of their brickyard west of Borough Road in 1899, also off Coniscliffe Road and on the Pierremont estate, as well as converting Pierremont to flats.[94] In 1928 the company was bought out by R. T. Snaith & Son Ltd., the companies merging in 1938. Between the wars, contracts included the training college

39. *Construction of the Sir E. D. Walker homes, 1926–8.*

extension, the Sir E. D. Walker Homes, and panelling and bookcases for Darlington library extension.[95] Other substantial firms engaged in house-building in the late 19th century were Ward & Airey, Watson Brothers, Thomas Thornton, and John Guthrie & Sons, whose principal was president of the Northern Master Builders Association.[96]

Another noteworthy business was the Darlington Construction Company of Albert Hill, which had its origins in the engineering industry. John Shewell, a former railway engineer, operated as a bridge builder and boiler-maker from the 1870s until his retirement in 1916. His company was taken over by the Darlington Construction Company, trading as J. Shewell & Co.'s Successors Ltd.. The new directors, Capt. E. H. Pease, formerly of the Cleveland Bridge Company, and E. Lloyd Pease, withdrew from bridge-building to concentrate on structural engineering and press work. Among the large steel buildings they constructed were bus sheds, and the stand at Stockton-on-Tees racecourse.[97]

The experience of Darlington's building trade during World War Two was at odds with the fortunes of the town's other main industries. Builders had been doing well, with a great deal of new housebuilding in progress during the 1930s. This stopped completely at the outbreak of war, and

40. *Post-war council house building.*

the only projects on offer were large government contracts which the main Darlington builders, despite forming into a group to tender, had little success in obtaining. Most of the workforce transferred to public sector contracting and, it was reported in 1942, 'the effect . . . has been very nearly to eliminate the small master builder'. There were fears that at the end of the war the number of firms and building workers would be inadequate to deal with the accumulated demand for building repairs and new homes.[98] In fact the list of builders and contractors in 1947 contains many of the same small firms as in the pre-war directory, and with the number slightly increased.[99]

6. THE MODERN TOWN, 1914–2000

TOWN CENTRE PLANS AND ROADS

Town planning in Darlington became more deliberate and purposeful around the time that the borough was extended in 1915. The new council produced plans and projections in 1916 allocating land for various uses, including parks, recreation grounds and cemeteries. Prospective residential sites were denoted for 'workmen's' or 'better class' houses. A total of 488 a. in the recently extended borough was identified as available for building, with another 688 a. considered suitable for development later, partly dependant upon the extension of the sewerage system.[1]

By the middle of the 1920s a town planning scheme had been drafted which designated areas for industry, for housing at various densities, and as open spaces, as well as laying out new roads on the outskirts of town.[2] There was opposition from land owners to what were seen as radical proposals, resulting in a public enquiry in March 1926. Objectors to the proposed town plan included the R. H. Allan estate, with 450 a. of land at issue; Hummersknott Ltd., which owned 283 a.; the executors of Alderman W. E. Pease, MP, who held 197 a.; Lord Barnard with 90 a.; and 19 smaller owners of land adjoining the Black Path. Residents of the Black Path – later to become a western extension of Cleveland Terrace – objected to the prospect of further traffic, and to funerals travelling along their road to reach the West Cemetery. Yet that was a minor issue in the scale of proposals covering 6,526 a., more than half of which was in the rural area, and with which the rural district council largely concurred.[3] It was proposed to build or widen 61 streets and roads, to allocate residential zones where no 'industries likely to injure the amenity of the area' would be permitted, and to limit certain districts on the north and east of town to industry. Limits were placed on housing density in areas where development was already underway. In the main this restricted houses to an average of 16 per acre, in the west end, Brinkburn and the NER estate, and various sites across the north of the town, between West Auckland Road and Stockton Road. Other planned developments were allowed to be more intensive: 630 houses were proposed on 21 a. at Cumberland Street, off the North, or Durham, Road; 180 on a six-acre site at Springfield; 210 to be built on seven acres in Langdale Road, off Neasham Road; and 120 on four acres at Chatsworth Terrace, between Bank Top and South Park. To counter this, open land would be maintained, some of it remaining in agricultural use, but other tracts designated for public spaces: in the Cockerbeck valley, Woodland Road, Staindrop Road, West Beck valley, Hundens recreation ground, Eastbourne, Chatsworth Terrace and an extension of South Park, a total of 134 a.[4] This plan involved the loss of allotments at West Beck valley and Eastbourne – over the war years the number of allotments in Darlington had risen to more than 2,500 – and by way of compensation, a new allotment site of 33 a. was to be created out of agricultural land at Hundens Lane.[5]

Darlington's town clerk justified the council's position to the planning enquiry. The corporation had in mind 'the paramount ideals' of town planning, the main one of which was to provide for the systematic development of the town in years to come. Development had been almost entirely to the north while there had been a ring of private landed estates around the south and west sides of town. These estates had been, or were in process of being, broken up, and a town plan was needed in order that development could be controlled. The council was also concerned that, while there were excellent railways and 'a very good system of radial roads', cross communications were poor. The town clerk praised the foresight of previous administrators for an Act of 1872 with powers to require any landowner to make up a road, and for the limit of 18 houses per acre, to be reduced to 12. The Allan estate representative disagreed with the council's estimate of future population growth. As the Durham coalfield declined, he argued, Darlington would follow: 'I suggest that the prosperity of Darlington is on the wane'. The town clerk replied that if no development took place, the roads would not be built. 'The plan simply laid down the lines the road should take when the development appeared'.[6]

41. *The Mead, part of Darlington garden suburb.*

The plan was timely, for the inter-war years saw the building of almost 8,000 new houses in and around the town.[7] By 1929 the main areas of new housing development were Brinkburn Road, Geneva Road, the Mead and the Fairway off Yarm Road, and streets east of the Durham Road at Harrowgate Hill. There were also substantial plans to extend the Cleveland estate further west, to develop sites behind the West Cemetery and south of South Park, and a further swathe of land east of Geneva Road and south of Yarm Road. Road improvements were also in progress. Part of Clay Row, which had been renamed Parkgate following a petition by residents in 1919, was widened between Borough Road and the railway bridge, and subsequently the bottleneck under the bridge relieved by extensive work which doubled the width of the roadway.[8] The council next turned its attention to the Great North Road, the passage of which through the town centre brought severe congestion, especially on market days. There were also concerns about poor quality ribbon development alongside the main road beyond the borough boundaries.[9] In 1930 three options were suggested for diverting the road: around the east of town, to rejoin its old route at Harrowgate Hill; to the west of Cockerton; or along Carmel Road and north via Cockerton.[10] By the time a Select Committee started to consider the Darlington Corporation Bill in 1934, the

council had come down in favour of a bypass from
Whessoe to Blackwell Bridge.[11]

The bypass plan fell into abeyance during the mid 1930s,
while a major redevelopment of the town centre was
contemplated. Competing architects were told that there
was no intention to implement the scheme immediately,
but that 'a definite plan' was sought 'with which future
municipal development shall conform'. Council depart-
ments had become dispersed around the town centre, and
there was a desire to gather offices and council accommodation under one roof. The old town hall buildings
contained the council chamber and committee room, and
borough surveyor's offices, on the south; the transport
superintendent's offices and clock tower on the north; and
the covered market in the middle. Architects were asked to
design premises to accommodate the borough accountant,
public assistance officer, education officer, the police,
weights and measures inspector, and markets superintendent on the ground floor, with the mayor's parlour,
reception rooms, council chamber, three committee rooms,
along with the town clerk, medical officer, borough
surveyor, magistrates, and gas department, above. Car-
etaker's quarters, and a car park, were also envisaged. If the
new development were to be on the market place, then an
alternative site for the market itself would be needed. A
scheme was required which would take account of market
and traffic problems, which had become severe: 'The Great
North Road, bearing a very large volume of traffic, passes
through the area via Grange Road, Blackwellgate and
Northgate and considerable congestion of traffic occurs,
particularly on market day. The market square is at present
used as a car park . . . The Lead Yard is used as a terminus for
omnibus traffic, and as this is likely to increase, the
provision of a properly designed terminus might well be
incorporated in a scheme.'[12] North Lodge Park was under
consideration as a location for the municipal building, its
two-acre site having been bought by the council in 1929.[13]

One of the more radical responses to the council's
challenge was a design to build upon the whole central
market area, including both banks of the Skerne. An
isometric view of this plan shows a dual carriageway 'Civic
Approach' sweeping across the river, with car parks where

the 1970 town hall now stands. Large blocks, presumably of flats, cover land on the former Low Park facing the town centre across the Skerne. Covered and open markets have been relocated south of the present town hall, along Feethams. A new municipal block occupies the top of the market place, alongside a police station, with a bus station adjoining at the Tubwell Row end. Small blocks of shops and arcades have been redeveloped around the former market place.[14] This ambitious and incongruous scheme did not proceed – whether on aesthetic or cost grounds is unclear – and Darlington's medieval street plan was spared obliteration. Discussions continued on the need for new municipal buildings, culminating in 1937 with an agreement with the London architect Charles Cowles-Voysey for a scheme on Feetham's Field.[15] This project fell victim to the war, as did a plan for an aerodrome on 200 a. of land off Yarm Road, bought by the council by compulsory purchase in 1937, on part of which site the 1960s Cummins factories now stand.[16]

The attention of the local authority at this time of national emergency instead turned to preparations for civil defence. The borough surveyor, Ernest Minors, was concerned in particular to identify sites for, and basements for conversion to, air raid shelters. Public shelters were formed in the town centre, as well as individual surface shelters in residential districts.[17] Communal shelters numbered more than 450 across the town, although there was a shortfall of several thousand places – the whole population could not be accommodated, especially in the northern industrial area of Darlington.[18] The war also brought A.R.P. buildings and posts, first aid and ambulance depots, and another great extension in allotments.[19] Later, during the term of office of Darlington's first Jewish mayor, Councillor Barnett Jackson, in 1941–3, a number of large halls were converted to billets for Jewish refugees.[20]

A long term town plan for the borough published in 1950 envisaged considerable expansion in housing, industry and schools over the following 20 years, with a concomitant halving of agricultural acreage. It anticipated the inner ring road, new courts and police station.[21] It was some time later, in 1956, that discussions resumed on the town centre problem and need for consolidated municipal buildings. A new town hall was finally completed in 1970, on Feethams, beyond the south-eastern corner of the market place, with a car park which covers the site of the bishop's palace. After consultation with the Royal Fine Art Commission, the five-storey main block was designed to be sensitive to its surroundings, and approximately the same height as the neighbouring St. Cuthbert's church. The architects, Williamson, Faulkner Brown and Partners, in collaboration with the borough architect, E. A. Tornbohm, envisaged the town hall as the first phase of a much larger central redevelopment scheme which would see civic buildings covering part of the market square and town hall car park, with a covered market facing the town hall across a new 'civic square' on Feethams.[22] This idea was developed as the 'Shepherd plan' in 1969, with two indoor shopping malls and a multi-storey car park. Most of the buildings on the north side of the market place were to be demolished. This plan was scrapped after a change in political control of the council from Conservative to Labour in 1971. The new council instructed Tornbohm to produce revised schemes, one of which proceeded as far as a public enquiry in 1973, when the proposed demolition of a number of listed buildings, including the Pease house, Bennett House and others in Horsemarket, the Central Hall, covered market and Waterhouse's old town hall, was rejected by the secretary of state. The council ultimately paid £380,000 in compensation to the original developers, Shepherds of York, for the aborted scheme.[23]

At the time of the development plan in 1950, a traffic census had revealed a peak flow of 650 vehicles an hour in Northgate. Earlier studies had suggested that 35 per cent of rush-hour traffic was long-distance, following the route of the Great North Road through the town centre.[24] Discussions on ways of bypassing Darlington were already underway in 1947. By 1950 a plan had been agreed in principle between the Ministry of Transport and the Durham county council to build a 'motor road' from Barton to Coatham Mundeville which would rejoin the existing A1 at Mainsforth, exactly the route of the recently closed Merrybent branch railway line. The road was costed at £5.5 million.[25] The scheme was delayed until the end of the decade, when the proposed bypass was expected to 'look like the [new M6] motorway and eradicate a lot of Darlington's traffic problems'.[26] Work on the 10½-mile stretch of road, on a similar route to the 1950 proposal and incorporating a six-mile section of the disused Merrybent line, began in 1961, and the A1 bypass opened in 1965.[27] By the time this was extended as motorway north past Durham in 1967, much heavy traffic had been taken away from Darlington town centre.[28]

Councillors had argued in 1950 that the bypass alone was not enough to deal with traffic problems in the town, and that an inner ring road was also needed to ease congestion.[29] Four such schemes were submitted for ministry approval between 1954 and 1961, without positive result.[30] From 1963, planning and construction of St Cuthbert's Way and other sections of the ring road proceeded in stages, concluded, though not completed, by 1973 – the final section, from Grange Road to Bondgate, was never

42. *St Cuthbert's Way, part of the inner ring road, under construction in 1963.*

constructed.[31] A new police station had been built in 1962 on the outer periphery of the new road, adjoining Park Place, to be joined by a fire station in 1972, and the Royal Mail house in 1981. In Northgate, the road attracted a multi-storey office block, Telegraph House, later Northgate House, but known as Darlington's Centre Point as it was planned in 1971, completed early in 1975, and thereafter stood empty for several years.[32] After the construction of the inner ring road came further debate on the matter of an outer road, called a relief road, linking the A66 from Stockton with the A1 motorway.[33] Arguments about the route took some years to resolve. Durham county council favoured a cross town route, while the borough council, backed by the Department of Transport, preferred a southern course from Great Burdon, turning west to Blands Corner, at the southern end of Grange Road.[34] The latter option was decided upon in 1982, went to public enquiry and was approved the following year.[35] Construction began in 1984, and the road opened ahead of schedule in 1985.[36] The new road attracted industrial and retail developments in its wake, notably the Lingfield estate, first planned in 1990, adjoining the McMullen Road trading estate, which dated from 1956, and close to the two factories of Cummins Ltd. built along Yarm Road, 1963–5.[37] The outer ring road lacked significant features until 1997, when it acquired a landmark in the shape of a brick train designed by the Scottish sculptor David Mach. Costing £760,000, the train, 39.6 metres in length, 7.05 metres high and containing more than 181,000 bricks, emerges from an embankment beside the road.[38]

PUBLIC BUILDINGS AND OTHER DEVELOPMENTS BEFORE 1939

The commitment to public open spaces made explicit in the 1920s town plan was followed seriously by the borough council. A number of additional parks and recreation grounds were dedicated. Almost 24 a. of land in Cockerbeck valley, acquired by the council in 1912 and used as allotments, became a park in 1925.[39] The Dene, shortly afterwards renamed Brinkburn Dene, opened in 1923.[40] Six acres of land on the south side of Yarm Road, donated to the council in 1930 by Ald. Tommy Crooks, was made into a recreation ground.[41] Three acres of land bequeathed by Dr John Waldy in Oakdene Avenue, off Coniscliffe Road, became Green Park, original site of the Tubwell Row fountain, which was moved in 1970.[42] Tennis courts opened at Hundens recreation ground in 1923.[43] Some of the older parks were equipped with new facilities. Stanhope Green acquired tennis courts and a putting green,[44] Eastbourne Park tennis courts.[45] South Park, already well-provided with facilities, underwent further improvement in the 1920s and 1930s: putting and bowling greens, and an aviary in 1936, as well as the transfer to the park of the Pierremont estate fountain, and of the Leadyard arch to become a feature in the grotto. In addition a 10 a. boating lake was constructed outside the park, on the south side of Parkside, using unemployed labour. Work started in 1921 and the lake opened in 1924.[46] Further alterations to South Park followed the second war, with the boating lake abandoned and some time later filled in as too expensive to restore, while the Skerne was diverted and landscaped, and new facilities provided for anglers.[47] Another long-standing public park, North Lodge, had its lake filled in and boathouse converted to a shelter during the 1930s, to be finally demolished in 1955.[48] While subsequently undergoing improvements, such as the restoration of its bandstand in 1989, North Lodge park's later history has been a sorry one, attracting complaints as a health hazard and

43. *North Lodge Park, with boat house and bandstand*

haunt of drug abusers.[49] In general, the inter-war years can be seen as the heyday of Darlington's public parks, and the period also saw new suburban cemeteries. The West Cemetery was extended by eight acres, and in the rapidly growing Geneva Road area, a new 36 a. Eastbourne Cemetery was established in 1926.[50]

While the council's town centre plans had come to little in the inter-war period, there were marked advances in shops and other privately sponsored public buildings. Eight cinemas, as well as the Hippodrome theatre and the Theatre Royal, then undergoing conversion to the Regal cinema, were in existence in 1937, joined by a tenth cinema, the Regent in Cobden Street, in 1939.[51] Binns' department store, which had undergone constant enlargement and modernisation since 1922, stretching 240 feet back from the High Row, was destroyed in a fire of 1925.[52] It was rebuilt on a larger scale after the company had bought adjoining sites to extend its frontage along High Row and halfway down Blackwellgate, in a style considered 'the last word in store architecture'.[53] Buildings housing the Midland bank in Prospect Place, which had replaced the Sun Inn in 1867, were themselves demolished in 1923. The bank was rebuilt by 1926, set back four feet from the street thus providing an opportunity for the road to be widened on the Northgate junction.[54] The Northern Echo opened new printing works

44. Binns' department store, the 'last word in store architecture', rebuilt from 1925 and extended in the 1930s.

and offices in 1934, replacing its old building in Priestgate.[55] A new Woolworth's store, involving alterations to the frontage of the King's Head Hotel, was built in 1939.[56]

Public transport developed to service new housing on the outskirts of town, with the paraphernalia of trams and trolley buses impacting upon street scenes. Tramcars were replaced by trolley buses from 1926. The new system, starting with routes to Barton Street and Haughton, was an immediate success, and a Cockerton service was added within weeks.[57] In 1942, 50 vehicles working for the corporation trolley bus service covered the whole town, while motor buses served the surrounding rural district.[58] Trolley buses were gradually replaced by motor buses from the end of 1950, with the last service, along Neasham Road, terminating in 1957 and trolley wires finally lost to the local landscape a year later.[59] After the council dropped plans to concentrate cattle markets at Feethams in favour of Bank Top, the vacant site instead, in about 1930, accommodated a new garage and workshops for United Automobile Services Ltd., provider of some of the rural motor bus services.[60]

Darlington's power station, located between Borough Road and the main railway line, came to dominate views of the town. The works had been extended in 1920, but it was the building of giant concrete cooling towers and large chimneys in 1939 which had greatest impact upon the townscape.[61] The town's eastern skyline was further marked in 1939 by the

45. *The impact of trolley buses on the street scene near the North Road locomotive works.*

46. View across the north of the town centre towards cooling towers under construction in Borough Road, 1939.

building of engine sheds with a coaling unit and water tower, on the Green Street side of the railway at Bank Top. This replaced 19th-century buildings which had been used to house locomotives and repair wagons, and was alongside a roundhouse, or circular shed, of 1864 which held up to 18 engines. When wagon repairs were transferred to Shildon in 1885, the workshop at Bank Top had been converted to an engine shed, but by the 1930s, when 119 steam locomotives were stationed at Darlington, facilities were no longer adequate.[62] After diesel engines came into service, a depot for servicing and maintaining them was opened in 1957, across the line from the engine sheds and on the route of the Stockton and Darlington Croft branch railway of 1829.[63]

HOUSING BETWEEN THE WARS

The national housing crisis of the immediate post-war period affected Darlington acutely. The council debated the issue in December 1918, when Cllr. Tommy Crooks received widespread support in emphasising an urgent need for more working-class accommodation, and arguing for an increase in local powers of compulsory land purchase.[64] A severe shortage of rented accommodation in the town was causing concern, with a county court judge criticising the large number of landlords seeking vacant possession in order to occupy houses themselves, or to increase the rent by re-letting.[65]

Darlington council had already begun to investigate the scale of the local housing problem, with George Winter, the borough surveyor, producing plans of working-class housing in the town and of potential building sites while the First World War was still in progress.[66] In response to a request from the local government board to consider 'the extreme urgency of the housing question', and also to develop a town planning strategy, joint meetings of the Health and Sanitary and Streets committees were inaugurated in 1919. This group started to search for housing sites and work out procedures through which the council might build its own houses. The borough surveyor was too busy to supervise construction, and after hearing a deputation of local architects – Moscrop, Hoskins, Pritchett, Lee, Chilton, Brown and Clayton, who offered to work for fees which would not exceed the cost of a directly employed architect – it was instead decided to appoint a qualified architectural assistant to the surveyor.[67]

The committee's first moves were unambitious. They looked around for large houses to convert to flats, but concluded that nothing suitable was available.[68] Another strategy was to convert wooden huts from military to domestic use. In 1919 the borough surveyor bought from the government a total of 10 huts at Haughton-le-Skerne searchlight station, Lingfield light station, and elsewhere in Haughton Road.[69] The first conversion to a dwelling, of an army hut re-erected at the cattle market, was inspected by the committee in February 1920, and permission given for a further four huts on that site to be made into houses. The remaining five conversions were in Haughton Road.[70] Priority in allocating these homes was given to applicants suffering from tuberculosis.[71]

Although by 1920 there had been a net increase of 1,341 houses in the town since 1911, it was estimated that the shortfall, taking account of population increase and overcrowding, was still almost 4,000.[72] A further 500 families were expected to move into Darlington during the following 18 months, as North Eastern Railways workers were transferred from Shildon and York to the Faverdale wagon works. The council managed to negotiate an arrangement with the company in August 1920 for an immediate loan of £250,000 for housing purposes, and a further £500,000 to be available in installments as required.[73] They also began investigating some of the rapid prefabricated building systems then on offer, receiving a visit in 1920, for instance, from William Airey, whose Leeds firm had patented such a method of house construction.[74] But system-building options were not pursued between the wars, nor did the council resort to building tenements or flats.[75]

The search for possible council housing sites produced an initial group of four, which were approved by the Housing Commissioner in 1919.[76] By far the largest was an area of 69 a. in Cockerton, with frontages on Newton Lane and West Auckland Road, between the Alma Hotel and the railway bridge.[77] Percy S. Worthington was engaged as architect to lay out the estate in August 1919 as the compulsory purchase of a then 82 a. site proceeded, and the first tenants were selected early in 1921.[78] The other schemes to proceed were much smaller: a plot of less than an acre called the St Paul's site, around Askrigg Street, off the North Road; and three acres of land on Crosby Street, Honeypot Lane (later renamed Longfield Road) and Thompson Street West, where initially 24 houses were built.[79] In 1920 three and a half acres near Hundens Lane, south of the Fighting Cocks railway branch line, were bought from the builder R. Blackett and Sons, along with land to form a new connection between Yarm and Haughton roads.[80] Soon afterwards, the council was offered 79 a. at Polam Hill Farm as housing land, and an estate plan, incorporating a new link between Grange Road to Neasham Road, was produced.[81] Building the radial roads which gave access to housing land on the edge of the built up area was suggested as suitable work for the unemployed. The Polam roads had been constructed by the middle of 1923, while the council's unemployment sub-committee attempted to organise labour to extend Park Lane, and to open up the Geneva site.[82]

By the end of that year, the committee, which in the light of its new range of responsibilities had become the Housing and Town Planning Committee, was able to record a total of 341 new council dwellings. Already complete were 27 houses at St. Paul's, 38 at Thompson Street and 200 on the Cockerton estate. A further 50 were completed or in progress at Polam Hill, and 26 in progress at Cockerton. Added to these were the 10 converted army huts.[83] Construction was carried out by 15 private building firms, most or all of whom were local.[84] The numbers of houses constructed, public and private, continued to grow through the 1920s: a total of 329 in 1924, 510 in 1925.[85] The borough surveyor noted that the main growth was in Cockerton, followed by Eastbourne and North wards.[86]

Like Cockerton, much of the Eastbourne expansion was in council housing. The first six houses in Geneva Road were ready for occupation in June 1926, by some of 538 applicants, 138 of whom claimed to be living in over-crowded conditions.[87] Rents were set at 7s. 6d. a week for a two-bedroomed house, and 8s. 6d. for one with three bedrooms.[88] The new road, named Geneva Road East between Neasham and Yarm Roads, and Geneva Road West (later changed to Parkside) from Neasham to Grange Roads, had street lighting installed in 1926.[89] Further land across Yarm Road, on Hundens Lane, had been acquired by the council in 1929, and by the end of 1932 a total of 200 houses, two- or three-bedroomed, stood there and on Geneva Road East.[90] A layout for a local shopping centre in Geneva Road East was approved in 1936.[91] Other land in the area took longer to develop. Part of Brankin Moor had been offered for council housing by a local builder, Mr S. Cohen, in 1919 and again in 1920.[92] It was finally bought by the council, for an estate of 400 houses, in the mid 1930s, by which time Cohen had apparently sold off individual plots fronting Yarm Road for £100 to £200 each for private housing.[93] Another major scheme at the time was the Harrowgate Hill estate, on the northern fringes of the town, laid out in 1936.[94]

By 1936, the borough had in total 733 council houses, two- and three-bedroomed, of which some had a separate parlour.[95] Despite the continuing pressure of population – in 1932 the town had to contend with the arrival of 500 additional families when LNER transferred the staff from its Gateshead locomotive works[96] – the council began to tackle another manifestation of its housing problem, that of unfit properties and insanitary areas. The first major demolition was of 141 houses around the notoriously unhealthy Leadyard and Park Street, on the bishop's Low Park, in 1935.[97] Many of the displaced inhabitants were re-housed in the new council dwellings of Geneva Road East and Hundens Lane.[98] In 1936, a three-year plan was approved to demolish areas of poor housing, by clearance order rather than purchase, allowing owners to rebuild on the site. The first phase included 91 houses east of Yarm Road at Bank Top: Green, Chancery and Silver Streets, Railway Terrace, Union Place, Silver Row, Studley Row, and the Penfold property.[99] A survey of 78 of these properties revealed that only eight had a rear access, while 43 had no kitchen, 15 no sink, 26 no form of food pantry, and 49 no facilities to wash clothes. None had a dampcourse, hot water on tap, or an indoor lavatory. For 12, the only water supply was in the yard; only one house had a bath, and only six a lavatory which was not shared with others.[100] The second and third phases of demolition, along with a further clearance scheme condemning 80 houses in 1938, appear to have been largely suspended for the duration of the war.[101] The plan for the second year had included 142 properties in the Neasham Road area of Bank Top – Albert Street, St John's Place, Princes, Victoria and Adelaide Streets, Garbutt's Square and Carter's Row – as well as Vulcan Street and Howard Street, with its 'front and back' houses, on the west side of Albert Hill. The third phase was the demolition of 155 houses, on the northern side of the town – in John, Low Wooler and Lowson Streets, Whessoe Road, South, Alliance and Foundry Streets – and others in the Commercial Street area, in Sun, King, Regent and Union Streets, some of which dated from the 1820s. Housing in Haughton and Cockerton was also condemned in this order, along with the four widows' almshouses built by Mary Pease in Post House Wynd in 1820.[102]

Other than some modest almshouses, there was no housing in Darlington designed specifically for old people. The first such development came in 1926. It was proposed to build 'a colony for the aged poor' at Salutation Corner, with a bequest of £60,000 from Sir Edward Walker. The plan met angry objections from residents of Linden Grove, Sylvan Grove and Coniscliffe Road who sent a petition to the council: 'Almshouses would be quite incongruous centred among the most costly residences of the town. . . . The erection of that class of houses would seriously depreciate the value of our residences'. The council said that it had no jurisdiction over the choice of site, while supporters of the project argued against the use of the term 'almshouses.'[103] A plan for 48 homes, including the widening of Coniscliffe Road, was approved later in the year, and the homes opened in 1928.[104] Walker, founder of one of the country's largest provincial newspaper distributors and three times mayor of Darlington, had died in 1919, leaving the residue of his estate to build homes for the elderly.[105] Building cost £30,000, with the balance held in trust for the upkeep of the houses. In blocks of two, four or six around a spacious quadrangle, 'in a friendly neo-Georgian', according to Pevsner, were bungalows with red-tiled roofs as well as a public hall, place of worship, laundry, and superintendent's house. The architect was Joshua Clayton of Darlington.[106]

It was not until a decade later that the first council houses were built for the elderly. These were 10 'cottages for the aged' in Hilda Street, Freeman's Place, opened in 1937. They were intended for couples 'dispossessed under slum clearance orders', cost £360 each to build, and were let at 3s. a week. At their opening, Cllr. W. Heslop, chairman of the Housing and Town Planning Committee, announced that the next scheme would be for 40 old people's houses on the Polam Hill estate.[107]

Although relatively late starters in council house building, Darlington borough council constructed a total of 978 houses between 1919 and 1939. Yet the ratio of council to private housing built during those twenty years was very low by regional standards, at only 12.3 per cent. In the same period, 6,954 private houses were built in Darlington.[108] The peak year for new houses was 1934, when over 1,000 private dwellings were completed.[109] Much of the immediate post-war private house-building was the continuation of schemes which had already been in progress before 1914, such as the revived model cottages project at

47. *Houses in Brinkburn Road,*
behind which terraces were
intensively developed between
1918 and 1930.

the Mead, and the intensive terrace housing south of Brinkburn Road, the bulk of which was built between 1918 and 1930.[110]

The Hummersknott estate of 283 a. along with Hummersknott, Uplands, Tees Grange, Wilton House, Ivycroft, Hill House Farm and Tees Grange Farm, was sold by A. F. Pease in 1919 to a development company, Hummersknott Ltd., of 92 Northgate, Darlington.[111] The property was split into 11 lots for auction in 1927, and housing development proceeded there shortly afterwards.[112] Four and a half acres of land in Nunnery Lane was retained as open space, let to the Hummersknott Allotments Association.[113] None of the existing houses on the estate was still in Pease occupation, most having been leased out for some time before the war. A survey of other former Quaker mansions in 1930 showed that many awaited a similar fate. Woodside stood empty, its estate in the process of being broken up for building. It was demolished shortly afterwards, although its kitchen garden and vinery survived as a market garden until 1984.[114] Beechwood too was empty.[115] Woodburn was demolished in 1935.[116] Elmfield and Woodlands had survived. Pierremont had been divided into three houses. A number of other large houses had found institutional uses: Polam Hall was a school; Feethams was council offices; North Lodge became the borough education office; West Lodge housed the YMCA; Southend, 'greatly added to', was a Roman Catholic school, and later became the Grange Hotel.[117] Elm Ridge was converted to a Methodist church in 1932.[118] Mowden Hall became a prep school in 1935, and later a corporate headquarters, while development of its estate proceeded from 1934 with the building of Staindrop Crescent.[119]

The west end continued its outward march to embrace many of these previously secluded estates, as the former glebe land was built up beyond Cleveland Avenue. Development had reached Elton Road by 1926.[120] Land adjacent to the Black Path west of Elton Parade was made into a builders' road in 1932, then surfaced and dedicated as a public highway, becoming Cleveland Terrace after construction was completed.[121] The track which had marked the northern boundary of the glebe land between Woodland Road and Carmel Road, and upon which the Glebe Farm stood, had been developed at its east and west ends as Milbank Road. In 1938 the road was driven through the full length, made up by Lord Barnard and adopted as a highway.[122] The Woodside estate, south of Coniscliffe Road, was also under development from the mid 1920s, with Woodvale Road and Hartford Road laid out, and street lighting installed in 1926.[123]

A more modest style of house was under construction in large numbers east of the Durham Road, in the Leyburn and Middleham Road area. Building was carried out in phases from the 1920s by J. E. Chilton, who was also responsible for much of the new housing in Brinkburn Road. Private

48. *Black Path, used as a builders' road from 1932 and afterwards forming an extension of Cleveland Terrace.*

housing was at the same time appearing near the new council estate in Cockerton, organised by the local builder Bussey and Armstrong, who had bought a 25 a. site from the council in 1928.[124]

DEVELOPMENT AND REDEVELOPMENT AFTER 1939

The Second World War exacerbated Darlington's continuing housing shortage. 'Key workers' for the Royal Ordnance Factory No. 28 at Aycliffe were accommodated in lodgings, and also on an estate of about 138 houses built by the Ministry of Supply on and to the west of Lingfield Lane.[125] Middle-class evacuees arriving in the town from Teesside drove up the cost of houses: a bungalow which had sold for £750 before the war was reported to have changed hands for £1,300 in 1942.[126] The borough council declined to reveal any information about their post-war housing development plans, even to the Board of Trade, lest speculation inflated site values.[127]

Despite the suspension of the slum clearance programme, the housing waiting list stood at 2,200 in 1945.[128] The council had opposed the building of temporary housing by the Ministry of Supply, taking the view that the Lingfield Lane estate was sub-standard and insisting it be demolished as soon as hostilities ceased. At the war's end, it was obliged to change policy and buy the whole estate as a partial response to the housing shortage. The council paid £15,660 for it in 1947, and the temporary homes survived for more than another decade, before being replaced by new and more permanent housing.[129] Further development in that area came as a result of Patons and Baldwins' new factory in McMullen Road, which was accompanied by the building of 60 houses for key workers in the Broadway and Estoril Road, north and south of Yarm Road, which were designed by the Newcastle architects Cackett, Burns, Dick and Mackellar.[130] Patons also converted the West Lodge YMCA hostel to accommodate some of their workers.[131] Carmel Gardens and Thornbury Rise, completed in 1948–9 in the west end, were built by the North Eastern Housing Development Association with Royal Ordnance Factory and Patons managers in mind.[132]

49. Prefabs under construction in Green Street, c. 1946.

The crisis forced the council to build its own prefabricated houses. The housing committee had in 1944 applied to the Ministry of Health for 200 prefabs, and in 1945 approved a design called 'Tarran', although delivery problems later led to another type, 'Arcon', being used in Green Street.[133] Site preparation and the digging of foundations were carried out by German prisoners. The building of 23 homes on the recently cleared Green Street, 59 at Burnside Road, off Geneva Road East, and 118 directly south of the Eastbourne Cemetery, also off Geneva Road, was complete by the beginning of 1947.[134] The prefabs remained for almost 20 years, before being demolished between 1963 and 1965.[135]

While prefabs helped in the short term, there remained a severe shortage of rented accommodation. In 1950 there were 3,500 applications for council houses, and the authority estimated that 1,310 households were in substandard housing, with 1,500, or 6,000 people, over-crowded.[136] A cartoon in the *Northern Despatch* suggested that the town clock tower, then under repair, should instead be converted to flats.[137] The council made rapid progress with its post-war housing. The Brankin Moor estate was under way in 1948.[138] Roads and sewers were laid for housing in Nickstream Lane, Cockerton, in 1950; for the Branksome estate in 1952; and for Firth Moor estate in 1953.[139] Branksome Hall, formerly Westfield, had been home to a branch of the Kitching family and was sold to the council in the 1950s. Its park, between Staindrop Road and Newton Lane, was developed for housing, including accommodation for the elderly and disabled; the hall itself was demolished to make way for housing in 1978.[140] The Springfield estate, consisting of 190 council dwellings, was built along Salters Lane, Springwell Terrace, Hutton Avenue, Alnwick Place, Belford Gardens, Belsay Walk, Morpeth Avenue and Corbridge Crescent, from 1955.[141] Skerne Park estate, south of Parkside, was planned with six different house types in 1958.[142] The Red Hall estate, between McMullen Road and Haughton-le-Skerne, was developed from the mid 1960s, its first phase system-built using pre-cast concrete panels.[143] Building there continued into the 1970s, with British Legion flats opened in 1972.[144] The Tudor Gothic mansion of 1830 from which the area took its name was demolished in 1984.[145]

Mowden Hall was the locus of a different kind of scheme. The hall, long detached from its 157 a. park, had served as headquarters of Summerson's Foundries from 1953, becoming Department of Education offices in 1966. The land was sold in 1961 to a Hartlepool builder, Cecil Yuill, for £241,000, 'with plans to build a small town on it'. Yuill submitted plans for 1,380 houses, ranging in price from £2,275 to over £6,000, along with shops, a public house, a school, and a site for a church which was never built.[146]

During the 1960s and 1970s extensive demolition took place, especially in the town centre.[147] Amidst much protest, the 17th-century Nag's Head was demolished in 1962 in favour of a modern version.[148] Larchfield was pulled down in 1978 and replaced by St Augustine's social club.[149] Some clearance was made necessary by road widening and new

50. *Brunswick Street demolition, photographed in 1961 by Joseph Coulthard.*

roads, especially the inner ring road, which cut a swathe through Northgate in particular. Brunswick Street, in the shadow of the Borough Road cooling towers, was flattened in 1960, and other unhealthy properties followed.[150] Yet by the time Havelock, Gurney and Henry Streets, near the North Road station, and Florence Street at Bank Top, were marked out for clearance and replacement by new houses in 1976,[151] a change in thinking was discernible. Albert Hill was declared a general improvement area, and the local authority issued a guide to home improvement.[152] The council's Policy and Resources Committee asked its own housing department to reconsider a decision to demolish 36 houses in Vulcan and Edward Streets, west of the railway at Albert Hill.[153] There was concern at a dramatic fall in population of Darlington's two central wards, from 17,400 in 1951, to 8,900 in 1971.[154] The final plan for mass demolition, though, was the largest ever, with the housing committee in March 1979 approving the clearance of more than 1,000 houses in the central, Yarm Road and North Road areas. Some opposition was reported, with residents asking instead for renovations.[155] The scheme was dramatically halted, for in May, while a newly-elected government asked for further demolition projects, the council had also changed its political control, and announced that the clearance plans would be revised.[156]

Other new approaches to housing were apparent at this time. One hundred new houses and flats near the town centre, in the Hargreave Terrace area, were planned to be energy-efficient, well-insulated and with small windows.[157] Improvement of older homes was given official support, as in the five-year housing action area in China Street.[158] Joint public and private building schemes were announced, for instance between the borough council and Wimpey Homes on the Brinkburn Road estate in 1979, and a scheme in conjunction with Cecil M. Yuill Ltd. at Whinfield Green in 1978.[159] Totals produced in 1983 show council housing at its peak: Cockerton had 601 council houses; Whinfield, 129; Woodland Terrace, 65; Coniscliffe Road, 18; Rise Carr, 236; Yarm Road, 101; Firth Moor, 891; Skerne Park, 546; Hundens Lane, 248; Parkside, 354; Brankin Moor, 417; Geneva Road, 292.[160] After that, through the 1980s, many were sold to their tenants, and later, many more were demolished. A total of 350 houses on Firth Moor, for instance, were cleared in 2001.[161]

House-building at the end of the 20th century was mainly private, much of it on former industrial land. The Coles Cranes site on Pendleton Road was planned as a 600-house estate from 1984, its roads named after Oxbridge colleges.[162] The borough council sold nine acres formerly occupied by the Phoenix Tubeman factory in Springfield Road to Wimpey Homes, who received a £500,000 derelict land grant for reclamation and extensive landscaping. Work on the first 100 houses on the newly named Springfield Park started in 1988.[163] The site of the former North Road railway workshops began to be re-developed at about the same time, with a scheme for 65 relatively low cost homes built by Wimpey around Westmoreland Street.[164] Previously industrial land at the old Cleveland Bridge works in Neasham Road was approved for house-building in 1990, and ambitious plans were submitted for a development of 600 houses in Clifton Road, involving a further proposal to move the cattle market.[165] In 1994, 327 new homes were approved on 33 a. of the former Whessoe works in Brinkburn Road.[166] A smaller development took place on the old railway forge site in Rocket Street.[167] Plans for a new village on the Neasham Road former brickworks caused controversy.[168]

A new estate constructed in the former grounds of the Carmel Convent during the late 1980s was relatively unusual in finding a vacant site in the west end. Covering 12 a., it provided sheltered accommodation at Worsley Park and Cardinal Gardens, sponsored by a local housing association, the Darlington Re-Roof.[169] The pressure to identify larger areas suitable for housing led to infill around other new housing, as with estates at Wylan Avenue in 1986, and Salters Lane and Whinfield Road in 1989.[170] Plots on the fringes of the existing built area, mainly on the northern side of town, proved attractive to developers – the reservoir site at Harrowgate Hill, land in Barmpton Lane[171] – though often less acceptable to planners and residents, as with a plan to build 300 houses at Harrowgate Farm, near Princess Road, in 1995, which brought protests from neighbours.[172]

THE MODERN TOWN

As suburban housing has taken the place of industrial sites, so too in the centre of Darlington the remains of industry have disappeared, to be replaced by new commercial and retail premises. The engine sheds at Bank Top closed in 1966, when only 10 steam locomotives remained in Darlington, and the roundhouse and coaling plant were demolished the following year.[173] On the west side of the tracks, the diesel engine depot closed in 1984 and was pulled down in 1990.[174] Closure of the power station was announced in 1975, and demolition first of the chimneys, then cooling towers and finally the works themselves, took place between 1977 and 1979.[175] The site became the Borough Road industrial estate. Nearby, the derelict Pease textile factory with its landmark chimney was subject to a compulsory purchase order in 1978, and after efforts to

51. *The continuing impact of railways on the town, pictured here in c. 1951, lessened from the 1960s.*

keep its rose garden, clock and other landmarks failed, that
site too was cleared, in 1983.[176]

Two prominent buildings brought new shape to the town
centre during the 1980s.[177] The first was a sports centre,
incorporating the Central Hall, and named the Dolphin
Centre, reflecting both a well-known former building there,
the Dolphin inn, and the site's new use as a swimming pool
and for other leisure purposes.[178] Designed by the borough
architect Gabriel Lowes, the centre was constructed between
1980 and 1982, at a cost of £23 million, and officially
opened in 1983 by Roger Bannister.[179] The second major
development, stretching from Tubwell Row to Northgate
via a covered bridge across Priestgate, though partly
concealed behind older shop frontages, was the Cornmill
shopping centre, planned from 1988 and completed in
1992.[180] Many of the 19th-century inns and shops which
had stood on Tubwell Row had already been lost in the
1960s, to Barclay's Bank and the Co-op, two large concrete
and glass buildings out of harmony with their surroundings. The Cornmill centre replaced these relatively new
constructions.[181]

The Dolphin and Cornmill centres, while significant
departures from what had gone before, sit reasonably
comfortably in an older Darlington, a town of medieval
market place, streets and wynds whose buildings date in the
main from the town's 19th-century heyday. The 20th
century's most radical efforts at transformation ultimately
failed, thwarted variously by world war, lack of funds and
public opposition, leaving the distinctive market town of
Darlington to a generation more inclined to appreciate its
historic assets.

Notes

CHAPTER 1

1 J. Granger, *General View of the Agriculture of the County of Durham* (1794), 32.
2 *The Review and Abstract of the County Reports to the Board of Agriculture* (1818), 13.
3 P. A. G. Clack and N. F. Pearson, *Darlington: A Topographical Survey* (1978), 3–4.
4 Clack and Pearson, *Darlington*, 1–2.
5 P. A. G. Clack, 'The origins and growth of Darlington', in P. Riden (ed.), *The Medieval Town in Britain* (1980), 67.
6 W. H. D. Longstaffe, *The History and Antiquities of the Parish of Darlington* (1854), 10.
7 Clack, 'Origins', 67–8.
8 Clack, 'Origins', 67.
9 Clack and Pearson, *Darlington*, 1.
10 E. Wooler and A. C. Boyde, *Historic Darlington* (1913), 2–9; C. P. Nicholson, *Those Boys o' Bondgate, and other contributions to the story of Darlington and neighbourhood* (1949), 47–8.
11 G. Flynn, *Darlington in Old Photographs: Second Selection* (1992), 85.
12 P. Abramson, 'River Skerne Restoration Project, Report NAA 95/12' (report in Durham SMR, 4817, 1995).
13 Clack and Pearson, *Darlington*, 3.
14 R. Young, 'Flint material from Darlington', in Clack and Pearson, *Darlington*, 38–9; Durham SMR, 1500, 1504, 1516.

15 M. Adams, 'Darlington Market Place: Archaeological Excavations, 1994' (report in Durham SMR, 4000, 4812), 14–15.
16 J. Robinson and J. Biggins, 'Morton Palms, Darlington, Co. Durham: geophysical survey, 1999', (report in Durham SMR, 5639).
17 Young, 'Flint material', 38.
18 P. Clack, 'Darlington's rural area', in Clack and Pearson, *Darlington*, 69–81.
19 See, for example, Durham SMR, 262, 912, 915, 917, 921, 924
20 Durham SMR, 322, 323.
21 Clack and Pearson, *Darlington*, 3–4.
22 Clack, 'Darlington's Rural Area', 71–81.
23 Robinson and Biggins, 'Morton Palms', 4.
24 D. W. Harding, *Holme House, Piercebridge: Excavations 1969–70: a summary report* (1984), 1, 18–20.
25 *VCH Durham*, ii. 175; T. H. Rowland, *Dere Street: Roman Road North* (1974), 9–12.
26 Durham SMR, 1536, 1537, 1539.
27 A. P. Fitzpatrick and P. R. Scott, 'The Roman bridge at Piercebridge, North Yorkshire – County Durham', *Britannia*, xxx (1999), 114.
28 Harding, *Holme House*, 16.
29 Fitzpatrick and Scott, 'Roman bridge at Piercebridge', 115, 117–18, 129.
30 W. Hutchinson, *The History*

and Antiquities of the County Palatine of Durham (1794), iii. 214.
31 Fitzpatrick and Scott, 'Roman bridge at Piercebridge', 129; N. Pevsner, rev. E. Williamson, *The Buildings of England: County Durham* (1985 edn.), 379.
32 Pevsner, *County Durham*, 379.
33 Longstaffe, *Darlington*, 352, 354.
34 Longstaffe, *Darlington*, 187; Durham SMR, 1517.
35 Wooler and Boyde, *Historic Darlington*, 27–8; Durham SMR, 1533, 180.
36 Durham SMR, 1518.
37 Fitzpatrick and Scott, 'Roman bridge at Piercebridge', 114–15; S. Lucy, 'Changing burial sites in Northumbria, AD 500–750' in J. Hawkes and S. Mills (ed.), *Northumbria's Golden Age* (1999), 16.
38 Clack and Pearson, *Darlington*, 7.
39 V. E. Watts, 'Place-names of the Darlington area', in Clack and Pearson, *Darlington*, 40.
40 *An Historical Atlas of County Durham* (1992), 16–17.
41 Watts, 'Place-names', 40–2.
42 *VCH Durham*, i, 211; Durham SMR, 1530; Lucy, 'Changing burial sites', 12–23, 33.
43 R. Miket and M. Pocock, 'An Anglo-Saxon cemetery at Greenbank, Darlington', *Med. Archaeol.*, xx (1976), 62.
44 Clack and Pearson, *Darlington*, 7.

45 *VCH Durham*, i. 216.

46 Miket and Pocock, 'Anglo-Saxon cemetery', 62–74.

47 Miket and Pocock, 'Anglo-Saxon cemetery', 73–4.

48 E. Wooler, 'The Saxon burgh of Darlington and its military defensive earthworks', *Proc. Soc. Antiq. Newcastle-upon-Tyne*, 3rd ser., v (1913), 185–6.

49 Durham SMR, 244.

50 Wooler and Boyde, *Historic Darlington*, 42–6.

51 Adams, 'Darlington Market Place excavations', 11–12.

52 R. Cramp, *Corpus of Anglo-Saxon Stone Sculpture* (1984) i. 62–3.

53 Durham SMR, 733, 734.

54 Durham SMR, 735.

55 Durham SMR, 736.

56 Cramp, *Corpus*, 62; C. D. Morris, 'The pre-Norman sculpture of the Darlington area', in Clack and Pearson, *Darlington*, 46.

57 Morris, 'Pre-Norman sculpture', 47; H. D. Pritchett, *The Story of the Church of St Cuthbert, Darlington* (1965), 12.

58 *VCH Durham*, i. 240; Wooler and Boyde, *Historic Darlington*, 48–9; Pritchett, *Story of the Church of St Cuthbert*, 12–13; Cramp, *Corpus*, 157.

59 Wooler and Boyde, *Historic Darlington*, 75–6; Pritchett, *Story of the Church of St Cuthbert*, 12.

60 P. F. Ryder, 'St Cuthbert Darlington: an archaeological assessment' (report in Durham Diocesan Office, DAC section, 1997), 14–15.

61 Pritchett, *Story of the Church of St Cuthbert*, 12.

62 Adams, 'Darlington Market Place excavations', 11–12.

63 E. Cambridge, 'The early church in County Durham: a reassessment', *Journ. Brit.*

Archaeol. Assoc., cxxxvii (1984), 79–80; B. K. Roberts, *The Green Villages of County Durham* (1977), 8, 13–18; *VCH Durham*, i. 263–8; Clack and Pearson, *Darlington*, 8; Clack, 'Origins', 68–70; R. Lomas, *North-east England in the Middle Ages* (1992), 105.

64 *Symeonis Monachi Opera Omnia*, ed. T. Arnold (Rolls Ser., 1882–5), i. 83, 212.

65 See *VCH, Durham*, i. 266.

66 Clack and Pearson, *Darlington*, 8; Watts, 'Place-names', 40–3.

67 Longstaffe, *Darlington*, 44–6; M. H. Dodds, 'The Bishops' Boroughs', *Archaeologia Aeliana*, 3rd ser., xii (1915), 84.

68 *Opera Omnia*, i. 123.

69 R. Surtees, *The History and Antiquities of the County Palatine of Durham* (1816–40), iii. 350.

70 Dodds, 'Bishops' Boroughs', 100.

71 *Boldon Buke: a survey of the possessions of the See of Durham made by order of Bishop Hugh Pudsey, 1183*, ed. W. Greenwell (Surtees Soc., xxv, 1852), 17; see also *VCH Durham*, i. 259–341; *Boldon Book: Northumberland and Durham*, ed. D. Austin (1982).

72 For discussions on the manuscript sources, see the detailed analysis by G. T. Lapsley in *VCH Durham*, i. 321–6. A modern translation of the oldest surviving text, dating from the 13th century (known as Manuscript A) appears in *Boldon Book: Northumberland and Durham*.

73 Clack and Pearson, *Darlington*, 9.

74 *Boldon Buke*, app., vi.

75 Dodds, 'Bishops' Boroughs', 86.

76 *Boldon Buke*, vii; *Boldon Book:*

Northumberland and Durham, 7. See however the discussion in *VCH Durham*, i. 312.

77 Longstaffe, *Darlington*, 62; Lomas, *North-east England*, 28–9.

78 *Boldon Buke*, 16, 54; *VCH Durham*, i. 270; Lomas, *North-east England*, 174.

79 DULASC, CCB, I/E2/1, Box 54 (188764).

80 *Boldon Buke*, liii; *VCH Durham*, i. 295; Longstaffe, c.

81 *Boldon Buke*, 17, 54.

82 *VCH Durham*, i. 297–8, 303.

83 W. J. Mountford, 'Biographical and historical notes on bygone Darlington' (Typescript in Darlington Lib., *c.* 1912), 93; Darlington Lib., U418a40, Plan of the Town of Darlington, 1826, surveyed by John Wood (reproduced in J. Wood, *Town Atlas of Northumberland and Durham, 1820–7* (1991)).

84 *VCH Durham*, i. 291–2, 318.

85 *Boldon Buke*, 17, 55.

86 *VCH Durham*, i. 300, 338.

87 Lomas, *North-east England*, 163.

88 Several entries in Boldon Book note the existence of the bishop's house and court: *Boldon Buke*, 17; *VCH Durham*, i. 339.

89 *VCH Durham*, i. 308; Dodds suggests that du Puiset may have granted the town a charter although no evidence of this survives: 'Bishop's Boroughs', 91.

90 *VCH Durham*, i. 312–3.

91 Dodds, 'Bishops' Boroughs', 91.

92 Longstaffe, *Darlington*, 271.

93 Longstaffe, *Darlington*, 55.

94 *VCH Durham*, ii. 114–5; *Cal. Pat.* 1549–51, 14, 17; Mountford, 'Biographical and historical notes', 48.

95 *Boldon Buke*, 17; *Bishop Hatfield's Survey. A Record of the Possessions of the See of Durham,*

made by order of Thomas de Hatfield, Bishop of Durham, ed.
W. Greenwell (Surtees Soc., xxxii.
1857), 11.
96 Longstaffe, *Darlington*, 191;
PRO, DURH 3/73, m. 5d.
97 Clack, 'Origins', 67–84.
98 Clack, 'Origins', 75–6.
99 Clack, 'Origins', 71; Lomas,
North-east England, 165.
100 *Bishop Hatfield's Survey*,
1–6.
101 *Bishop Hatfield's Survey*, 6.
102 *Bishop Hatfield's Survey*, 4.
103 *Bishop Hatfield's Survey*, 5;
V. Chapman, *Rural Darlington:
Farm, Mansion and Suburb*
(1975), 4.
104 *Bishop Hatfield's Survey*, 9.
105 Lomas, *North-east England*,
150–9.
106 *VCH Durham*, ii. 183.
107 *Bishop Hatfield's Survey*,
1–6.
108 *Bishop Hatfield's Survey*,
1–3; Longstaffe, *Darlington*, 87.
109 Dodds, 'Bishops' Boroughs',
120–1, 136–7.
110 Nicholson, *Boys o'
Bondgate*, 49.
111 DULASC, SDD 94; DRO,
D/X 666/216; Mountford, 'Biographical and historical notes',
48, 166.
112 *VCH Durham*, ii. 211;
Bishop Hatfield's Survey, app.,
247–8.
113 F. Bradshaw, 'The Black
Death in the Palatinate of
Durham', *Archaeologia Aeliana*,
3rd ser., iii (1907), 157.
114 R. Lomas, 'The Black Death
in County Durham', *Journ. Med.
History*, xv (1989), 128–30, 135.
115 See also the discussions in
R. H. Britnell, 'Feudal Reaction
after the Black Death in the Pala-
tinc of Durham', *Past and Present*, cxxviii (1990), 28–47;
'The Black Death in Durham',

Cleveland Hist., lxxvi (1999),
42–51.
116 DULASC, CCB, I/E2/1, Box
54 (188764); CCB (Box 54)
I/E2/2 (188772).
117 A. J. Pollard , *North Eastern
England during the Wars of the
Roses* (1990), 43–80.
118 J. Leland, *Itinerary*, ed. L
Toulmin Smith (1907), i. 69.
119 Leland, *Itinerary*, i. 69.
120 Dodds, 'Bishops'
Boroughs', 109.
121 Clack and Pearson, *Darlington*, 1.
122 Surtees, *Durham*, iii. 350.
123 Longstaffe, *Darlington*, 351.
124 *Wills and Inventories of the
Northern Counties of England, i*,
ed. J. Raine (Surtees Soc., ii,
1835), 23.
125 *Bishop Hatfield's Survey*, 5.
126 Leland, *Itinerary*, i. 70.
127 N. Sunderland, *Tudor
Darlington* (1974), i. 6.
128 *Durham Quarter Sessions
Rolls, 1471–1625*, ed. C. M. Fraser
(Surtees Soc., cxcix, 1987–8),
257.
129 Longstaffe, *Darlington*, 38.
130 Sunderland, *Tudor Darlington*, i. 6.
131 *Darlington Wills and Inventories, 1600–25*, ed. J. A. Atkinson,
B. Flynn, V. Portass,
K. Singlehurst and H. J. Smith
(Surtees Soc., ccl, 1993), 53, 126.
132 Detailed accounts of the
architectural history of St Cuthbert's appear in J. P. Pritchett, *An
Architectural History of St Cuthbert, Darlington* (1902); H. D.
Pritchett, *History of the Parish
Church of St Cuthbert, Darlington*
(1924); Pevsner, *County Durham*,
140–1.
133 Cunningham, 'Hugh of Le
Puiset', 163, 167.
134 Ryder, 'St Cuthbert,
Darlington', 1.

135 Pevsner, *County Durham*,
141.
136 Pritchett, *Story of the Church
of St Cuthbert*, 25.
137 Longstaffe, *Darlington*, 218.
138 Longstaffe, *Darlington*, 218;
Pritchett, *Story of the Church of St
Cuthbert*, 25; Pevsner, *County
Durham*, 141.
139 Cunningham, 'Hugh of Le
Puiset', 164; Longstaffe, *Darlington*, 213.
140 Leland, *Itinerary*, i. 69.
141 DRO, DX/1351.
142 N. J. G. Pounds, *A History of
the English Parish* (2000), 392–4.
143 B. Flynn, 'The chantries of
St Cuthbert's Church, Darlington', *Durham Archaeological Journal*, i, (1984), 66–71.
144 Longstaffe, *Darlington*,
198–9; *Bishop Hatfield's Survey*, 2.
145 *VCH Durham*, i. 388; J. J.
Vickerstaffe, 'A gazetteer of
Durham county schools,
1400–1640', *Durham County
Local Hist. Soc. Bull.*, xli (1988),
3–14.
146 *VCH Durham*, i. 387–93;
Longstaffe, *Darlington*, 256.
147 Longstaffe, *Darlington*,
195–6.
148 Longstaffe, *Darlington*,
37–8, 196; Sunderland, *Tudor
Darlington*, i. 5; *Registrum Palatinum Dunelmense*, ed. T. D.
Hardy (Rolls Ser., 1873–8), ii.
1163.
149 Sunderland, *Tudor Darlington*, i. 5; Longstaffe, *Darlington*,
222; Clack and Pearson, *Darlington*, 17.
150 Durham SMR, 1519.
151 Hutchinson, *History and
Antiquities*, iii. 188.
152 Longstaffe, *Darlington*, 198.
153 Longstaffe, *Darlington*,
188–9; Sunderland, *Tudor
Darlington*, i. 4.
154 *Boldon Buke*, 18.

155 N. Sunderland, *A History of Darlington* (1967), 26.
156 PRO, DURH 3/13 f. 38; *Parliamentary Surveys of the Bishopric of Durham*, ed. D. A. Kirby (Surtees Soc., clxxxiii, 1971), 90.
157 Mountford, 'Biographical and historical notes', 45.
158 Longstaffe, *Darlington*, 188–9.
159 T. D. Hardy, *A Description of the Patent Rolls in the Tower of London: to which is added an Itinerary of King John* (1835).
160 *Pat. R.* 1225–32, 207.
161 *Cal. Chart. R.* 1257–1300, 421; *Cal. Close* 1290–1302, 580; 1333–7, 406, 468; 1337–9, 397, 398; Longstaffe, *Darlington*, 71, 73, 78–9.
162 Longstaffe, *Darlington*, 96.
163 *L. & P. Hen. VIII*, xiii, 2, 157, 431–2; xviii, passim.
164 DULASC, CCB (Box 68), 1/F1/14 (188865); Sunderland, *Tudor Darlington*, i. 4.
165 Sunderland, *Tudor Darlington*, i. 4; DULASC, will dated 6 Aug. 1564, II, 148–148v.; inventory, 148v.-150.
166 Longstaffe, *Darlington*, 143–4; Sunderland, *Tudor Darlington*, i. 5.
167 Durham SMR, 4028.
168 *Ecclesiastical Proceedings of Richard Barnes, Bishop of Durham, 1576–87*, ed. J. Raine (Surtees Soc., xxii, 1850), app. 1, xxviii; Longstaffe, *Darlington*, 196–7.
169 Longstaffe, *Darlington*, 278; DULASC, CCB I/D2/12 (Box 48) 188796–188798.
170 *L. & P Hen. VIII*, xiii (1), 221, 318.
171 *L. & P. Hen. VIII*, xiii (1), 221.
172 M. J. Tillbrook, 'Aspects of the Government and Society of County Durham, 1558–1642'

(Univ. of Liverpool, Ph. D. thesis, 1981), 23–4.
173 *Ecclesiastical Proceedings of Bishop Barnes*, app. 1, lxx–lxxi.
174 Longstaffe, *Darlington*, 201.
175 Longstaffe, *Darlington*, 200.
176 *Cal. Pat.* 1563–6, 150–1; 1566–9, 137–8.
177 *Wills and Inventories from the Registry at Durham, ii*, ed. W. Greenwell (Surtees Soc., xxxviii, 1860), 5.
178 *Wills and Inventories*, i. 273.
179 PRO, C 3/69/26.
180 Longstaffe, *Darlington*, 120.
181 *Cal. Pat.* 1566–9, 137–8.
182 PRO, E 178/736.
183 Longstaffe, *Darlington*, 193.
184 *Cal. Pat.* 1566–9, 137–8.
185 PRO, E 178/736.
186 *Wills and Inventories*, ii. 127–8.
187 *Wills and Inventories*, ii. 127–8.
188 *Wills and Inventories*, ii. 168–70.
189 PRO, CP 43/146, m.14; Birmingham City Archive, MS. 351735.
190 DRO, Da/ DM/1/165; Longstaffe, *Darlington*, 269; see also Raby Castle, Deeds Room, Press 11, boxes 5 and 6.
191 Durham Chapter Lib., Allan, xv, p. 173.
192 See in particular Darlington Lib., Sowerby's Plan of Darlington, 1848.
193 *Bishop Hatfield's Survey*, 5.
194 DULASC, CCB, Box 48, I/D2/5 (190199).
195 Longstaffe, *Darlington*, 283; North Yorks. RO, ZDG (A) IV/7/7.
196 See for example Durham Chapter Lib., Allan, xv, pp. 173, 199–207.
197 Durham Chapter Library, Allan, xv, pp. 218–223.
198 *Reg. Palat. Dunelmense*, ii. 205, 662–3.

199 DULASC, CCB (Box 48) I/D2/2 (188788).
200 Durham SMR, 1514; Sunderland, *Tudor Darlington*, i. 7.
201 *Bishop Hatfield's Survey*, 3; Clack, 'Origins', 78.
202 DULASC, CCB (Box 68) I/F1/7 (188921); I/F1/1 (188916).
203 Sunderland, *Tudor Darlington*, i. 7.
204 M. Bonney, *Lordship and the urban community: Durham and its overlords, 1250–1540* (1990), 82–3; see also H. Swanson, *Medieval Artisans: An Urban Class in Late Medieval England* (1989), 83.
205 Swanson, *Medieval Artisans*, 88–9.
206 Sunderland, *Tudor Darlington*, i. 40.
207 See for example DULASC, CCB (Box 68), 1/F1/2 (188918).
208 C. Sharp, *The 1569 Rebellion: being a reprint of the Memorials of the Rebellion of the Earls of Northumberland and Westmorland* (1975 edn.), 133–4; Longstaffe, *Darlington*, 109–10.
209 Longstaffe, *Darlington*, 122–4; 'Historical Sketches of Missions', *Northern Catholic Calendar* (1927), 76.
210 See for example Durham Chapter Lib., Allan, xv, interleaved, pp. 39–40.
211 *VCH Durham*, ii. 254; Sunderland, *Tudor Darlington*, i. 8.
212 Sunderland, Tudor Darlington, i. 7–8; Clack and Pearson, Darlington, 10–11.
213 Mountford, 'Biographical and historical notes', 19
214 *Boldon Buke*, 17; *Bishop Hatfield's Survey*, 5.
215 DULASC, CCB (Box 68), 1/F1/1 (188916).
216 DULASC, CCB (Box 68), 1/F1/7 (188921); Sunderland, *Tudor Darlington*, i. 7.

217 Durham Chapter Lib., Allan, xv, p. 12.
218 Durham Chapter Lib., Allan, xv, interleaved, pp. 39–40; Sunderland, *Tudor Darlington*, i. 6–7, 37–8.
219 *Bishop Hatfield's Survey*, 5.
220 Durham Chapter Lib. Allan, xv, pp. 152–3.
221 Surtees, *Durham*, iii. 357.
222 BL, Add. Ch. 66341; DULASC, CCB (Box 68) 1/F1/14 (188865).
223 Clack, 'Origins', 76–7; L. Addis, 'The Pottery', in Clack and Pearson, *Darlington*, 54, 57.
224 *Records of Anthony Bek, Bishop and Patriarch, 1283–1311*, ed. C. M. Fraser (Surtees Soc., clxii, 1947), 50; Longstaffe, *Darlington*, 196.
225 *Reg. Palat. Dunelmense*. ii. 1163; *Bishop Hatfield's Survey*, 3.
226 Durham SMR, 1515; Longstaffe, *Darlington*, 195.
227 A. H. Thompson, 'The Clervaux Chartulary', *Archaeologia Aeliana*, 3rd ser., xvii (1920), 186–228; see Longstaffe, *Darlington*, lvix–lxxx; Pollard, *North Eastern England*, 88–9.
228 Thompson, 'Clervaux Chartulary', 200–1, 209, 21–2; Clack, 'Origins', 76.
229 Longstaffe, *Darlington*, 86.
230 Longstaffe, *Darlington*, 37.
231 *Cal. Pat.* 1566–9, 137–8.
232 Clack and Pearson, *Darlington*, 14.
233 Surtees, *Durham*, iii. 357.
234 PRO, DURH 3/14, 541r.; DURH 3/16, 27v.
235 *VCH Durham*, ii. 130–1.
236 DULASC, CCB (Box 54), I/E2/4 (188752).
237 Lomas, *North-east England*, 165.
238 Thompson, 'Clervaux Chartulary', 207, 209, 215.

239 Bonney, *Lordship and the Urban Community*, 69–70.
240 Clack, 'Origins', 77.
241 *App. to the 45th Report of the Deputy Keeper of the Public Records*, 190–1; Thompson, 'Clervaux Chartulary', 204.
242 Longstaffe, *Darlington*, 85.
243 Clack, 'Origins', 77; A. M. Oliver, 'The Blagroves law roll', *Proc. Soc. Antiq. Newcastle-upon-Tyne*, 4th ser., i (1924), 323–4.
244 Bonney, *Lordship and the Urban Community*, 72.
245 *Bishop Hatfield's Survey*, 164–6.
246 BL, Harl. MS 594, ff.186–95; for a transcript of the Durham return, see B. J. D. Harrison, 'A Census of households in County Durham, 1563', *Cleveland and Teesside Local Hist. Soc. Bull.*, xi (1970), 16; see also R. I. Hodgson, *Demographic Trends in County Durham, 1560–1801*, (1978), 4.
247 D. A. Kirby, 'Population density and land values in County Durham during the mid 17th century', *Trans. Inst. Brit. Geog.*, lvii (1972), 92.
248 Pevsner, *County Durham*, 158; Durham SMR, 304.
249 Sunderland, *Tudor Darlington*, i. 12.
250 Sunderland, *Tudor Darlington*, i. 13.
251 Chapman, *Rural Darlington*, 18–19; Durham SMR, 891.
252 Chapman, *Rural Darlington*, 19; Durham SMR, 890.
253 Durham Chapter Lib., Allan, xv, pp. 78–88; Sunderland, *Tudor Darlington*, i. 12.
254 *Wills and Inventories from the Registry at Durham, iii*, ed. J. C. Hodgson (Surtees Soc., cxii, 1906), 85–6.

255 *Wills and Inventories*, ii. 127–8.
256 *Wills and Inventories*, ii. 168–70.
257 *Lamentable N[ewes] from the Towne of Darnton in the Bishopricke of Durham* (1585) (copy in BL); Sunderland, *History of Darlington*, 35–6; *Tudor Darlington*, i. 13.
258 Thompson, 'Clervaux Chartulary', 204.
259 *Cal. S. P. Dom.* 1598–1601, 459, where it is dated 1600; cf. Tillbrook, 'Aspects of Government and Society', 23–4.
260 PRO, SP 12/275/44.
261 Sunderland, *Tudor Darlington*, i. 13.
262 PRO, DURH 13/223 m 2, 4d, 7.
263 *Lamentable N[ewes] from the Towne of Darnton*, 5–6.
264 H. J. Smith, 'John Vaux, parson and astrologer, 1575–1651', *Trans. Arch. and Archaeol. Soc. Durham and Northumberland*, new ser., vi (1982), 83–8.

CHAPTER 2

1 Longstaffe, *Darlington*, 266, 268; Darlington Lib., U418b E800004800; DRO, D/XD 66.
2 *Darlington Wills*, 21.
3 PRO, E 179/106/28.
4 A. G. Green, 'Houses and households in Co. Durham and Newcastle, c. 1570–1730' (Univ. of Durham, Ph. D. thesis, 2000), 87, also 67, 75.
5 DRO, D/Ki 439; Darlington Lib., U418a E800004760.
6 Darlington Lib., E810024034; U418a750, E800004006; North Yorks. RO, ZDG (A) IV/7. Longstaffe, *Darlington*, 299, presents totals for the census which

cannot be reconciled with the original.

7 Pevsner, *County Durham*, 144.

8 Durham Chapter Lib., Allan, xv, p. 364.

9 Darlington Lib., E810002723.

10 Longstaffe, *Darlington*, 126; Mountford, 'Biographical and historical notes', 66.

11 H. Spencer, *Men that are gone from the Households of Darlington* (1862), 458.

12 Mountford, 'Biographical and historical notes', 31.

13 Spencer, *Men that are gone*, 341–2.

14 'List of buildings of special historical or architectural interest' (Dept. of the Environment, 1977).

15 Spencer, *Men that are gone*, 217; Mountford, 'Biographical and historical notes', 82; Longstaffe, *Darlington*, 223; 'Old Elizabethan House, Darlington', *The Builder*, xlviii (1885), 549.

16 'Elizabethan House', 549; D. H. Heslop, B. Jobling and G. McCombie, *Alderman Fenwick's House: The History of a Seventeenth-century House in Pilgrim Street, Newcastle upon Tyne, and its Owners* (2001).

17 Longstaffe, *Darlington*, 131–2; DRO, D/Whes 12/2.

18 Adams, 'Darlington Market Place Excavations', 22–5; see also Darlington Lib., U418a40, 'Plan of the Town of Darlington, 1826, surveyed by John Wood'.

19 Longstaffe, *Darlington*, 222–3.

20 DULASC, 1/23, Darlington St Cuthbert Glebe terrier.

21 Longstaffe, *Darlington*, 268.

22 Mountford, 'Biographical and historical notes', 74.

23 Longstaffe, *Darlington*, 112; Durham Chapter Lib., Allan, xv, p. 404.

24 Longstaffe, *Darlington*, 271;

Mountford, 'Biographical and historical notes', 19.

25 Guildhall Lib., RE MS. 7253/5, no.79176; 7253/1, no.64490; 7253/12, no.100219.

26 *Darlington Wills*, 55–7; Durham Chapter Lib., Allan, xv, pp. 60–1.

27 Durham Chapter Lib., Allan, xv, pp. 60–1; *Darlington Wills*, 65, 55–7, 87–8.

28 Longstaffe, *Darlington*, 353–4.

29 Longstaffe, *Darlington*, 40, 291. A plan of 1755 shows only a single-arch bridge: North Yorks. RO, ZDG(A) IV/1/8.

30 Durham Chapter Lib., Allan, xv, pp. 352–3.

31 Longstaffe, *Darlington*, 292–3.

32 Longstaffe, *Darlington*, 354; DULASC, Darlington Turnpike Deeds.

33 DRO, D/St X2/6/1.

34 Darlington Lib., E810077147.

35 *Durham Quarter Sessions Rolls*, 258–9.

36 Longstaffe, *Darlington*, 38–9.

37 Longstaffe, *Darlington*, 39; Durham Chapter Lib., Allan, xv, p. 404; Hutchinson, *History and Antiquities*, iii. 183–96.

38 Longstaffe, *Darlington*, 39.

39 Spencer, *Men that are gone*, 145–6.

40 Longstaffe, *Darlington*, 125–6.

41 *Darlington Wills*, 93.

42 Longstaffe, *Darlington*, 125.

43 Adams, 'Darlington Market Place excavations', 24.

44 Mountford, 'Biographical and historical notes', ix.

45 Durham Chapter Lib., Allan, xv, pp. 173–92.

46 Durham Chapter Lib., Allan, xv, p. 14.

47 Longstaffe, *Darlington*, 293.

48 Durham Chapter Lib., Allan, xv, pp. 173–92.

49 Durham Chapter Lib., Allan, xv, p. 411.

50 North Yorks. RO, ZDG (A) IV 7/7.

51 For illustrations of this and other pre 19th-century properties, see Durham Chapter Lib., Longstaffe scrapbook on Darlington, and Box F; Darlington Lib., E810002723; Wooler and Boyde, *Historic Darlington*, 35, 52, 103, 108, 143, 154, 207; Darlington Lib., sketches and watercolour paintings including L56B; L203; L100B; L566A; L1084A; L407B.

52 PRO, C 54/3669/7.

53 W. H. Longstaffe, 'Ruins of the north of England: Darlington Episcopal Mansion', *Church of England Magazine* (18 Sept. 1847), 177–9; Longstaffe, *Darlington*, 143–4, also ciii.

54 Spencer, *Men that are gone*, 260.

55 Longstaffe, 'Ruins of the north of England', 178.

56 Longstaffe, *Darlington*, 152.

57 Longstaffe, *Darlington*, 153; see also Hutchinson, *History and Antiquities*, iii. 189.

58 Darlington Lib., E810002723.

59 DULASC, CCDBED, 321771/3; Spencer, *Men that are gone*, 297.

60 DRO, Da/ DM/1/165.

61 Raby Castle, Deed Room, Chest of drawers, drawer 1.

62 Darlington Lib., E810024034; North Yorks. RO, ZDG (A) IV/7.

63 Durham Chapter Lib., Allan, xv, p. 365.

64 Spencer, *Men that are gone*, 299–303.

65 Darlington Lib., Durham Record, DR 08221; Mountford, 'Biographical and historical notes', 41.

66 DRO, D/X 666/220, lots 2, 3 and 4.

67 DRO, D/Ki 317; Durham Chapter Lib., Allan, xv, p. 404.

68 Longstaffe, *Darlington*, ciii.

69 Spencer, *Men that are gone*, 270–85.
70 Longstaffe, *Darlington*, 292.
71 Longstaffe, *Darlington*, 129n.
72 Longstaffe, *Darlington*, 283n. See above.
73 Longstaffe, *Darlington*, 283n.; Darlington Lib., E810029121.
74 *Darlington Pamphlet*, 17 July 1772.
75 Longstaffe, *Darlington*, 129.
76 Longstaffe, *Darlington*, ci.
77 Longstaffe, *Darlington*, 296.
78 Longstaffe, *Darlington*, 296.
79 Mountford, 'Biographical and historical notes', 137–9; Guildhall Lib., Sun MS. 11936, 10/55 no. 14853; 19/165 no. 33283.
80 Guildhall Lib., Sun MS. 11936, 32/542. The date at which the Post House, known alternatively as the Talbot from the 1770s, became an inn is not known.
81 Mountford, 'Biographical and historical notes', 15–6; see also Longstaffe, *Darlington*, 295; Durham Chapter Lib., Longstaffe Box F, view of the market place in 1843; Darlington Lib., Durham Record DR 07949.
82 DULASC, SDD 114–16.
83 Longstaffe, *Darlington*, 299; Darlington Lib., picture 143A.
84 Adams, 'Darlington Market Place excavations', 22–5.
85 Adams, 'Darlington Market Place excavations', 19; Durham Chapter Lib., Longstaffe Box F.
86 Spencer, *Men that are gone*, 392.
87 *Darlington Wills*, 170–3.
88 *Darlington Wills*, 91–2.
89 *Darlington Wills*, 126–9.
90 *Darlington Wills*, 155–7.
91 *Darlington Wills*, 55–7.
92 *Darlington Wills*, 87–91.
93 *Darlington Wills*, 83–5; 95; 25.
94 For instance *Darlington Wills*, 89, 126–9.

95 *Darlington Wills*, 197–200.
96 *Darlington Wills*, 111–5.
97 *Darlington Wills*, 151–4; 128.
98 *Darlington Wills*, 178–80.
99 *Darlington Wills*, 70–2; see also DULASC, A1 CHU BAA 654; Misc. Books M.64, CCB (1981) 185000B.
100 *Darlington Wills*, 191–5.
101 PRO, E 179/106/28.
102 Green, 'Houses and households', 87.
103 Revealed during the Second World War search for air raid shelters: Darlington Lib., acc. 40895.
104 DRO, D/XD 108/1/A/116–117; also D/XD 108/1/A/144.
105 DULASC, Janson deeds, 1–7.
106 DRO, D/XD 108/1/A/118–120.
107 DULASC, SDD 92–3.
108 DULASC, Janson deeds, 15/1–2.
109 DULASC, SDD 94.
110 DRO, D/XD 108/1/A/162.
111 DULASC, SDD 100–1.
112 DRO, D/XD 108/1/A/132.
113 DRO, D/XD 108/1/A/134.
114 DRO, D/XD 108/1/A/131.
115 DRO, D/XD 108/1/A/110–115.
116 DRO, D/XD 108/1/A/133.
117 DRO, D/XD 108/1/A/135.
118 DULASC, SDD 90; also DRO, D/XD 108/1/A/159.
119 DULASC, SDD 106, 109.
120 See for instance DRO, D/Whes 12/2.
121 DRO, D/X 666/220.
122 *Darlington Pamphlet*, 29 May 1772.
123 DRO, D/Ki 31.
124 Darlington Lib., U418eSTE, bankruptcy notice issued against Daniel Stewart, 1771; Guildhall Lib., RE MS. 7253, Redstone index.

125 Spencer, *Men that are gone*, 332–3.
126 DRO, D/Ki 317; Lancs. RO, MF/1/18.
127 Darlington Lib., U418a40, Plan of the Town of Darlington, 1826, surveyed by John Wood.

CHAPTER 3

1 J. Ogilby, *Britannia* (1675), i. 8; M. J. Armstrong, *An Actual Survey of the Great Post-roads between London and Edinburgh* (1776), 22.
2 B. J. Barber, 'The Economic and Urban Development of Darlington, 1800–1914' (Univ. of Leicester M. A. dissertation, 1969) (copy in Darlington Lib.), 1.
3 See OS Map 1:10,560, Durham LV (1858 edn.).
4 F. Mewburn, *The Larchfield Diary: Extracts from the Diary of the late Mr Mewburn, first railway solicitor* (1876), 5.
5 Longstaffe, *Darlington*, 335, 252.
6 Longstaffe, *Darlington*, 125.
7 Mewburn, *Larchfield Diary*, 5.
8 Spencer, *Men that are gone*, 346.
9 Spencer, *Men that are gone*, 69–70.
10 Darlington Lib., E810029121; DULASC, CCDBED 321771/1–2; Darlington Lib., E810077148; DULASC, CCDBED 321771/26; for leases of Low Park, see DRO, D/XD 108/1/A/92–96.
11 DULASC, CCDBED, 321771/3.
12 Mewburn , *Larchfield Diary*, 5.
13 DRO, D/Ki 317, 61.
14 Mewburn, *Larchfield Diary*, 5; Mountford, 'Biographical and historical notes', 10; *Parson and White's Dir. Northumberland and*

Durham (1827) i. 241; Long-staffe, *Darlington*, 317–18; Tees-side Archives, U/OME 4/10; DRO, D/Ki 313, p. 106.

15 Nicholson, *Boys o' Bondgate*, 82; Spencer, *Men that are gone*, 86.

16 *Parson and White's Dir. Northumberland and Durham* (1827) i. 241.

17 Spencer, *Men that are gone*, 366.

18 Longstaffe, *Darlington*, 188; Spencer, *Men that are gone*, 259–60; also DRO, D/Ki 313, p. 106; Barclays Bank Archives, 388/730.

19 Pevsner, *County Durham*, 144; Spencer, *Men that are gone*, 452–3.

20 Pevsner, *County Durham*, 143–4; Spencer, *Men that are gone*, 429–30.

21 Spencer, *Men that are gone*, 244.

22 Spencer, *Men that are gone*, 258.

23 North Yorks. RO, ZDG (A) IV/7/6.

24 Durham Chapter Lib., Allan, xv, copy of vestry minute, 12 Nov. 1788; DRO, D/X 666/225; Longstaffe, *Darlington*, 321.

25 Spencer, *Men that are gone*, 187–9.

26 DRO, D/XD/16/33; Spencer, *Men that are gone*, 188–9.

27 Spencer, *Men that are gone*, 179–87.

28 Spencer, *Men that are gone*, 206.

29 Spencer, *Men that are gone*, 179–80.

30 See Darlington Lib., E810033811, with *Reference to the Plan of Darlington Township, by Anthony Reed, Land-surveyor* (1829) (copies in Durham Univ. Lib. and Darlington Lib.).

31 Barclays Bank Archives, 388/566, 571, 574; Darlington Lib., E810037064; Pevsner, *County Durham*, 154; Chapman, *Rural Darlington*, 37–40.

32 Mewburn, *Larchfield Diary*, 5; Darlington Lib., E810024882; Chapman, *Rural Darlington*, 40–2.

33 Chapman, *Rural Darlington*, 42–3.

34 Pevsner, *County Durham*, 153; Chapman, *Rural Darlington*, 44–5.

35 Mewburn, *Larchfield Diary*, 5; Chapman, *Rural Darlington*, 43.

36 Darlington Lib., U418a40, Plan of the Town of Darlington, 1826, surveyed by John Wood; E810024882; Chapman, *Rural Darlington*, 47; Barclays Bank Archives, 388/391–392.

37 Chapman, *Rural Darlington*, 47–8; Pevsner, *County Durham*, 151; also *Leeds Mercury*, 6 Oct. 1838.

38 Chapman, *Rural Darlington*, 48; Pevsner, *County Durham*, 151.

39 Chapman, *Rural Darlington*, 49; also DRO, D/HO/F 111.

40 Mewburn, *Larchfield Diary*, 5.

41 Darlington Lib., U418a40, Plan of the Town of Darlington, 1826, surveyed by John Wood.

42 Spencer, *Men that are gone*, 358.

43 Spencer, *Men that are gone*, 150.

44 Darlington Lib., E810031377.

45 Longstaffe, *Darlington*, 311.

46 Longstaffe, *Darlington*, 249, 251; Spencer, *Men that are gone*, 449.

47 *Pigot's Dir. Ireland, Scotland and Northern Counties* (1820), 265–8.

48 *Census*, 1801–21.

49 *Parson and White's Dir. Northumberland and Durham* (1827) i. 246–53.

50 Darlington Lib., U418a40, Plan of the Town of Darlington, 1826, surveyed by John Wood; *Parson and White's Dir. Northumberland and Durham* (1827) i. 246–53.

51 Nicholson, *Boys o' Bondgate*, 78.

52 M. W. Kirby, *The Origins of Railway Enterprise: the Stockton and Darlington Railway, 1821–1863* (1993), 40.

53 *Parson and White's Dir. Northumberland and Durham* (1827) i. 244; *Pigot's Dir. Durham, Northumbs. and Yorks.* (1834), 11.

54 *Pigot's Dir. Durham, Northumbs. and Yorks.* (1834), 11

55 Darlington Lib., E810026864.

56 Nicholson, *Boys o' Bondgate*, 54, 47.

57 Nicholson, *Boys o' Bondgate*, 51; M. H. Pease, *Henry Pease: a Short Sketch of his Life* (1898 edn.), 33.

58 DRO, D/Ho/F 123/2; Darlington Lib., E810033877.

59 Darlington Lib., E810024176.

60 D. W. Hockin, *Whessoe: Two Centuries of Engineering Distinction* (1994).

61 Pevsner, *County Durham*, 149.

62 Darlington Lib., E810033813; DRO, D/XD 27/4; OS Map 1:2500, Durham LV.6 (1858 edn.).

63 Longstaffe, *Darlington*, 335.

64 DRO, D/Ho/F 123/4; Darlington Lib., E810041663; DRO, D/Ho/F 123/6 and 9; Darlington Lib., E810033886; E810049719.

65 Kirby, *Origins of Railway Enterprise*, ch. 5.

66 Darlington Lib., E810033813; *Newcastle Courant*, 17 July 1840.

67 OS Map 1:2500, Durham LV.10 (1858 edn.).

68 Longstaffe, *Darlington*, 248.
69 Spencer, *Men that are gone*
191–3, 396–8; Nicholson, *Boys o'*
Bondgate, 59.
70 DRO, D/XD 108/1/A/1;
Durham SMR, 1513; DRO,
D/XD 108/1/A/148; Darlington
Lib., E810033884.
71 Barber, 'Development of
Darlington', 8; DRO,
D/XD/16/34.
72 *Parson and White's Dir.*
Northumberland and Durham
(1827) i. 241–4.
73 Darlington Lib., U418a40,
Plan of the Town of Darlington,
1826, surveyed by John Wood;
Spencer, *Men that are gone*, 431.
74 Darlington Lib., U418a40,
Plan of the Town of Darlington,
1826, surveyed by John Wood;
E810026864; *Kelly's Dir. Stock-*
ton-on-Tees, Darlington and Sub-
urbs (1885), 228.
75 Darlington Lib., E810033820.
76 DRO, D/X 666/220; D/X
666/221; Darlington Lib.,
E810031299–300.
77 DRO, D/X 666/220.
78 Mewburn, *Larchfield*
Diary, 35.
79 Spencer, *Men that are gone*,
500, 47.
80 J. R. Kellett, *The Impact of*
Railways on Victorian Cities
(1969).
81 Longstaffe, *Darlington*, 335–7,
326–7.
82 G. Flynn, *The Book of*
Darlington (1987), 87–8; Spencer,
Men that are gone, 85, 122–9,
332–3; Pevsner, *County Durham*,
146.
83 Longstaffe, *Darlington*, 335–7,
326–7; Spencer, *Men that are*
gone, 189; Pevsner, *County*
Durham, 154.
84 Darlington Lib., E810026864.
85 Mewburn, *Larchfield Diary*,
28, 73.

86 *Report to the General Board of*
Health on Darlington, 1850, ed.
H. J. Smith (1967), 1.
87 Longstaffe, *Darlington*, 336.
88 *Report to the General Board of*
Health, 19
89 *Report to the General Board of*
Health, 24
90 *Report to the General Board of*
Health, 11.
91 *Census*, 1821–51.
92 Mewburn, *Larchfield Diary*,
66; Darlington Lib., E810033828;
Pevsner, *County Durham*, 151–2;
Chapman, *Rural Darlington*,
50–2; DRO, D/X 656/2; D/X 666.
93 Longstaffe, *Darlington*, 336.
94 Chapman *Rural Darlington*,
50–2.
95 Mewburn, *Larchfield*
Diary, 66.
96 *Census*, 1851–71.
97 Barber, 'Development of
Darlington', 9.
98 *Northern Echo*, 7 Aug. 1872;
R. A. Barnby, 'Darlington's Railway Workshops', *Durham County*
Local Hist. Soc. Bull., x (1969),
22–5.
99 Barber, 'Development of
Darlington', 12.
100 Barber, 'Development of
Darlington', 17.
101 Barber, 'Development of
Darlington', 26.
102 DRO, D/XD 108/1/A/73;
D/Ki 15A; North Yorks. RO,
ZDG(A)IV/1/9.
103 J. S. Jeans, *Jubilee Memorial*
of the Railway System: a History of
the Stockton and Darlington Rail-
way and a Record of its Results
(1875), 280.
104 Jeans, *Jubilee Memorial*,
281.
105 J. K. Harrison, 'The development of a distinctive Cleveland
blast furnace practice, 1866–75',
in C. A. Hempstead (ed.), *Cleve-*
land Iron and Steel (1979), 129.

106 J. S. Jeans, *Pioneers of the*
Cleveland Iron Trade (1875),
192–3.
107 North Yorks. RO, ZDG (A)
IV/7/7; Jeans, *Jubilee Memorial*,
285–6.
108 OS Map 1:10,560, Durham
LV (1858 edn.).
109 North Yorks. RO, ZDG (A)
IV/7/7.
110 North Yorks. RO, ZDG (A)
IV/1/9 and IV/7/7.
111 North Yorks. RO, ZDG (A)
IV/1/9; IV/7/7; Darlington Lib.,
U418a E800004866.
112 Barber, 'Development of
Darlington', 26; Building Plans,
124/1864; 185/1864; North
Yorks. RO, ZDG (A) IV/7/7.
113 Barber, 'Development of
Darlington', 27.
114 Darlington Lib., U418a
E800004866.
115 Building Plans, 401/1865;
421/1866; 71/1899; 223/1904.
116 Darlington Lib.,
E810037008.
117 Darlington Lib.,
E810032629.
118 Darlington Lib.,
E810032627.
119 R. Benson, 'Darlington
Forge and Albert Hill' (typescript
in Darlington Lib., 1976).
120 Nicholson, *Boys o' Bondgate*,
59; Pevsner, *County Durham*,
147.
121 Jeans, *Jubilee Memorial*, 280;
Barber, 'Development of Darlington', 27.
122 Darlington Lib.,
E810033880.
123 DRO, D/XD 108/13; Building Plans, 1561/1875; 1946/1877;
73/1882; 38/1906.
124 DRO, D/Whes 12/3.
125 PRO, RG 10/4884, passim.
126 OS Map 1:10,560, Durham
LV (1858 edn.); Darlington Lib.,
E810031474. Foundry Street later

disappeared into the Whessoe site.

127 See for instance Building Plans, 475/1866 and 226/1905.

128 Building Plans, 69/1863; 268/1865; 269/1865; 270/1865; Darlington Lib., E810032540–1.

129 Darlington Lib., E810032539.

130 Darlington Lib., E810032542.

131 Building Plans, 63/1897; 144/1903; 216/1903; 99/1905; 73/1906.

132 DRO, D/DL/1/164.

133 Darlington Lib., E810034536; Building Plans, 62, 153 and 154/1902.

134 *Darlington and Stockton Times*, 7 Feb. 1908; G. W. May, *British Industry and Commerce: 5. Teesside* (c. 1965), 44–5.

135 Building Plans, 189/1867; 226/1868; 605/1870.

136 Building Plans, 2145/1878; 92/1896.

137 Darlington Lib., E810026831; Building Plans, 2145/1878.

138 Building Plans, 134 and 201/1906.

139 Spencer, *Men that are gone*, 399; Nicholson, *Boys o' Bondgate*, 61, 63.

140 Building Plans, 972/1873.

141 DRO, D/X 854/1 and /2.

142 PRO, RG 10/4884.

143 Darlington Building Society, abstract of title of John Harris and Michael Middleton, 1851; Darlington Lib., E810030517, E810030539 and E810028164.

144 M. Chase, 'Out of radicalism: the mid-Victorian freehold land movement', *Eng. Hist. Rev*, cvi (1991), 319–45.

145 Darlington Lib., E810030517.

146 Darlington Lib., E810037714.

147 DRO, Da/A5/1/1.

148 Darlington Lib., E810034519, E810037715; OS Map 1:10,560, Durham LV (1858 edn.).

149 See for instance Building Plans, 91/1894; 21/1896.

150 Darlington Lib., E810034519.

151 Flynn, *Book of Darlington*, 68.

152 Darlington Lib., E810033878, E810033879; DRO, D/Ho/F 123/12–13.

153 DRO, D/XD 108/1/A/125–130; D/Ho/F 123/8.

154 Darlington Lib., E810033881; DRO, D/Ho/F 123/14–15; D/XD 108/7/7.

155 DRO, Da/A5/1/1; information on bridge.

156 Building Plans, 194/1867; Teesside Archives, U/OME (2) 6/85; also U/OME (2) 6/82.

157 DRO, D/Ho/F 123/1.

158 DRO, D/XD 100; D/DL/2/50–52; Building Plans, 221/1865.

159 Building Plans, 90/1867; 563/1870; DRO, D/XD 10/19.

160 Mountford, 'Biographical and historical notes', 256.

161 Building Plans, 92/1885; 95/1885; Darlington Lib., E810028177, lots 4–10; also E810034536, E810034534 and E810034530–1.

162 Teesside Archives, U/OME (2) 5/40.

163 Darlington Lib., E810002723.

164 Building Plans, 254/1865; 693/1871; 699/1871; 1239/1874; PRO, RG 10/4879, passim.

165 G. G. Hoskins, *An Hour with a Sewer Rat; or, a Few Plain Hints on House Drainage and Sewer Gas* (1879), 9.

166 DRO, Da/A5/1/1; Nicholson, *Boys o' Bondgate*, 88; Spencer, *Men that are gone*, 167.

167 DRO, Da/A5/1/1.

168 DRO, Da/A5/1/1, Nov. 1859; Spencer, *Men that are gone*, 365–6; Mountford, 'Biographical and historical notes', 10.

169 Teesside Archives, U/OME 4/10.

170 Teesside Archives, U/OME 4/10.

171 Teesside Archives, U/OME 4/10; for Dunning, see W. Lillie, *History of Middlesbrough* (1868), 168–9.

172 Pevsner, *County Durham*, 145.

173 Spencer, *Men that are gone*, 271.

174 Longstaffe, *Darlington*, cvii–cviii.

175 Darlington Lib., E810032485–518; also E810032519; Pevsner, *County Durham*, 148.

176 V. Chapman, 'George Gordon Hoskins, J. P., F. R. I. B. A.: a Darlington architect and his work, 1864–1907. Part 1: Hoskins and his Darlington Buildings', *Durham Archaeol. Jour.*, iv (1988), 64–8.

177 Information on bridge.

178 Darlington Lib., E810034281; E810036074; E810043913–15; E810009621–4; also E810033179–87; *Northern Echo*, 6 Mar. 1894; Chapman, 'George Gordon Hoskins', 65.

179 Darlington Lib., Wooler cuttings book no. 2, p. 77.

180 *North Star*, 10 Apr. 1894; 14 Apr. 1894.

181 *Northern Echo*, 13 Jan. 1894.

182 Darlington Lib., Wooler cuttings book no. 2, p. 78.

183 Darlington Lib., Wooler cuttings book no. 2, pp. 75, 78.

184 Building Plans, 158/1864.

185 Spencer, *Men that are gone*, 209.

186 Teesside Archives, U/OME 4/1; also DRO, D/XD 108/1/A/153–4.

187 Teesside Archives, U/OME (2) 6/77.

188 Teesside Archives, U/OME (2) 5/40; Building Plans, 943/1872; 2037/1877; 92/1885; 95/1885; 7/1896; DRO, D/XD 108/1/A/182, /183 and /188.

189 DRO, D/Wa 5/7/47.

190 DRO, D/XD 108/1/A/153.

191 Darlington Lib., E810032850–2.

192 Darlington Lib., E810034536, E810028177.

193 DRO, D/XD 108/1/A/188.

194 Building Plans, 151/1867; see also 1372/1875; 1611/1876.

195 Pevsner, *County Durham*, 149–50.

196 Darlington Lib., E810057496; Nicholson, *Boys o' Bondgate*, 80.

197 OS Map 1:2500, Durham LV.10 (1898 edn.).

198 Darlington Lib., E810032550–2.

199 Darlington Lib., E810024882; E810033886.

200 Pease, *Henry Pease*, 2; see also DULASC, SDD 130.

201 Darlington Lib., E810024882.

202 Darlington Lib., E810023897.

203 M. W. Kirby, *Men of Business and Politics: the Rise and Fall of the Quaker Pease Dynasty of North-east England, 1700–1943* (1984), 50; Darlington Lib., E810024882.

204 *Gardeners' Chronicle*, Aug. 1879; Chapman, *Rural Darlington*, 50–2; Pease, *Henry Pease*, 95; *The Diaries of Edward Pease*, ed. A. E. Pease (1907), 217.

205 *Diaries of Edward Pease*, 212.

206 Darlington Lib., E810024882; P. Meadows and E. Waterson, *Lost Houses of County Durham* (1993), 65; Chapman, *Rural Darlington*, 49–50; Durham Chapter Lib., Longstaffe, Darlington scrapbook, sale notice of 1871.

207 Darlington Lib., E810033794; Building Plans, 368/1869.

208 C. Cunningham and P. Waterhouse, *Alfred Waterhouse, 1830–1905: Biography of a Practice* (1992), 255; Chapman, *Rural Darlington*, 52–5.

209 Darlington Lib., E810024882; *The Builder*, xxvii (1869), 306–7; Pevsner, *County Durham*, 148; Meadows and Waterson, *Lost Houses*, 64; Chapman, *Rural Darlington*, 36, 54, 55–6; Chapman, 'George Gordon Hoskins', 65.

210 Pevsner, *County Durham*, 152–3; Chapman, *Rural Darlington*, 56–8; also Teesside Archives, U/OME (2) 5/41; DRO, D/XD 108/7/2.

211 Cunningham and Waterhouse, *Alfred Waterhouse*, 255; DRO, Da/NG2/2386; Pevsner, *County Durham*, 152.

212 Darlington Lib., E810085068); Chapman, *Rural Darlington*, 58.

213 Barber, 'Development of Darlington', 24.

214 Mewburn, *Larchfield Diary*, 137.

215 For example Building Plans, 34/1891.

216 Chapman, *Rural Darlington*, 48.

217 Building Plans, 1369/1874; 1534/1875; 1723/1876; 1808/1876; also 92/1863; Chapman, *Rural Darlington*, 42–3.

218 *Slater's Dir. Northern Counties* (1876–7), 71; Building Plans, 1369/1874; 1534/1875; 1723/1876; 1808/1876; 1870/1876.

219 V. Chapman, '"Front house and back house" houses and small terraced houses in Darlington', *Durham County Local Hist. Soc. Bull.*, xxix (Dec. 1982), 21–9.

220 PRO, BT 31/ 2753/ 14926.

221 *Kelly's Dir. Stockton and Darlington* (1887), 275–6; see Building Plans, 118/1894; 14/1895; 146/1895; 79/1896.

222 Darlington Lib., E810032446; cuttings book 1884, pp. 20–8, 58, 60, 65; Chapman, *Rural Darlington*, 43; Flynn, *Book of Darlington*, 68.

223 Building Plans, 14/1893; 15/1897; also 24/1882; 89/1882; 20/1883; 47/1885; 60/1889; 148/1894; 125/1896; 187/1903; 133/1904.

224 Chapman, *Rural Darlington*, 48–9.

225 Building Plans, 94/1892; 170/1894; 51/1895; 32/1896; 82/1896; 16/1897; 71/1898; 149/98; 171/1899; 76/1900; 171/1900.

226 OS Map 1:2500, Durham LV.6 (1915 edn.); see also Building Plans, 85/1891; 145/1899; 86/1901.

227 Kirby, *Men of Business and Politics*, 54.

228 Teesside Archives, U/OME (2) 6/79.

229 PRO, BT 31/7436/52834; Darlington Lib., E810034852.

230 Chapman, 'George Gordon Hoskins', 68; Building Plans, 83/1899; 98/1899; 106/1900; 124/1902; 54/1903.

231 Building Plans, 170/1912; also 243/1911; 247/1911; 23/1912; 103/1912; DRO, D/XD 108/7/4–5.

232 DRO, D/HH 2/3/8; D/St/C4/3/13.

233 North Yorks. RO, ZDG (A) IV/7/6; Darlington Lib., E800004867; M. Phillips, *A History of Banks, Bankers and Banking in Northumberland, Durham and North Yorkshire* (1894), 353–60; Spencer, *Men that are gone*, 60–1.

234 Darlington Lib., E800004867; Chapman, *Rural Darlington*, 18–19.

235 Spencer, *Men that are gone*, 405–6; Pevsner, *County Durham*, 148.

236 Longstaffe, *Darlington*, 323.

237 Darlington Lib., E810031135.

238 OS Map 1:10,560, Durham LV (1858 edn.).

239 Mewburn, *Larchfield Diary*, 66.

240 Barber, 'Development of Darlington', 34.

241 See A. J. Kenwood, 'Residential building activity in north eastern England, 1853–1913', *Manchester School of Econ. and Soc. Studies*, xxxiii (1965), 115–28.

242 Darlington Lib., E810034853, E810029501; Building Plans, 255/1865; also 1971/1877.

243 DRO, D/X 666/224; Darlington Lib., E810034850; Building Plans, 189/1864; 265/1865.

244 Building Plans, 224/1865; also 43/1909; Pevsner, *County Durham*, 151.

245 Teesside Archives, U/OME (2) 6/81.

246 Darlington Lib., E810032618; OS Map 1:2500, Durham LV.9 (1897 edn.); Building Plans, 19/1911.

247 For example, Building Plans, 1940/1877; 23/1890; 29/1896;

58/1897; 83/1898; 113/1898; 119/1900; 15/1903; 106/1903.

248 Barber, 'Development of Darlington', 34.

249 Raby Castle, Steward's Room, box 71.

250 Longstaffe, *Darlington*, 247; Pevsner, *County Durham*, 147.

251 Nicholson, *Boys o' Bondgate*, 82.

252 Raby Castle, Deed Room, press 8/35.

253 Cleveland Estate Act, 31 Vic., c. 1 (Private).

254 Building Plans, 254/1868; 257/1868; 763/1871; 869/1872; 1061/1873; 1237/1874; 1292/1874; 1331/1874; 1353/1874; 1506/1875; 1528/1875; 1732/1876; 2099/1878.

255 Barber, 'Development of Darlington', 29.

256 DRO, U/Da 829, pp. 13–17; U/Da 830, pp. 14–20; U/Da 831, pp. 16–17, 20–3.

257 Darlington Lib., E810029502; Raby Castle, plan 188.

258 Darlington Lib., E810032879.

259 L. Strutt, 'An architectural and historical survey of the housing of Darlington between 1850 and 1918', (Newcastle-upon-Tyne Polytechnic, B. A. dissertation, 1982) (copy in Darlington Lib.).

260 DRO, D/Wa 5/9/7–12.

261 Building Plans, 1147/1873; 1580/1875.

262 Raby Castle, plan 203.

263 Barber, 'Development of Darlington', 28; Building Plans, 1331/1874.

264 Raby Castle, Steward's Room, Box 68; Schedule of Purchases, 1899; also DRO, D/Wat, boxes 40–43; Building Plans, 32/1894; 29/1897; 131/1897;

122/1898; 128/1898; 129 and 130/1898; 26/1899; 111/1899; 141/1899; 216/1902.

265 Raby Castle, Steward's Room, Box 68, Particulars of roads made, 1901–1910.

266 Raby Castle, Steward's Room, box 68, letters from John H. Watson of Ryedale, Darlington.

267 Raby Castle, Steward's Room, box 68, Edward Wooler to Lord Barnard, 10 Mar. 1902.

268 OS Map 1:2500, Durham LV.5 (1915 edn.); Raby Castle, Steward's Room, Box 68, correspondence, 1906–10.

269 DRO, D/DL/1/38/2.

270 *Northern Echo*, 4 July 1902.

271 Darlington Lib., E810029411–2.

272 Darlington Lib., E810026797, E810031165; DRO, Da/TR/4/7–8.

273 DRO, Da/DM/7/27/7.

274 Darlington Lib., E810032427.

275 Building Plans, 435/1866; 24/1879; 87/1885; 11/1888; 62/1890; 123/1893; 14/1894; 68/1894; 71/1894; 21/1897; 35/1898; 90/1898; 4/1901; 9/1901; 12/1903; 112/1905; 135/1901.

276 Building Plans, 408/1865; 39/1867; 153/1867; 484/1869; 720/1871; 1520/1875; 1521/1875; 1909/1877; 1947/1877; 34/1880; 85/1889; 73/1893; 58/1896; 15/1901; 186/1903; 111/1904; 269/1905.

277 Building Plans, 2062/1877; 20/1892; 172/1899.

278 *Northern Echo*, 18 Dec. 1900; *North Star*, 21 Nov. 1900; *Darlington and Stockton Times*, 16 Mar. 1901.

279 *Darlington and Stockton Times*, 16 Mar. 1901.

280 DRO, D/XD 27/4, plots 709–713.

281 *Northern Echo*, 18 Nov. 1908; 8 Jan. 1909; *Darlington and Stockton Times*, 21 July 1934; Flynn, *Book of Darlington*, 101.

282 *Darlington and Stockton Times*, 3 Dec. 1859.

283 Darlington Lib., cuttings book 1885, p. 31.

284 *North Star*, 10 Nov. 1887.

285 *Darlington and Stockton Times*, 21 July 1934; 7 Jan. 1893; *North Star*, 4 July 1893; 5 July 1893.

286 *Northern Echo*, 5 Sept. 1901; *Darlington and Stockton Times*, 6 June 1908; 17 July 1954.

287 *Darlington and Stockton Times*, 30 Aug. 1884.

288 Teesside Archives, U/OME (2) 5/40, p. 40.

289 *Darlington and Stockton Times*, 9 Sept. 1899; 7 July 1906; *Northern Echo*, 6 July 1903; Darlington Lib., cuttings books 1959, p. 2; 1976, p. 8.

290 *Darlington and Stockton Times*, 18 Apr.1953; 8 Mar. 1879.

291 *Darlington and Stockton Times*, 3 May 1879; 19 Aug. 1899.

292 *Darlington and Stockton Times*, 3 Feb. 1894; 16 May 1896; 23 May 1896; 20 Jun. 1903.

293 *Northern Echo*, 23 May 1901.

294 *Northern Echo*, 19 May 1902; 29 May 1908.

295 *Darlington and Stockton Times*, 24 May 1902.

296 *Northern Echo*, 5 Sept. 1925.

297 Spencer, *Men that are gone*, 393–5.

298 Nicholson, *Boys o' Bondgate*, 87.

299 *Kelly's Dir. Stockton-on-Tees, Darlington and suburbs* (1885), 230–1.

300 Nicholson, *Boys o' Bondgate*, 123.

301 Companies House, no. 121679, incorporated 1912, dissolved 1968; the company's file does not survive.

302 Darlington Lib., E810033793.

303 T. Fordyce, *Local Records* (1876), iv. 240; *Northern Echo*, 2 Feb. 1872; 23 Mar. 1872; 27 Mar. 1872; 18 Dec. 1874; *Darlington and Stockton Times*, 25 Mar. 1911.

304 *Darlington and Stockton Times*, 18 Apr. 1903.

305 Raby Castle, Deed Room, plan 79.

306 *Northern Echo*, 7 Oct. 1912.

307 Building Plans, 130/1912; 131/1913.

308 *Northern Echo*, 7 Oct. 1912.

309 *Northern Echo*, 7 Oct. 1912.

310 DRO, D/DL/1/73; see also D/DL/1/103.

311 Darlington Lib., E810033816.

312 Building Plans, 4/1909; 141/1910; 127/1911; 68/1912; 36/1913; also DRO, D/DL/1/133.

313 DRO, Da/DM/11.

314 DRO, Da/DM/11; Darlington Lib., Wooler cuttings book no. 8, p. 35; OS Map 1:2500, Durham LV.5 (1915 edn.).

315 DRO, D/Whes 3/35.

316 Darlington Lib., E810032188–9; E810032197; Wooler cuttings book no. 5, pp. 290, 297.

317 OS Map 1:2500, Durham LV.5 (1915 edn.); Pevsner, *County Durham*, 150. For earlier transactions relating to Stooperdale, see DRO, D/Whes 3/66, 101, 107–8, 110, 112–20, 131, 12/35, 3/3–23, 12/7–9, 11–13.

CHAPTER 4

1 H. M. Colvin, *A Biographical Dictionary of British Architects 1600–1840* (1995 edn.).

2 DRO, D/Ki 317, p. 61; Mewburn, *Larchfield Diary*, 5; Longstaffe, *Darlington*, 299 and n., 317; Teesside Archives, U/OME 4/10; F. Graham, *Northumberland and Durham: A Social and Political Miscellany* (1979), 93; N. McCord and D. T. Rowe, *Northumberland and Durham: An Industrial Miscellany* (1971), 54.

3 Fordyce, *Durham*, i. 471; G. W. Dolby, *The Architectural Expression of Methodism: the First Hundred Years* (1964), 177–8; Colvin, *Biographical Dictionary*, 543–4.

4 Spencer, *Men Who Are Gone*, 449; Fordyce, *Durham*, i. 469–70.

5 L. Wilkes, *John Dobson, Architect and Landscape Gardener* (1980), 104.

6 Fordyce, *Durham*, i. 469; J. Crosby, *Ignatius Bonomi of Durham: Architect* (1987), 55.

7 Crosby, *Ignatius Bonomi*, 81.

8 A. F. Sealey and D. Walters, 'First railway architect', *Architectural Rev.*, cxxxv, no. 807 (1964), 364–6.

9 T. Faulkner and A. Greg, *John Dobson: Architect of the North East* (2001), 169.

10 *Newcastle Chronicle*, 9 June 1832; H. Haggar, 'The bridges of John Green', *Northern Architect*, viii (April 1976), 25–31.

11 Longstaffe, *Darlington*, illustration opp. 247; J. Allibone, *Anthony Salvin: Pioneer of Gothic Revival Architecture* (1988), 110–11, 162.

12 DRO, Da/A5/1/2.

13 R. Scarr, 'Darlington's First Architect', *Darlington and Stockton Times*, 11 Aug. 1951.

14 A. G. Chamberlain, 'North-

eastern architects and the building trade up to 1865' (Typescript in Newcastle Central Library, 1986); B. Fawcett, *A History of North Eastern Railway Architecture: 1. the Pioneers* (2001).

15 *Newcastle Courant,* 10 Apr. 1840; *Newcastle Chronicle,* 5 June 1841; illustrated in D. and S. Dean, *Darlington in the 1930s and 40s* (1984), 52; C. Stell, *Nonconformist Chapels and Meeting Houses in the North of England* (1994), 61–2.

16 *Newcastle Chronicle,* 23 May 1840; *Newcastle Courant,* 17 July 1840.

17 *Builder,* xlviii (1885), 266 (obit.); Scarr, 'Darlington's First Architect'.

18 Fawcett, *Railway Architecture,* ch. 7.

19 J. Latimer, *Local Records* (1857), 252.

20 Pevsner, *County Durham,* 147.

21 *Newcastle Courant,* 16 Apr. 1847; *Builder,* viii (1850), 425.

22 Inf. from the Revd. B. Torode, Cheltenham.

23 *Directory of British Architects 1834–1900,* eds. A. Brodie, A. Felstead, J. Franklin, L. Pinfield and J. Oldfield (2001 edn.), ii. 414–15.

24 Colvin, *Biographical Dictionary,* 784–6.

25 *Builder,* xii (1854), 635.

26 *Builder,* ci (1911), 375 (obit.).

27 *Yorkshire Notes and Queries,* ii (1890), 122–34, 163–7.

28 *Builder,* xix (1861), 739, 901; xx (1862), 771; *Illustrated London News,* xxxix (1861), 625–7.

29 *British Architect,* iv (1875), 63.

30 *Sunderland Daily Echo,* 20 Apr. 1881; 25 Jan. 1883.

31 *Builder,* xiv (1856), 122.

32 DRO, Da/NG2.

33 *British Architect,* i (1874), 11; xxxi (1886), vii; DRO, Da/NG2/122, 1944, 2655.

34 *Northern Echo,* 25 Sept. 1911 (obit.).

35 Chapman, *Rural Darlington,* 32.

36 V. Chapman, 'James Pigott Pritchett', in G. R. Batho (ed.), *Durham Biographies,* i. (2000), 99–104.

37 DRO, Da/NG2/281; *Builder,* xxviii (1870), 531.

38 DRO, Da/NG2/1185; W. Pike, *Darlington Illustrated* (1905), 5.

39 DRO, Da/NG2/341; *Builder,* xxx (1870), 732.

40 Pevsner, *County Durham,* 140; J. P. Pritchett, *An Architectural History of St Cuthbert, Darlington* (1902), reprinted from the *Journal of the British Archaeological Association* (1886); H. D. Pritchett, *An Ecclesiastical, Archaeological and Architectural History of St Cuthbert's Church, Darlington* (n.d.).

41 Fawcett, *Railway Architecture,* 126.

42 DRO, Da/NG2/208.

43 V. Chapman, 'Thomas Pease, Son & Co.: a family business and its premises in Darlington market place', *Durham County Local Hist. Soc. Bull.,* xxxi (1983), 82 and plan.

44 Cunningham and Waterhouse, *Alfred Waterhouse,* 271.

45 Fordyce, *Durham,* i. 475; Latimer, *Local Records,* 325; Fawcett, *Railway Architecture,* 126; Longstaffe, *Darlington,* cviii.

46 Fawcett, *Railway Architecture,* 116, 126–7.

47 Cunningham and Waterhouse, *Alfred Waterhouse,* 9–10.

48 Cunningham and Waterhouse, *Alfred Waterhouse,* 211, 213; Barclays Bank Archives, 388/391; 388/111.

49 Barclays Bank Archives, 388/392; Cunningham and Waterhouse, *Alfred Waterhouse,* 213.

50 Cunningham and Waterhouse, *Alfred Waterhouse,* 22.

51 Cunningham and Waterhouse, *Alfred Waterhouse,* pl. 200–1; Darlington Lib., E810033800–3; Teesside Archives, U/OME 4/10.

52 Spencer, *Men that are gone,* 475–7.

53 DRO, D/Whes 14/46.

54 Cunningham and Waterhouse, *Alfred Waterhouse,* 165, 215.

55 Cunningham and Waterhouse, *Alfred Waterhouse,* 222; Pevsner, *County Durham,* 147.

56 Cunningham and Waterhouse, *Alfred Waterhouse,* 218, 244, 255; DRO, Da/NG2/2386.

57 Cunningham and Waterhouse, *Alfred Waterhouse,* 96, 219 and pl. 109.

58 Cunningham and Waterhouse, *Alfred Waterhouse,* 222, pl. 108; 93, 240, pl.107; 93, 244, pl.100.

59 Cunningham and Waterhouse, *Alfred Waterhouse,* 144, 215.

60 Cunningham and Waterhouse, *Alfred Waterhouse,* 144–5.

61 Pevsner *County Durham,* 148.

62 *Kelly's Dir. Durham* (1910), 272.

63 *Kelly's Dir. Durham* (1894), 361.

64 DRO, Da/NG2/62.

65 *Kelly's Dir. Durham* (1894), 361; *British Architect,* iv (1875), 217; *Builder,* xxxv (1877), 642.

66 *Builder,* xliv (1883), 48–9 and pl.; *Newcastle Monthly Chronicle,* Mar. 1889, 110–12; C. Cunningham, *Victorian and Edwardian Town Halls* (1981), 244, pl. 31, 200.

67 DRO, D/Ad/1/3/64; *Architect,* xix (1878), 368.

68 *Builder,* xxxiii (1875), 306.

69 A. T. C. Targett, 'G. G. Hoskins in Darlington' (Newcastle Univ. B. A. dissertation, 1991) 12–19 (copy in Darlington Lib.).

70 DRO, Da/NG2/1222.

71 DRO, Da/NG2/2016.

72 Targett, 'G. G. Hoskins', 20–5.

73 *British Architect,* xvii (1882), 13; DRO, Da/NG2/2560.

74 DRO, Da/NG2/1954.

75 DRO, Da/NG2/1582, /1661.

76 *Northern Echo,* 13 Dec. 1911 (obit.); *Darlington and Stockton Times,* 16 Dec. 1911 (obit.); V. Chapman, 'George Gordon Hoskins JP, FRIBA', parts 1 and 2.

77 For instance Barclays Bank Archives, 388/392.

78 Darlington Lib., E810023897.

79 Cunningham and Waterhouse, *Alfred Waterhouse,* 215, 255; Chapman, *Rural Darlington,* 32.

80 DRO, Da/NG2/88; *Builder,* xxvii (1869), 273.

81 *Builder,* xxv (1867), 923, 925 and pl.

82 *Architect,* x (1873), 111.

83 *Directory of British Architects,* i. 378; ii. 219.

84 DRO, Da/NG2.

85 *Builder,* lxvi (1894), 189–90; *Architect,* liii (1895), 282; Pevsner, *County Durham,* 144.

86 G. R. Potts, 'A biographical guide to Darlington architects, 1840–1914', (Typescript in Darlington Lib., 2002).

87 M. Hussain, 'Development of Saltburn' (Sunderland Univ. BA dissertation, 1998), 5 and app.

88 DRO, Da/NG2/1741, /3068.

89 *Directory of British Architects,* i. 226.

90 Building plans, 130/1912;

131/1913; *Northern Echo,* 7 Oct. 1912.

91 *Directory of British Architects,* ii. 92.

92 Hussain, 'Development of Saltburn', 5; G. Biddle and O. S. Nock, *Railway Heritage of Britain* (1983), 40.

93 DRO, Da/NG2/283.

94 Pevsner, *County Durham,* 149.

95 Darlington Civic Society, *Darlington and District: Buildings and Places* (1975), 64.

96 *Proc. Inst. Civil Engineers,* cxxxiv (1898), 415–16 (obit.).

97 *Darlington and Stockton Times,* 2 Aug. 1924; *Northern Echo,* 2 Aug. 1924.

98 DRO, Da/A42/1/1, p. 50.

99 A. Quiney, *John Loughborough Pearson* (1979), 160–2, 249; Pevsner, *County Durham,* 147.

100 *Durham Chronicle,* 27 July 1883; DRO, Da/NG2/1208.

101 *Builder,* lxxxiv (1903), 120; DRO, Da/NG2/2810.

102 Pevsner, *County Durham,* 148.

103 DRO, Da/NG2/1398, 1428.

104 *Darlington and Stockton Times,* 9 Apr. 1904; Targett, 'G. G. Hoskins', 26–32.

105 DRO, Da/NG2/3164, 3174; L. F. Pearson, '"The Architecture of Entertainment Run Riot": William Hope of Newcastle, 1862–1907', *Northern History,* xxvii (1991), 184–97.

106 I. Mackintosh and M. Sell (ed.), *Curtains!!! or a New Life for Old Theatres* (1982), 214; Targett, 'G. G. Hoskins', 26–32.

107 *Proc. Inst. Civil Engineers,* cxvii (1894), 367.

CHAPTER 5

1 PRO, DURH 3/14, f.541r.; 3/16, f.27v.

2 *Cal. S. P. Dom.* 1598–1601, 459; Tillbrook, 'Aspects of Government and Society', 23–4.

3 Nicholson, *Boys O' Bondgate,* 73.

4 Durham Chapter Lib., Allan, xv, pp. 56–8; 228–36.

5 Longstaffe, *Darlington,* 143–5.

6 Mountford, 'Biographical and historical notes', 45.

7 Longstaffe *Darlington,* 293.

8 'Old Elizabethan House, Darlington', *The Builder,* xlviii (1885), 549.

9 Green, 'Houses and households', 270–1.

10 Longstaffe, *Darlington,* xcii.

11 See for instance Durham Chapter Lib., Allan, xv, p. 12; also Longstaffe, *Darlington,* 144.

12 *An Historical Atlas of County Durham* (1992), 58–9; Durham Chapter Lib., Allan, xv, Whitworth's canal plan of 1768; List of buildings of special historical or architectural interest.

13 North Yorks. RO, ZDG (A) IV/7/7.

14 D. Defoe, *A Tour through the Whole Island of Great Britain* (1983 edn.), iii. 124.

15 Longstaffe, *Darlington,* 39.

16 Guildhall Lib., RE MS. 7253/5, no. 77461, 1780; 7253/11, no. 96689, 1786; 7253/11, no. 100015, 1786; 7253/12, no. 101221, 1787; 7253/12, no. 101220, 1787.

17 Guildhall Lib., RE MS. 7253/1, no. 62827, 1774; 7253/1, no. 64258, 1774.

18 Guildhall Lib., RE MS. 7253/8, no. 88157, 1783; 7253/9, 92565, 1785; 7253/1, no. 60421, 1775.

19 Guildhall Lib., RE MS. 7253/11, no. 97285, 1786; 7253/9, 93185, 1785; 7253/1, no. 54372, 1775; 7253/1, no. 64259, 1774.

20 Guildhall Lib., RE MS. 7253/5, no. 79176, 1780.
21 Guildhall Lib., RE MS. 7253/1, no. 64490.
22 Guildhall Lib., RE MS. 7253/12, no. 100219.
23 DRO, D/XD 116/1; see DULASC, DHC 1/II/59, f.207.
24 DRO, D/XD 108/1/A/95 and /96.
25 Guildhall Lib., Sun MS. 11936, 9/310 no. 14294; 30/179; DRO, D/BR/D2467; D/X 667/117; D/HH 2/3/8; Spencer, *Men that are gone,* 269; Longstaffe, *Darlington,* 245, ciii.
26 DRO, D/XD 108/1/A/159–161.
27 DRO, D/XD 116/1.
28 Barclays Bank Archives, 388/390.
29 DRO, D/XD 27/4.
30 DRO, D/XD 12/1; D/St/C4/3/13; D/XD 5/313/3.
31 DRO, D/Ki 439.
32 Longstaffe, *Darlington,* civ.
33 DULASC, 321771/26.
34 Chapman, *Rural Darlington,* 50; Spencer *Men that are gone,* 56.
35 *The Journeys of Sir Richard Colt Hoare through Wales and England 1793–1810,* ed. M. W. Thompson (1983), 145.
36 *Universal British Dir.* (1791), ii. 759; *Pigot's Dir. Ireland, Scotland and Northern Counties* (1820), 266; P. J. Davison, *Brickworks of the North East* (1986), 270–8.
37 *Parson and White's Dir. Northumberland and Durham* (1827) i. 248.
38 Teesside Archives, U/MSB (3) 1–4; *Parson and White's Dir. Northumberland and Durham* (1827) i. 248.
39 *Parson and White's Dir. Northumberland and Durham* (1827) i. 248.
40 Darlington Lib., E810033811;

Reference to the Plan of Darlington Township, by Anthony Reed, Land-surveyor (1829) (copies in Durham Univ. Lib. and Darlington Lib.).
41 DRO, D/X 666/220.
42 *Pigot's Dir. Durham, Northumbs. and Yorks.* (1834), 13.
43 DRO, D/XD 27/4.
44 OS Map 1:1050, Durham LV.6.3 and LV.6.5 (1856).
45 North Yorks. RO, ZDG (A) IV/7/7.
46 Davison, *Brickworks,* 4.
47 Strutt, 'Architectural and historical survey', 27; Chapman, *Rural Darlington,* 32.
48 *Slater's Dir. Northern Counties* (1876–7), 80; Darlington Lib., E810034525; DRO, D/XD 108/7/6.
49 OS Map 1:2500, Durham LV.6 (1898 and 1915 edns.); May, *British Industry and Commerce,* 44–5; Davison, *Brickworks,* 270, 274.
50 Davison, *Brickworks,* 270–3; *Ward's Dir. Darlington* (1935), 162; *Darlington Year Book and Business Dir.* (1947), 131.
51 OS Map 1:2500, Durham LV.2 (1898 and 1915 edns.).
52 Davison, *Brickworks,* 270–3.
53 *Northern Despatch,* 4 Apr. 1946.
54 See *VCH Durham,* iv, forthcoming.
55 DRO, EP/Da SC33.
56 *Universal British Dir.*(1791), ii. 759.
57 Spencer, *Men that are gone,* 300–3; Mewburn, *Larchfield Diary,* 5.
58 *Pigot's Dir. Ireland, Scotland and Northern Counties* (1820), 266–7; *Parson and White's Dir. Northumberland and Durham* (1827) i. 246–53; *Pigot's Dir. Durham, Northumbs. and Yorks.* (1834), 13.

59 Spencer, *Men that are gone,* 3–4; *Parson and White's Dir. Northumberland and Durham* (1827) i. 246–53; *Pigot's Dir. Durham, Northumbs. and Yorks.* (1834), 13.
60 Longstaffe, *Darlington,* 243; Spencer, *Men that are gone,* 3; *Leeds Mercury,* 6 Oct. 1838.
61 Strutt, 'Architectural and historical survey', 25; Darlington Lib., E810024882; Kirby, *Men of Business and Politics,* 26.
62 Raby Castle, Deed Room, Press 8/27.
63 See for instance DRO, D/XD 108/1/A/79–80, 82, 84–6; W. Stokes, 'John Botcherby: a victim of the railway age?', *Durham County Local Hist. Soc. Bull.,* lxi (May 2000), 3–17.
64 See for instance DRO, D/XD 108/1/A/87; D/XD 108/1/A/88; D/XD 108/1/A/89.
65 Spencer, *Men that are gone,* 69–70.
66 Spencer, *Men that are gone,* 11–12; also DRO, D/XD 108/1/A/169.
67 Spencer, *Men that are gone,* 42; see also DRO, D/X 666/130.
68 Spencer, *Men that are gone,* 92–3.
69 Spencer, *Men that are gone,* 93; *Slater's Dir. Northern Counties* (1854–5), 17–22.
70 Spencer, *Men that are gone,* 187–8.
71 DRO, D/XD/16/33; Da/A3.
72 Spencer, *Men that are gone,* 189.
73 DRO, D/ X 666/220; D/XD 27/4; North Yorks. RO, ZDG (A) IV/7/7.
74 Barclays Bank Archives, 388/390.
75 Darlington Building Society, scrapbook; DRO, D/X 943/2.
76 For instance DRO, D/Whes

3/121; 3/46–50; *Slater's Dir. Northern Counties* (1876–7), 80.

77 See May, *British Industry and Commerce*, 21. W. Richardson should not be confused with the building contractor J. W. Richardson & Sons Ltd., founded in 1905, who moved from Quebec Street to the Darlington Forge site on the Cleveland Trading Estate in 1973 and wound up in 1984: *Northern Echo*, 1 June 1973; Darlington Lib., cuttings book, 1984, p. 42.

78 Darlington Lib., E810023897.

79 Drawings of heating schemes from over 80 years were deposited at Beamish museum in 1971.

80 May, *British Industry and Commerce*, 21; Darlington Lib., E810010002.

81 *Northern Despatch*, 20 Oct. 1961; *Northern Echo*, 6 May 1965.

82 *Northern Echo*, 19 June 1889; 6 Nov. 1894.

83 DRO, Da, DM/7/27/7.

84 May, *British Industry and Commerce*, 21.

85 Darlington Lib., cuttings books, 1970, p. 88; 1980, pp. 34, 44, 51; *Evening Despatch*, 19 Mar. 1980.

86 Darlington Lib., cuttings book 1986, p. 172.

87 *North Star*, 17 Feb. 1906; inf. from records in the possession of Mr D. Brown of Latimer, Hinks, solicitors, Priestgate, Darlington; W. T. Pike, *A Descriptive Account of Darlington* (1894), 38.

88 *Northern Echo*, 6 Mar. 1908.

89 DRO, D/Whes 14/47; *Sawmill Magazine*, Jan.-Feb. 1926; *Northern Despatch*, 28 Sept. 1956.

90 Pike, *Descriptive account*, 36–7; Darlington Lib., proposed new articles of association, 1899; reports of the directors, 1896–1929; *Newcastle Jour.*, 6

Sept. 1962; 4 Sept. 1964; 8 Sept. 1966; PRO, BT 31/2145/9913.

91 DRO, Da/DM/7/27/7; D/Whes 14/47.

92 Pike, *Descriptive Account*, 39–40.

93 May, *British Industry and Commerce*, 44–5.

94 Building Plans, 172/1899; 119/1899; 243/1911; 247/1911; 23/1912; 103/1912; 170/1912.

95 May, *British Industry and Commerce*, 44–5.

96 Information collected by Graham Potts from building plans in DRO.

97 *Northern Echo*, 12 Oct. 1916; May, *British Industry and Commerce*, 42–3.

98 PRO, BT 64/3120, pp. 9–10.

99 *Ward's Dir. Darlington* (1935), 162–3; *Darlington Year Book and Business Dir.* (1947), 131–3.

CHAPTER 6

1 Darlington Lib., E810026797, E810031165, E810032523; DRO, Da/TR/4/ 7–27; Da/TR/5.

2 DRO, D/DL/1/87 and 89, map no. 2.

3 *Darlington and Stockton Times*, 20 Mar. 1926.

4 DRO, D/DL/1/87/1; D/DL/1/88, map no. 2.

5 DRO, D/DL/1/87/1; D/DL/1/88, map no. 2; Darlington Lib., Wooler cuttings book no. 7, p. 22.

6 *Darlington and Stockton Times*, 20 Mar. 1926; DRO, D/DL/1/87; D/DL/1/96.

7 R. Ryder, 'Council house building in County Durham, 1900–1939: the local implementation of national policy', in M. J. Daunton (ed.), *Councillors and Tenants: Local Authority Housing*

in English Cities, 1919–1939 (1984), 46, 48.

8 Darlington Lib., E810032198–201; E810032414–7; E810032545–9; Wooler cuttings book no. 7, p. 115.

9 DRO, Da/ DM/7/31, p. 10.

10 DRO, D/DL/1/95; D/DL/1/92.

11 DRO, Da/DM/ 7/31, p. 10; D/DL/1/95.

12 DRO, D/DL/1/104; D/DL/1/103, pp. 105–6.

13 DRO, D/DL/1/104; *Industrial Daily News*, 9 Jan. 1929; Darlington Lib., E810033175.

14 Darlington Lib., E810033119–20.

15 DRO, D/DL/1/105; D/DL/1/106; Darlington Lib., E810006352; E810033466; E810033520–1; E810032945–7.

16 Darlington Lib., cuttings book, 1978, p. 38; Pevsner, *County Durham*, 155.

17 Darlington Lib., E810040895, E810040923, E810040901, E810041089; also *Northern Despatch*, Sept. 1939, passim.

18 Darlington Lib., E810041103, E810040913.

19 Darlington Lib., E810040903; E810040918; E810040915; E810040920.

20 *Darlington and Stockton Times*, 25 Sept. 1965.

21 *Northern Despatch*, 13 Sept. 1950; see also 10 Mar. 1951.

22 'Design in detail: new Town Hall, Darlington, Co. Durham', *Building*, 19 Mar. 1971, 79–86; Pevsner, *County Durham*, 144–5.

23 DRO, D/XD/73/4; *Evening Despatch*, 5 Sept. 1969; 12 Sept. 1969; *Darlington and Stockton Times*, 29 June 1974.

24 *Northern Despatch*, 13 Sept. 1950.

25 *Northern Despatch*, 3 May 1950.

26 *Northern Echo*, 16 Oct. 1957; *Northern Despatch*, 6 May 1959.

27 *Northern Despatch*, 23 Feb. 1961; *Northern Echo*, 15 May 1965.

28 *Northern Echo*, 9 May 1967.

29 *Northern Despatch*, 3 May 1950.

30 *Northern Despatch*, 23 Feb. 1961.

31 Darlington Lib., cuttings book, 1963, p. 167; DRO, D/XD/73/4.

32 *Evening Despatch*, 15 Mar. 1975; 11 Nov. 1975; 7 Apr. 1976.

33 *Evening Despatch*, 5 Apr. 1978.

34 *Darlington and Stockton Times*, 9 Aug. 1980.

35 *Evening Despatch*, 2 Nov. 1982; 9 June 1983; 9 Sept. 1983.

36 *Evening Despatch*, 11 June 1984; *Evening Gazette*, 25 Nov. 1985.

37 *Northern Echo*, 28 Sept. 1990; Darlington Lib., cuttings books, 1990, p. 15; 1991, p. 61; DRO, Da/NG/6/12; Pevsner, *County Durham*, 155.

38 *Northern Echo*, 18 Nov. 1996; 23 June 1997; *Darlington and Stockton Times*, 27 June 1997.

39 *Northern Echo*, 5 Sept. 1925.

40 *Darlington and Stockton Times*, 15 Sept. 1923; 5 June 1926.

41 *Northern Despatch*, 25 July 1930; 4 July 1935; *Darlington and Stockton Times*, 26 July 1930; 6 July 1935.

42 *Northern Echo*, 18 Oct. 1937; *Darlington and Stockton Times*, 23 Oct. 1937; Darlington Lib. cuttings book, 1983, p. 10; C. Lloyd, *Memories of Darlington*, ii (1995), 6–7, 73.

43 *Darlington and Stockton*

Times, 15 Sept. 1923; also 16 July 1927; *Evening Despatch*, 11 Sept. 1973.

44 *Northern Despatch*, 8 Aug. 1925; *Darlington and Stockton Times*, 10 July 1926; *Northern Echo*, 13 May 1999.

45 *Northern Despatch*, 23 June 1927.

46 *Northern Echo*, 6 Sept. 1923; *Darlington and Stockton Times*, 19 Apr. 1924; 19 Feb. 1938; *Northern Despatch*, 22 Apr. 1924; 30 May 1925; 5 May 1930; 29 Feb. 1936.

47 *Northern Despatch*, 18 June 1954; *Darlington and Stockton Times*, 20 Dec. 1958.

48 *Darlington and Stockton Times*, 25 June 1932; 25 May 1935; *Northern Despatch*, 29 Jan. 1955; Darlington Lib., cuttings book, 1931–40, p. 59.

49 Darlington Lib., cuttings book, 1989, p. 464; *Northern Echo*, 20 July 2000; 29 Aug. 2001.

50 Darlington Lib., Wooler cuttings book, no. 8, pp. 9, 37.

51 *Northern Despatch*, 30 March 1937.

52 *Northern Echo*, 26 Jan. 1925; *North Star*, 12 Sept. 1923.

53 *Evening Despatch*, 3 Aug. 1925.

54 *North Star*, 18 Dec. 1923; *Darlington and Stockton Times*, 13 Mar. 1926; Darlington Lib., cuttings books, 1956, p. 104; 1959, p. 65.

55 *Northern Echo*, 9 May 1934.

56 Darlington Lib., E810032438–44.

57 Darlington Lib., Wooler cuttings book no. 8, p. 14.

58 PRO, BT 64/3120, p. 44.

59 *Darlington and Stockton Times*, 28 Oct. 1950; 4 Nov. 1950; *Northern Despatch*, 29 Oct. 1951; I. Wood, *Darlington Transport* (1996), 29.

60 Darlington Lib., Wooler cuttings book no. 7, p. 136; DRO, Da/ NG/4/7.

61 Darlington Lib., Wooler cuttings book no. 7, p. 136.

62 K. Hoole, *North Eastern Locomotive Sheds* (1972), 171–5.

63 Darlington Lib., cuttings book, 1956, p. 64.

64 Darlington Lib., Wooler cuttings book no. 7, p. 58.

65 Darlington Lib., Wooler cuttings book no. 7, p. 145, 7 July 1920.

66 Darlington Lib., E810026797, E810032520, E810031165; also E810033470.

67 DRO, Da/A42/1/1, p. 13, 28 July 1919; p. 50, 24 Feb. 1920.

68 DRO, Da/A42/1/1, p. 24, 22 Sept. 1919.

69 DRO, Da/A42/1/1, pp. 11, 21, 23–4.

70 DRO, Da/A42/1/1, p. 44; Da/A42/1/2, p. 20.

71 DRO, Da/A42/1/1, p. 45.

72 DRO, Da/A42/1/1, p. 71a.

73 Darlington Lib., Wooler cuttings book no. 7, p. 150.

74 DRO, Da/A42/1/1, p. 116.

75 Inf. from Stuart Muckle of Darlington Borough Council.

76 Darlington Lib., Wooler cuttings book no. 7, p. 85.

77 DRO, Da/A42/1/1, p. 6.

78 DRO, Da/A42/1/1, pp. 21–2.

79 DRO, Da/A42/1/1, pp. 21–2; also pp. 11, 16, 30.

80 DRO, Da/A42/1/1, p. 39.

81 DRO, Da/A42/1/1, pp. 70, 143; Da/DM/1/173.

82 DRO, Da/A42/1/2, p. 1; D/DL/1/137.

83 DRO, Da/A42/1/2, p. 20.

84 DRO, Da/A42/1/2, p. 9.

85 Darlington Lib., Wooler cuttings book no. 8, p. 14.

86 Darlington Lib., Wooler cuttings book no. 8, p. 15.

87 DRO, Da/A42/1/2, p. 46;

Darlington Lib., Wooler cuttings book no. 8, p. 24.

88 Darlington Lib., Wooler cuttings book no. 8, p. 35.

89 Darlington Lib., Wooler cuttings book no. 8, pp. 4, 47.

90 DRO, Da/A42/1/2, pp. 96, 178; Darlington Lib., E810038258; DRO, D/DL/1/103.

91 DRO, Da/A42/1/2, p. 379.

92 DRO Da/A42/1/1, pp. 19, 103.

93 DRO, Da/A42/1/2, p. 303; Darlington Lib., E810031385; E810033209.

94 DRO, Da/A42/1/2, p. 334.

95 DRO, Da/A42/1/2, p. 352.

96 DRO, Da/A42/1/2, p. 163.

97 Darlington Lib., E810032434; E810032232–7.

98 PRO, BT 64/3120, p. 45; Darlington Lib., cuttings book, 1990, p. 67; *Northern Echo*, 14 Feb. 1990.

99 DRO, Da/A33/1/7.

100 *Northern Despatch*, 3 Feb. 1937.

101 PRO, BT 64/3120, p. 45.

102 DRO, Da/A33/1/7; Spencer, *Men that are gone*, 454.

103 *Darlington and Stockton Times*, 4 Aug. 1926.

104 Darlington Lib., Wooler cuttings book no. 8, p. 53.

105 Lloyd, *Memories of Darlington*, ii. 78–9.

106 Pevsner, *County Durham*, 149; *Northern Echo*, 30 Oct. 1926.

107 *Northern Despatch*, 13 Oct. 1937.

108 Ryder, 'Council house building', 46, 48; Flynn, *Book of Darlington*, 89.

109 PRO, BT 64/3120, p. 45; *Northern Despatch*, 20 Jan. 1937.

110 DRO, Da/DM/11.

111 Teesside Archives, U/OME (2) 5/41.

112 Darlington Lib.,

E810033838; see for instance DRO, Da/NG/4/2.

113 Teesside Archives, U/OME (2) 5/41

114 Darlington Lib., E810024882; Meadows and Waterson, *Lost Houses*, 65.

115 Darlington Lib., E810024882.

116 Meadows and Waterson, *Lost Houses*, 65.

117 Darlington Lib., E810024882; Pevsner, *County Durham*, 152.

118 Pevsner, *County Durham*, 148.

119 Darlington Lib., E810085068; DRO, Da/NG/4/4 and 5.

120 Darlington Lib.,Wooler cuttings book no. 8, p. 37; DRO, D/Wat, boxes 40–43; D/Wat P13; Da/ NG/4/3.

121 Raby Castle, Deed Room, Press 15/63 and 64.

122 Raby Castle, Deed Room, press 15/69.

123 Darlington Lib., Wooler cuttings book no. 8, pp. 4, 47, 58.

124 Darlington Lib., Wooler cuttings book no. 8, pp. 35, 47, 58.

125 PRO, BT 64/3120, p. 45; additional inf. from Robin Coulthard.

126 PRO, BT 64/3120, pp. 45–6.

127 PRO, BT 64/3120, p. 10.

128 Flynn, *Book of Darlington*, 89.

129 Inf. from Robin Coulthard.

130 DRO, Da/ NG/4/9/12; *Northern Despatch*, 5 Mar. 1946.

131 *Northern Despatch*, 21 Mar. 1946.

132 Inf. from Robin Coulthard.

133 Darlington Borough Council, Housing Committee mins., 22 Dec. 1944; 30 Oct. 1945.

134 Darlington Borough Coun-

cil, Housing Committee mins., 13 Sept. 1946; 14 Nov. 1946; 13 Feb. 1947.

135 Darlington Borough Council Minutes, H133, Jan. 1964; H126, Jan. 1965; H144, Jan. 1966.

136 *Northern Despatch*, 13 Sept. 1950.

137 *Northern Despatch*, 18 Aug. 1950.

138 DRO, D/DL/1/117; Darlington Lib., E810033211.

139 DRO, Da/NG/6/2–3, 5.

140 Darlington Lib., E810053583–90; Meadows and Waterson, *Lost Houses*, 64.

141 Darlington Lib., E810015297–8.

142 Darlington Lib., E810033792.

143 Darlington Lib., E810038254; inf. from Stuart Muckle of Darlington Borough Council; Darlington Lib., E810002029, E810034851.

144 Darlington Lib., cuttings books, 1970, p. 78; 1972, p. 47.

145 Meadows and Waterson, *Lost Houses*, 69.

146 Darlington Lib., E810085068.

147 Darlington Lib., E810032532–4; E810075680; E810057729.

148 Pevsner, *County Durham*, 146.

149 Flynn, *Book of Darlington*, 86.

150 *Northern Echo*, 14 Feb. 1990; also *Northern Despatch*, 5 Mar. 1966; DRO, Da/DM/1/1–163; DM/1/301–396; DM/1/977–1177.

151 *Evening Despatch*, 18 Nov. 1976.

152 Darlington Lib., E810040909.

153 *Evening Despatch*, 22 Jan. 1977.

154 *Evening Despatch*, 13 Apr. 1978.

155 *Evening Despatch*, 9 Mar. 1979.
156 *Evening Despatch*, 15 May 1979; 17 May 1979.
157 *Evening Despatch*, 14 Apr. 1978.
158 Darlington Lib., cuttings book, 1982, p. 107.
159 Darlington Lib., cuttings book, 1979, pp. 20, 4; E810047782.
160 *Evening Despatch*, 5 Sept. 1983.
161 Inf. from Stuart Muckle.
162 Darlington Lib., cuttings books, 1984, p. 50; 1985, pp. 19, 27, 74; 1987, p. 94; *Darlington and Stockton Times*, 27 Apr. 1985; *Evening Despatch*, 25 Apr. 1985.
163 Darlington Lib., cuttings books, 1984, pp. 110, 115, 113, 117; 1985, pp. 7, 11; 1987, p. 80; 1988, p. 31; *Darlington and Stockton Times*, 2 May 1987; 12 Mar. 1988.
164 Darlington cuttings books, 1988, pp. 193, 253, 270, 281; 1990, p. 346; 1992, pp. 13, 23; *Darlington and Stockton Times*, 8 Feb. 1992.
165 Darlington Lib., cuttings books, 1988, p. 305; 1989, p. 443; 1990, pp. 44, 207; *Darlington and Stockton Times*, 10 Feb. 1990; 23 Jun. 1990; 18 Jan. 1992.
166 *Darlington and Stockton Times*, 24 Sept. 1994; *Northern Echo*, 21 Mar. 1995.
167 Darlington Lib., cuttings book, 1984, pp. 99, 100, 142.
168 Darlington Lib., cuttings book, 1992, p. 9.
169 Darlington Lib., cuttings books, 1987, pp. 5, 6, 29, 211; 1988, p. 321; *Evening Despatch*, 31 Jan. 1985; 25 Apr. 1985; *Northern Echo*, 9 Dec. 1988.
170 Darlington Lib., cuttings books, 1986, pp. 23, 59; 1987, pp. 19, 21; 1989, p. 456.
171 Darlington Lib., cuttings book, 1984, p. 108; *Evening Despatch*, 25 Apr. 1985.
172 *Northern Echo*, 14 Feb. 1995.
173 K. Hoole, *North Eastern Locomotive Sheds* (1972), 173–5.
174 Darlington Lib., cuttings books, 1984, p. 56; 1990, p. 17.
175 Darlington Lib., cuttings books, 1975, pp. 78, 92; 1976, p. 100; 1977, pp. 83, 84; 1978, pp. 59–89; 1979, p. 8.
176 Darlington Lib., cuttings books, 1978, p. 25; 1983, p. 47 et passim.
177 Darlington Lib., E810051382.
178 *Evening Despatch*, 11 Jan. 1978; Darlington Lib., cuttings book, 1979, pp. 78–80, 190–1.
179 Pevsner, *County Durham*, 145; Darlington Lib., cuttings books, 1980, p. 99; 1982, pp. 161, 177, 178, 181, 190, 193; 1983, pp. 56, 75, 78.
180 Darlington Lib., cuttings books, 1988, pp. 31, 60, 112; 1992, p. 119.
181 Lloyd, *Memories of Darlington*, ii. 26–7.

Sources

The main collections of documents consulted for this study are kept in Durham and Darlington. The Durham County Record Office (DRO) holds records of the Darlington Borough Council (Da) and archival material previously kept in Darlington Library (D/DL). The county record office has other miscellaneous papers relating to Darlington at D/X and D/XD, as well as the papers of various influential Darlington Quaker families, including Hodgkin, Kitching, Pease and Wallis.

Durham University Library Archives and Special Collections (DULASC) has important material relating to the bishop of Durham's holdings in Darlington from the medieval period, in the Church Commission Durham Bishopric deposit and Halmote court records. DULASC's collections of significance to Darlington's modern history include South Durham (SDD) and turnpike deeds and Backhouse family papers. Barclays Bank, which on its foundation incorporated Backhouses Bank, holds other Backhouse family records at its archive in Manchester.

The papers of the antiquary George Allan of Blackwell are at the Durham Chapter Library. Allan's vol. xv, a rich miscellany of transcripts and pasted scraps of information covering several hundred pages and accumulated around the end of the 18th century, has provided a wealth of information. Without Allan's interest, much of this would not now be available as many of the original documents he consulted have since disappeared. The Durham Chapter Library also holds notes, illustrations and scrapbooks collected by Darlington's 19th-century historian, W. H. D. Longstaffe.

While past reorganisations of local government have meant the transfer of material to Durham, Darlington Library's collection remains substantial, including some unpublished sources, embracing dissertations, typescripts and other holdings. The miscellaneous material there includes scrapbooks, a picture collection and well-indexed newspaper cuttings. Darlington Town Hall holds building plan registers (Building Plans) from 1862, while any surviving plans to which the register refers can be found at the DRO in Da/NG.

The Durham Sites and Monuments Record (SMR) at County Hall has a list of archaeological material. Teesside Archives, Middlesbrough, holds records of the Owners of the Middlesbrough Estate (OME) relevant to the Pease family's interests in Darlington. The North Yorkshire Record Office in Northallerton keeps further Allan material (ZDG), though much of it is more accessible in the form of photocopies in Darlington Library. At Raby Castle, Lord Barnard has records relating to the Vane family's development of the west end of Darlington from the mid 19th century.

The earliest manuscript maps of Darlington date from the 1770s. Between 1776 and the end of the 18th century a number of plans were produced of the bishop's and George Allan's possessions in the town, including the High and Low parks, Feethams and Clay Row. These can be found in DULASC in the Church Commission Durham Bishopric deposit, or in Darlington Library. An outline of the market place layout in 1807, before the tollbooth was demolished, survives in the Halmote court records in DULASC. The first of many printed maps of Darlington, a well-drawn and detailed one of the whole town centre by John Wood in 1826, has been an exceptional resource, reflecting the extent of the town at the very time the railway arrived. Anthony Reed's plan of 1829, now in Darlington Library, covers a wider area and matches a published schedule listing owners and occupiers of land, available in Durham University Library. After Reed came a number of estate plans, some drawn when properties were being sold, and others, such as a series made for the Pease family now in Darlington Library, to record the extent of individual holdings. Significant printed maps before the Ordnance Survey in 1856 include those by Thomas Dixon in 1837 and 1840 and by Sowerby in 1842 and 1848. Copies of the tithe award of the township (1847) can be found in the DRO.

PRINTED SOURCES
PRIMARY SOURCES

Boldon Buke: a Survey of the Possessions of the See of Durham made by Order of Bishop Hugh Pudsey, 1183, ed. W. Greenwell (Surtees Soc., xxv, 1852).

Boldon Book: Northumberland and Durham, ed. D. Austin (1982).

Bishop Hatfield's Survey. A Record of the Possessions of the See of Durham, made by Order of Thomas de Hatfield, Bishop of Durham, ed. W. Greenwell (Surtees Soc., xxxii, 1857).

Darlington Wills and Inventories, 1600–25, ed. J. A. Atkinson, B. Flynn, V. Portass, K. Singlehurst and H. J. Smith (Surtees Soc., ccl, 1993).

The Diaries of Edward Pease, ed. A. E. Pease (1907).

Directory of British Architects 1834–1900, ed. A. Brodie, A. Felstead, J. Franklin, L. Pinfield and J. Oldfield, ii (2001 edn.).

Durham Quarter Sessions Rolls, 1471–1625, ed. C. M. Fraser (Surtees Soc., cxcix, 1987–8).

Ecclesiastical Proceedings of Richard Barnes, Bishop of Durham, 1576–87, ed. J. Raine (Surtees Soc., xxii, 1850).

The Itinerary of John Leland in or about the years 1535–1543, ed. L. Toulmin Smith (1907).

The Journeys of Sir Richard Colt Hoare through Wales and England 1793–1810, ed. M. W. Thompson (1983).

Parliamentary Surveys of the Bishopric of Durham, ed. D. A. Kirby (Surtees Soc., clxxxiii, 1971).

Records of Anthony Bek, Bishop and Patriarch, 1283–1311, ed. C. M. Fraser (Surtees Soc., clxii, 1953).

Registrum Palatinum Dunelmense, ed. T. D. Hardy (Rolls Ser., 1873–8).

Report to the General Board of Health on Darlington, 1850, ed. H. J. Smith (1967).

Symeonis Monachi Opera Omnia, ed. T. Arnold (Rolls Ser., 1882–5).

Wills and Inventories of the Northern Counties of England, i, ed. J. Raine (Surtees Soc., ii, 1835).

Wills and Inventories from the Registry at Durham, ii, ed. W. Greenwell (Surtees Soc., xxxviii, 1860),

Wills and Inventories from the Registry at Durham, iii, ed. J. C. Hodgson (Surtees Soc., cxii, 1906), 85–6.

BOOKS AND ARTICLES

L. Addis, 'The pottery', in Clack and Pearson, *Darlington*, 54–63.

J. Allibone, *Anthony Salvin: Pioneer of Gothic Revival Architecture* (1988).

M. J. Armstrong, *An Actual Survey of the Great Post-roads between London and Edinburgh* (1776).

R. A. Barnby, 'Darlington's railway workshops', *Durham County Local Hist. Soc. Bull.*, x (1969), 22–5.

G. Biddle and O. S. Nock, *Railway Heritage of Britain* (1983).

M. Bonney, *Lordship and the Urban Community: Durham and its Overlords, 1250–1540* (1990).

F. Bradshaw, 'The Black Death in the Palatinate of Durham', *Archaeologia Aeliana*, 3rd ser., iii (1907).

R. H. Britnell, 'Feudal reaction after the Black Death in the Palatinate of Durham', *Past and Present*, cxxviii (1990), 28–47.

R. H. Britnell, 'The Black Death in Durham', *Cleveland Hist.*, lxxvi (1999), 42–51.

E. Cambridge, 'The early church in County Durham: a reassessment', *Journ. Brit. Archaeol. Assoc.*, cxxxvii (1984), 65–85.

V. Chapman, *Rural Darlington: Farm, Mansion and Suburb* (1975).

V. Chapman, '"Front house and back house" houses and small terraced houses in Darlington', *Durham County Local Hist. Soc. Bull.*, xxix (Dec. 1982), 21–9.

V. Chapman, 'Thomas Pease, Son & Co.: a family business and its premises in Darlington market place', *Durham County Local Hist. Soc. Bull.*, xxxi (1983), 77–86.

V. Chapman, 'George Gordon Hoskins JP, FRIBA: a Darlington architect and his work, 1864–1907. Part I. Hoskins and his Darlington buildings', *Durham Archaeol. Jour.*, iv (1988), 61–8.

V. Chapman, 'George Gordon Hoskins JP, FRIBA: a Darlington architect and his work, 1864–1907. Part II. Hoskins's buildings in the north-east of England', *Durham Archaeol. Jour,* v (1989), 65–9.

V. Chapman, 'James Pigott Pritchett', in G. R. Batho (ed.), *Durham Biographies*. I. (2000), 99–104.

M. Chase, 'Out of radicalism: the mid-Victorian freehold land movement', *Eng. Hist. Rev*, cvi (1991), 319–45.

P. A. G. Clack, 'The origins and growth of Darlington', in P. Riden (ed.), *The Medieval Town in Britain* (1980), 67–84.

P. A. G. Clack and N. F. Pearson, *Darlington: A Topographical Survey* (1978).

H. M. Colvin, *A Biographical Dictionary of British Architects 1600–1840* (1995 edn.).

R. Cramp, *Corpus of Anglo-Saxon Stone Sculpture* (1984).

J. Crosby, *Ignatius Bonomi of Durham: Architect* (1987).

C. Cunningham, *Victorian and Edwardian Town Halls* (1981).

C. Cunningham and P. Waterhouse, *Alfred Waterhouse, 1830–1905: Biography of a Practice* (1992).

J. A. Cunningham, 'Hugh of Le Puiset and the church of St Cuthbert, Darlington', in N. Coldstream and P. Draper (ed.), *Medieval Art and Architecture at Durham Cathedral* (1980).

Darlington and District: Buildings and Places (1975).

P. J. Davison, *Brickworks of the North East* (1986).

D. and S. Dean, *Darlington in the 1930s and 40s* (1984)

D. Defoe, *A Tour through the Whole Island of Great Britain* (1983 edn.).

M. H. Dodds, 'The Bishops' Boroughs', *Archaeologia Aeliana*, 3rd ser., xii (1915), 1.

G . W. Dolby, *The Architectural Expression of Methodism: the First Hundred Years* (1964).

T. Faulkner and A. Greg, *John Dobson: Architect of the North East* (2001).

B. Fawcett, *A History of North Eastern Railway Architecture: 1, the Pioneers* (2001).

A. P. Fitzpatrick and P. R. Scott, 'The Roman Bridge at Piercebridge, North Yorkshire – County Durham', *Britannia*, xxx (1999), 111–32.

B. Flynn, 'The chantries of St Cuthbert's church, Darlington', *Durham Archaeol. Journ.*, i (1984), 67–71.

G. Flynn, *The Book of Darlington* (1987).

G. Flynn, *Darlington in Old Photographs: Second Selection* (1992).

T. Fordyce, *Local Records* (1876).

F. Graham, *Northumberland and Durham: A Social and Political Miscellany* (1979).

J. Granger, *General View of the Agriculture of the County of Durham* (1794).

H. Haggar, 'The bridges of John Green', *Northern Architect*, viii (April 1976), 25–31.

188   SOURCES

D. W. Harding, *Holme House, Piercebridge: Excavations 1969–70: a Summary Report* (1984).

T. D. Hardy, *A Description of the Patent Rolls in the Tower of London: to which is added an Itinerary of King John* (1835).

B. J. D. Harrison, 'A census of households in County Durham, 1563', *Cleveland and Teesside Local Hist. Soc. Bull.*, xi (1970).

J. K. Harrison, 'The development of a distinctive Cleveland blast furnace practice, 1866–75', in C. A. Hempstead (ed.), *Cleveland Iron and Steel* (1979), 81–115.

An Historical Atlas of County Durham (1992).

D. H. Heslop, B. Jobling and G. McCombie, *Alderman Fenwick's House: The History of a Seventeenth-century House in Pilgrim Street, Newcastle upon Tyne, and its Owners* (2001).

D. W. Hockin, *Whessoe: Two Centuries of Engineering Distinction* (1994).

R. I. Hodgson, *Demographic trends in County Durham, 1560–1801* (1978).

K. Hoole, *North Eastern Locomotive Sheds* (1972).

G. G. Hoskins, *An Hour with a Sewer Rat; or, a Few Plain Hints on House Drainage and Sewer Gas* (1879).

W. Hutchinson, *The History and Antiquities of the County Palatine of Durham* (1794).

J. S. Jeans, *Jubilee Memorial of the Railway System: a History of the Stockton and Darlington Railway and a Record of its Results* (1875).

J. S. Jeans, *Pioneers of the Cleveland Iron Trade* (1875).

J. R. Kellett, *The Impact of Railways on Victorian Cities* (1969).

A. J. Kenwood, 'Residential building activity in north eastern England, 1853–1913', *Manchester School of Econ. and Soc. Studies*, xxxiii (1965), 115–28.

D. A. Kirby, 'Population density and land values in County Durham during the mid 17th century', *Trans. Inst. Brit. Geog.*, lvii (1972), 83–98.

M. W. Kirby, *Men of Business and Politics: the Rise and Fall of the Quaker Pease Dynasty of North-east England, 1700–1943* (1984).

M. W. Kirby, *The Origins of Railway Enterprise: the Stockton and Darlington Railway, 1821–1863* (1993).

J. Latimer, *Local Records* (1857).

W. Lillie, *History of Middlesbrough* (1868).

C. Lloyd, *Memories of Darlington*, ii (1995).

R. Lomas. 'The Black Death in County Durham', *Journ. Med. History*, xv (1989), 127–40.

R. Lomas, *North-east England in the Middle Ages* (1992).

W. H. D. Longstaffe, 'Ruins of the north of England: Darlington episcopal mansion', *Church of England Magazine*, 18 Sept. 1847, 177–9.

W. H. D. Longstaffe, *The History and Antiquities of the Parish of Darlington* (1854).

S. Lucy, 'Changing burial sites in Northumbria, AD 500–750', in J. Hawkes and S. Mills (ed.), *Northumbria's Golden Age* (1999), 12–43.

I. Mackintosh and M. Sell (ed.), *Curtains!!! or a New Life for Old Theatres* (1982).

G. W. May, *British Industry and Commerce: 5. Teesside* (c. 1965).

N. McCord and D. T. Rowe, *Northumberland and Durham: An Industrial Miscellany* (1971).

P. Meadows and E. Waterson, *Lost Houses of County Durham* (1993).

F. Mewburn, *The Larchfield Diary: Extracts from the Diary of the Late Mr Mewburn, First Railway Solicitor* (1876).

R. Miket and M. Pocock, 'An Anglo-Saxon cemetery at Greenbank, Darlington', *Med. Archaeol.*, xx (1976), 62–74.

C. D. Morris, 'The pre-Norman sculpture of the Darlington area', in Clack and Pearson, *Darlington*, 44–51.

C. P. Nicholson, *Those Boys o' Bondgate, and other Contributions to the Story of Darlington and Neighbourhood* (1949).

J. Ogilby, *Britannia* (1675).

'Old Elizabethan House, Darlington', *The Builder*, xlviii (1885), 549.

A. M. Oliver, 'The Blagroves law roll', *Proc. Soc. Antiq. Newcastle upon Tyne*, 4th ser., i (1924), 323–4.

L. F. Pearson, '"The Architecture of Entertainment Run Riot": William Hope of Newcastle, 1862–1907', *Northern History*, xxvii (1991), 184–97.

M. H. Pease, *Henry Pease: a Short Sketch of his Life* (1898 edn.).

N. Pevsner, rev. E. Williamson, *The Buildings of England: County Durham* (1985 edn.).

M. Phillips, *A History of Banks, Bankers and Banking in Northumberland, Durham and North Yorkshire* (1894).

W. Pike, *Darlington Illustrated* (1905).

W. T. Pike, *A Descriptive Account of Darlington* (1894).

A. J. Pollard, *North Eastern England during the Wars of the Roses* (1990).

N. J. G. Pounds, *A History of the English Parish* (2000).

H. D. Pritchett, *History of the Parish Church of St Cuthbert, Darlington* (1924).

H. D. Pritchett, *The Story of the Church of St Cuthbert, Darlington* (1965).

H. D. Pritchett, *An Ecclesiastical, Archaeological and Architectural History of St Cuthbert's Church, Darlington* (n.d.).

J. P. Pritchett, *An Architectural History of St Cuthbert, Darlington* (1902).

A. Quiney, *John Loughborough Pearson* (1979).

B. K. Roberts, *The Green Villages of County Durham* (1977).

T. H. Rowland, *Dere Street: Roman Road North* (1974).

R. Ryder, 'Council house building in County Durham, 1900–1939: the local implementation of national policy', in M. J. Daunton (ed.), *Councillors and Tenants: Local Authority Housing in English Cities, 1919–1939* (1984), 40–100.

R. Scarr, 'Darlington's first architect', *Darlington and Stockton Times*, 11 Aug. 1951.

A. F. Sealey and D. Walters, 'First railway architect', *Architectural Rev.*, cxxxv, no. 807 (1964), 364–6.

C. Sharp, *The 1569 Rebellion: being a Reprint of the Memorials of the Rebellion of the Earls of Northumberland and Westmorland* (1975 edn.).

H. J. Smith, 'John Vaux, parson and astrologer, 1575–1651', *Trans. Arch. and Archaeol. Soc. Durham and Northumberland*, new ser., vi (1982), 83–8.

H. Spencer, *Men that are Gone from the Households of Darlington* (1862).

C. Stell, *Nonconformist Chapels and Meeting Houses in the North of England* (1994).

W. Stokes, 'John Botcherby: a victim of the railway age?', *Durham County Local Hist. Soc. Bull.*, lxi (May 2000), 3–17.

N. Sunderland, *A History of Darlington* (1967).

N. Sunderland, *Tudor Darlington* (1974).

R. Surtees, *The History and Antiquities of the County Palatine of Durham*, (1816–40).

H. Swanson, *Medieval Artisans: an Urban Class in Late Medieval England* (1989).

A. H. Thompson, 'The Clervaux Chartulary', *Archaeologia Aeliana*, 3rd ser., xvii (1920), 186–228.

J. J. Vickerstaffe, 'A gazetteer of Durham county schools, 1400–1640', *Durham County Local Hist. Soc. Bull.*, xli (1988), 3–14.

Victoria County History of Durham, i–iii (1905–28).

V. E. Watts, 'Place-names of the Darlington area', in Clack and Pearson, *Darlington*, 40–3.

L. Wilkes, *John Dobson, Architect and Landscape Gardener* (1980).

I. Wood, *Darlington Transport* (1996).

J. Wood, *Town Atlas of Northumberland and Durham, 1820–7* (1991).

E. Wooler, 'The Saxon burgh of Darlington and its military defensive earthworks', *Proc. Soc. Antiq. Newcastle upon Tyne*, 3rd ser., v (1913), 185–7.

E. Wooler and A. C. Boyde, *Historic Darlington* (1913).

R. Young, 'Flint material from Darlington', in Clack and Pearson, *Darlington*, 38–9.

UNPUBLISHED MATERIALS

P. Abramson, 'River Skerne Restoration Project, Report NAA 95/12' (report in Durham SMR, 4817, 1995).

M. Adams, 'Darlington Market Place: archaeological excavations, 1994' (report in Durham SMR, 4000, 4812).

B. J. Barber, 'The economic and urban development of Darlington, 1800–1914' (Univ. of Leicester M. A. dissertation, 1969) (copy in Darlington Lib.).

R. Benson, 'Darlington Forge and Albert Hill' (typescript in Darlington Lib., E810041851, 1976).

A. G. Chamberlain, 'North-eastern architects and the building trade up to 1865' (Typescript in Newcastle Central Library, 1986).

A. G. Green, 'Houses and households in Co. Durham and Newcastle, *c.* 1570–1730' (Univ of Durham, Ph. D. thesis, 2000).

M. Hussain, 'Development of Saltburn' (Sunderland Univ. B.A. dissertation, 1998).

W. J. Mountford, 'Biographical and historical notes on bygone Darlington' (Typescript in Darlington Lib., *c.* 1912).

G. R. Potts, 'A biographical guide to Darlington architects, 1840–1914' (Typescript in Darlington Lib., 2002).

J. Robinson and J. Biggins, 'Morton Palms, Darlington, Co. Durham: geophysical survey, 1999' (report in Durham SMR, 5639).

P. F. Ryder, 'St Cuthbert, Darlington: archaeological assessment' (Report in Durham Diocesan Office, DAC section, 1997).

L. Strutt, 'An architectural and historical survey of the housing of Darlington between 1850 and 1918' (Newcastle-upon-Tyne Polytechnic, B. A. dissertation, 1982) (copy in Darlington Lib.).

A. T. C. Targett, 'G. G. Hoskins in Darlington' (Newcastle Univ. B. A. dissertation, 1991) (copy in Darlington Lib.).

M. J. Tillbrook, 'Aspects of the government and society of County Durham, 1558–1642' (Univ. of Liverpool, Ph. D. thesis, 1981).

Index

Unless otherwise specified, place references are to Darlington.

Printed and bound by CPI Group (UK) Ltd, Croydon, CR0 4YY

09/06/2025

14685720-0002